PATHWAYS TO RECONCILIATION

For Tilly, Nina, Frida and Ilya

Pathways to Reconciliation
Between Theory and Practice

Edited by

PHILIPA ROTHFIELD
La Trobe University, Australia

CLEO FLEMING
Monash University, Australia

PAUL A. KOMESAROFF
Monash University, Australia

ASHGATE

Published by
Ashgate Publishing Limited
Gower House
Croft Road
Aldershot
Hampshire GU11 3HR
England

Ashgate Publishing Company
Suite 420
101 Cherry Street
Burlington, VT 05401-4405
USA

www.ashgate.com

British Library Cataloguing in Publication Data
Pathways to reconciliation : between theory and practice
  1. Reconciliation - Political aspects
  I. Rothfield, Philipa II. Fleming, Cleo III. Komesaroff,
  Paul A.
  303.6'9
  Pathways to reconciliation : between theory and practice
  1. Reconciliation - Political aspects
  I. Rothfield, Philipa II. Fleming, Cleo III. Komesaroff,
  Paul A.
  303.6'9

Library of Congress Cataloging-in-Publication Data
Pathways to reconciliation : between theory and practice / [edited] by Philipa Rothfield, Cleo Fleming and Paul A. Komesaroff.
    p. cm.
  Includes index.
  ISBN 978-0-7546-7513-6
  1. Conflict management--Cross-cultural studies. 2. Culture conflict--Cross-cultural studies. 3. Reconciliation--Cross-cultural studies. I. Rothfield, Philipa. II. Fleming, Cleo. III. Komesaroff, Paul A.

  HM1126.P383 2008
  303.6'9--dc22

2008028144

ISBN: 978 0 7546 7513 6

Mixed Sources
Product group from well-managed
forests and other controlled sources
www.fsc.org Cert no. SA-COC-1565
© 1996 Forest Stewardship Council
FSC

Printed and bound in Great Britain by
MPG Books Ltd, Bodmin, Cornwall.

Contents

Part II: Sites of Reconciliation

Notes on Editors and Contributors

Patrick Burgess is an Australian barrister specializing in international human rights and criminal law. He is currently Asia Director for the International Centre for Transitional Justice. From 1999 to 2005 he worked in East Timor for the UNTAET and UNMISET missions and was Principal Legal Counsel for the East Timor Commission for Reception, Truth and Reconciliation (CAVR).

Helena Cobban is a writer and internationally syndicated columnist on global affairs. Since 1990 she written a column for The Christian Science Monitor and she contributes a regular column to the London-based Arabic-language daily, Al-Hayat. She is a Contributing Editor of Boston Review. Ms. Cobban has published five books, most recently, *Re-engage! America and the World After Bush* (2008).

Cleo Fleming has a BA (Politics) and a Graduate Diploma of Arts (International Relations) from Monash University, Melbourne and, a MA (International Development) from RMIT University, Melbourne. She is a founding member of the Global Reconciliation Network and has coordinated two of the network's four conferences (London 2003 and Sarajevo 2005).

Vince Gamberale is the Country Director for CHF International in Serbia, and the former Country Director for Bosnia and Herzegovina. Mr Gamberale has experience in implementing emergency assistance, post-conflict rehabilitation and transitional development programs gained in: Iraq, Bosnia and Herzegovina, Azerbaijan, Kosovo, FYR Macedonia and Albania.

Daphna Golan-Agnon is a sociologist who teaches human rights at the Hebrew University of Jerusalem and a Research Associate at the Harry S. Truman Institute. She is the author of *Separation, Normalization and Occupation: The Dilemmas of a Joint Venture by Palestinian and Israeli Women* (1995) and *Where Am I in this Story?* (2002). Dr Golan-Agnon is co-founder of B'Tselem: The Israeli Information Centre for Human Rights in the Occupied Territories.

Damian Grenfell is a Post-doctoral Fellow and Research Project Manager with the Globalism Research Centre, RMIT University. An interest in social movements and resistance politics has provided an impetus for research into forms of nationalist insurrection and post-conflict reconstruction, especially in terms of how we understand the nation-state in a period of intense globalisation. An RMIT-based project titled 'Sources of Insecurity' provides the basis for this research in which Timor L'Este is the focus.

Andrew Gunstone is Head of the Centre for Australian Indigenous Studies in the School of Humanities, Communications and Social Sciences at Monash University, Melbourne. His research focus is on the Australian reconciliation process and the history of Indigenous and non-Indigenous political relationships. He is the Foundation Editor of the *Journal of Australian Indigenous Issues*, and the author of *Unfinished Business: The Australian Formal Reconciliation Process* (2007).

Jackie Huggins AM is a woman of the Bidjara/Birri-Gubba Juru peoples. She is the former Co-Chair of Reconciliation Australia, a non-government organization dedicated to ending Indigenous disadvantage. She is Deputy Director of the Aboriginal and Torres Strait Islander Studies Unit at the University of Queensland. Historian and published author, she is one of Australia's most prominent Indigenous leaders and was a member of the Council for Aboriginal Reconciliation for six years.

Paul James is Director of the Globalism Research Centre, RMIT University. He is an editor of *Arena Journal*, and sits on the Council of the Institute of Post-colonial Studies. Professor James is the author or editor of nine books including, *Nation Formation: Towards a Theory of Abstract Community* (1996) (with T. Nairn), *Global Matrix: Nationalism, Globalism and State-Terror* (2005) and *Globalism, Nationalism Tribalism: Bringing Theory Back In* (2005).

Julian Jonker lives in Cape Town, South Africa. He teaches legal history and rhetoric at the Department of Private Law, University of Cape Town, and has written about law and memory in post-apartheid Cape Town, intellectual property and indigenous knowledge. Mr Jonker has also exhibited sound art on the subject of memory and identity and has produced community arts projects in Cape Town.

Paul A. Komesaroff is a physician, philosopher and medical researcher in the Faculty of Medicine at Monash University, Melbourne. Professor Komesaroff is the author of more than 250 articles and author or editor of ten books, including *Objectivity, Science and Society* (1986 and 2008), *Troubled Bodies: Critical Perspectives on Post-modernism, Medical Ethics and the Body* (1996), *Reinterpreting Menopause: Cultural and Philosophical Issues* (1997) (ed. with P. Rothfield and J. Daly), *Sexuality and Medicine: Bodies, Practices, Knowledges* (2004) (with P. Rothfield and J. Wiltshire) and *Experiments in Love and Death* (2008). Professor Komesaroff is the convener of the Global Reconciliation Network.

Alphonso Lingis is an American philosopher, writer and translator, Professor Emeritus of Philosophy at Pennsylvania State University. His areas of specialisation include phenomenology, existentialism, modern philosophy and ethics. He has translated the work of Merleau-Ponty, Levinas and Klossowski. Professor Lingis is the author of 12 books, most recently, *First Person Singular* (2006).

David Pettigrew is a member of the International Association for Genocide Scholars and a Professor of Philosophy at Southern Connecticut State University.

His research interests include Heidegger studies, contemporary French thought, and psychoanalysis, particularly the work of Parisian psychoanalyst JD Nasio. Professor Pettigrew has co-translated and co-edited a number of books, most recently, a translation of J.D. Nasio's *The Book of Love and Pain: Thinking at the Limit with Freud and Lacan*.

Philipa Rothfield is a Senior Lecturer in Philosophy at La Trobe University, Melbourne. Dr Rothfield publishes on philosophy of the body and dance, through the work of Merleau-Ponty, Nietzsche, Klossowski and Deleuze. She has recently published on reconciliation in *Trauma, Historicity, Philosophy*, edited by M. Sharpe et al. (2007). She is a founding member of the Global Reconciliation Network and helped organize three of the network's conferences (Melbourne 2002, London 2003, Sarajevo 2005). She also dances and reviews dance for *RealTime* arts magazine.

Modjtaba Sadria is an Iranian-born philosopher and Professor at the Institute for the Study of Muslim Civilisations at the Aga Khan University (International) in the United Kingdom. Professor Sadria holds doctorate degrees in philosophy from the University of Paris and in international relations from the University of Quebec at Montreal, and Master's degrees in literature, history and philosophy from the University of Paris. Professor Sadria has published over 50 articles and books, most recently, *Prayer for Lost Objects: A Non-Weberian Approach to the Birth of Modern Society* (2003, in Persian).

Kay Schaffer is an Adjunct Professor in the Gender Studies at Adelaide University and at the Hawke Research Centre for Sustainable Development at the University of South Australia. Her research areas include cultural studies, post-colonial and global formations and life writing. Presently, her main area of research involves the role of storytelling in human rights campaigns. She is co-author with Sidonie Smith of *Human Rights and Narrated Lives: The Ethics of Responsibility* (2004).

Geraldine Smyth O.P. has worked in the fields of education, theology and psychotherapy in Ireland. She is a Senior Lecturer in the Irish School of Ecumenics (now integrated into Trinity College) and Coordinator of the Research Degrees Programme. Her research interests include reconciling memories in post-conflict societies, peace theology and ecumenical ecclesiology. She has authored and edited a number of books, most recently, *The Critical Spirit: Theology at the Crossroads of Faith and Culture*, co-edited with Andrew Pierce (2003).

Derick Wilson is the Assistant Director of the UNESCO Centre at the University of Ulster and a Commissioner with the Equality Commission for Northern Ireland. He has been involved in reconciliation activity since 1965 and was awarded the MBE for services to Community Relations in Northern Ireland. A detached youth worker, he established professional courses for indigenous youth workers, directed the Corrymeela Centre, was a Research Fellow and established Future Ways, a university action research team supportive of reconciliation, organisational change and public policy development.

Foreword

Archbishop Desmond Tutu

It is a sad fact that alienation and disharmony, conflict and turmoil, enmity and hatred characterize so much of life today. Indeed, the last hundred years have been the bloodiest in human history. In spite of this, we are often able to catch glimpses of better things: for example, after natural disasters and in other conditions of terrible adversity we can see how it is possible for people to work together cooperatively, with compassion and generosity, bound together by caring humanity.

The work of the South African Truth and Reconciliation Commission signifies a remarkable capacity for good, and has become a model which many other countries have taken up in their own ways, in relation to their own problems. Because of this it is possible today to discern a movement at the heart of things to reverse the awful centrifugal forces of alienation, brokenness, division and hostility and to begin to move forward to peace and harmony. To give this process added force it is important to take stock of the various approaches to reconciliation and to understand their relative strengths and weaknesses. It is important to use this combined experience as a resource that can be drawn upon by all people struggling for reconciliation in their own settings.

This book provides a useful, accessible and balanced guide to the experiences of reconciliation around the world and will help build a global resource of experience and insight. It covers many topics, including forgiveness, justice, conflict resolution and the recognition of human rights. It shows how the relative importance of these varies according to the circumstances of individual countries and different cultures and histories. It also shows how ultimately if they are to be successful they must all lead to some form of forgiveness. This does not involve forgetting or condoning what has happened in the past: on the contrary, it includes remembering atrocities so that we can prevent them from happening again; it involves taking what has happened seriously and not minimising it, drawing out the sting in the memory that threatens to poison our entire existence; it involves dealing with the past, all of the past, to look forward to the future.

Reconciliation will always be a long and complex process. It will require ongoing study and reflection and different approaches to practice. No doubt there will be many disappointments and failures. However, at least today it is firmly on the agenda. In a tired, disillusioned, cynical world which has hurt so frequently and so grievously this is of crucial importance because it provides inspiration and hope that a peaceful and harmonious future is possible.

The Human Face of Indigenous Australia

Jackie Huggins AM

As descendants of one of the oldest surviving cultures on earth, superseding the arrival of Europeans in 1788 by some 40,000 years, the Indigenous people of Australia have every right to expect equality and respect. As someone who has spent much of her life engaged in the long and often difficult reconciliation process, it has been my duty to help meet that expectation by putting health, education, and quality of life at the centre of Australia's reconciliation agenda. Now more than ever, this duty is critical. Almost all key indicators of wellbeing and equality – most notably health and education – show Indigenous Australians at the end of the line, lost in the distance.

Successive governments have applied band-aid solutions to Indigenous disadvantage with limited success. Finally, it seems awareness is emerging of the inextricable linkages between the different aspects of Indigenous disadvantage: one problem predisposes us to the next, in a cycle that can often appear impossible to break. I would like to believe that in addition to this deeper comprehension of the nature of disadvantage, the perception of how to begin to address it has also matured. I would like to believe that we are past the point where people cloistered in capital cities think they can solve the problems facing black people. I hope that in Australia, government, business, civil society and anyone else trying to encourage good governance, dispense justice, end welfare dependence and combat substance abuse or family violence understands that they need the close, constant and respected cooperation of Aboriginal and Torres Strait Islander communities. Without our involvement they are on a road to nowhere. Working together respectfully is the foundation of reconciliation – both practical and symbolic.

The first important steps towards a new national approach to reconciliation that engages both symbolic and practical elements were made in early-2008 when the new Australian Prime Minister, Kevin Rudd, offered a formal apology to members of the Stolen Generations. It was a moment when the nation held its collective breath and exhaled in a shared outpouring of emotion and joy. This apology has generated a sense of hope, healing, forgiveness and unity. It fosters the kind of mutual respect that is essential for tackling the tough issues of Indigenous disadvantage.

Seeing is Believing

While some advances have been made in the state of Indigenous health, education and wellbeing, the reality is that overwhelming numbers of Indigenous Australians continue to live in poverty in a country that ranked third in the United Nations Development Program's Human Development Index (HDI) in 2006. And I continue to find myself on panels as the sole Indigenous voice trying to explain issues that should be better understood by now. The overdue insight about the need to put control into the hands of Indigenous people is starting to produce common ground between the main stakeholders. For this to lead to improved outcomes in Indigenous disadvantage, and tangible progress in terms of reconciliation, there must also be a multifaceted approach that accounts for all aspects of disadvantage – social, spiritual and physical.

The failure to gain headway on indicators of Indigenous disadvantage is a sign of the limitations of 'practical reconciliation'. For many years the predominant government policy was informed by the view that practical measures of overcoming disadvantage can operate in isolation from the spiritual aspects of reconciliation. In reality, it is impossible to separate attempts to better the employment, housing, education, health or income status of Indigenous Australians from the attainment of greater respect for and recognition of differences in culture, historical perspective and priorities. How you feel about yourself – the sense you have of who you are – is intrinsic to how you behave. If you believe you're beaten, then you're beaten. If you believe you're an outsider, then you're an outsider. For all intents and purposes, if you believe that the rest of Australia has no respect for you or your culture, then it does not.

The daily reporting of the high incidence of violent crime and substance abuse in our communities has sadly come to constitute what many non-Indigenous Australians associate with 'being Aboriginal'. For many, it defines us. It encourages some people to believe that we are somehow genetically predisposed to violence and alcoholism, or that this behaviour is simply part of our culture. It allows others to blame us for these problems or to write us off as a lost cause. For too long this perspective has relegated to the fringe of the mainstream consciousness the enormous contributions that we make to the nation. More tragically, it numbs people, both non-Indigenous and Indigenous, to the human significance of shocking statistics. The issues then become candidates for the 'too hard basket', where they are left to worsen until they reach crisis point. If you believe you're beaten, then you're beaten. These things are self-fulfilling. To overcome them, we need to work on both practical and symbolic solutions for bringing out the best in Indigenous communities.

Promoting Reconciliation in Australia

Australia's first peoples need and deserve a special place in the psyche of the country and rights that are recognized and enshrined in the nation's laws and symbols. The formal recognition of the special place of Indigenous people, the kind of recognition that has been extended to the Indigenous peoples of the United States, Canada and New Zealand, has enormous practical implications. It is the basis on which people can begin to take control of their lives, and it is the only real basis for lasting reconciliation.

In 2007, Australia celebrated the 40th anniversary of the 1967 referendum, in which over 90 percent of Australians voted to remove discriminatory clauses in the Constitution. As a result of that referendum, Aboriginal and Torres Strait Islander peoples were counted as Australians for the first time since Australia became a nation in 1901. In the decade before the vote was taken, Indigenous and non-Indigenous people campaigned side by side to ensure the referendum was passed. That period is often described as the start of the reconciliation movement and much has been changed for the better over the four decades since, but the job is far from done. That in an undeniably 'lucky country' the life expectancy of an Indigenous baby is some 17 years less than a non-Indigenous baby is unacceptable. That we are so dramatically over represented on all indicators of disadvantage is a national disgrace.

Many commentators still view the year 2000 as the high point of reconciliation in Australia. Vivid images of success are conjured up by the Sydney Olympics, where the Indigenous female athlete, Cathy Freeman, took centre stage; the memorable *Walk for Reconciliation* across Sydney Harbour Bridge, in which half a million people participated, followed by other *Corroboree 2000* bridge walks and; the culmination of Australia's 10-year formal process of reconciliation with the handing over to the Prime Minister and the Commonwealth Parliament of the Final Report of the Council for Aboriginal Reconciliation (CAR). In reality, a great deal remained to be done. Perhaps one of the biggest pieces of 'unfinished business' was the need to bring public attitudes into step with CAR's final recommendations, and sustain the reconciliation process beyond 2000. It was in the context of this need that Reconciliation Australia was founded.

I spent many years involved with CAR before joining the board of Reconciliation Australia, an organization with a vision of Australia as one that recognizes the special place and culture of Aboriginal and Torres Strait Islander peoples as the First Australians, values their participation and provides equal chances in life for all citizens. At its essence, reconciliation in Australia is about:

- Recognizing the right of Aboriginal and Torres Strait Islander peoples, as the First Australians, to express their cultures and participate on an equal footing in all aspects of Australian life;
- Achieving respectful and productive relationships between Indigenous and non-Indigenous people in all spheres; and
- Being able as a society, through the way institutions and communities operate, to acknowledge, value and allow for difference.

With limited resources and a long period of government absence from the reconciliation process, achieving progress toward our mission has been difficult. However, significant changes have also occurred during this period, which present us with a substantial opportunity. Central to these changes has been the emergence of a radically different way of thinking by government regarding Indigenous affairs, based on acknowledgement of the failure to address Indigenous disadvantage and recognition of the importance of Indigenous engagement to any tangible hope for progress. A gap has also been created in Indigenous representation by the politically bi-partisan decision to close the Aboriginal and Torres Strait Islander

Commission (ATSIC). While ATSIC was not an Indigenous creation, it operated as, and was considered by many to be, the voice of Indigenous Australia. These changes have created an environment which requires renewed commitment towards reconciliation and makes it incumbent on all Australians to help find solutions to end the disadvantage suffered by Indigenous people. Aboriginal and Torres Strait Islander communities must be given the power to make our own decisions. This means supporting communities to build the capacity to effectively engage with government and express their views publicly and, impressing upon government the need to develop the cultural competence to work meaningfully with Indigenous communities. At the new Labor Government's 2020 'Ideas' Summit held in April 2008, the idea of a new national representative body was voiced, so too was the issue of a treaty.

The absence of a treaty between the Australian Government and its Indigenous peoples is unusual in the world of Indigenous relations. Support for such an agreement at the end of the reconciliation process in 2000 echoed similar campaigns at the end of the 1970s and 1980s. Its persistence is a reminder that large and enduring problems call for large and enduring solutions. The Australian Constitution is the fundamental law of Australia. The document was drafted during two conventions in the 1890s at which Aboriginal people were not represented. While the Constitution could recognise Indigenous peoples in a number of ways, for example in the preamble, it does not. As a broad-based, civil society organization Reconciliation Australia does not take a particular position on a treaty but it does believe it to be an issue worthy of discussion and encourages informed debate.

I am a positive person and that is partly because I have worked for reconciliation for so long. I have seen great things happen across Australia when Indigenous and non-Indigenous people work together to weaken obstacles. A particularly encouraging moment was the historic declaration in February 2006 at the Australian Future Directions Forum that ending Aboriginal and Torres Strait Islander disadvantage needed to be the nation's first priority. To hear this acknowledged by Australia's emerging leaders made me feel that we have every reason to be optimistic. In their words:

We stand diminished as a nation unless we act immediately and decisively to address the marginalization of Indigenous people across all areas of life. This is not only desirable, it is achievable. It would be outrageous for this level of alienation and disparity to continue into the next decade. As future leaders we are determined to take all efforts to address this legacy ... We will do this because it is right. The manifest disadvantage of Indigenous people is intolerable. By doing nothing we stand to witness the irreversible loss of one of the most ancient cultures in the world.

I look forward to a true and lasting reconciliation, where the life chances and expectations of children all over Australia are equal. We have a real opportunity to make all of this possible, it is time to begin working together as equals and grasp it.

Acknowledgements

The Editors would like to express their gratitude to the Monash Institute for the Study of Global Movements at Monash University, Melbourne, for making this collection possible. We would also like to acknowledge the support that numerous organizations and individuals have given over the years to the Global Reconciliation Network. This support has enabled the network to hold four international conferences, at which some of the papers in this collection were initially presented.

There are a number of individuals who have given generously of their time, skills and knowledge to this project and to them we also owe a debt of thanks: Robert Beattie, Catherine Morris, Joanne Shiells, Christopher Scanlon and Jackie Yowell. Thanks also to Kirstin Howgate and her team at Ashgate for their belief in the viability of the collection and their assistance in seeing it to publication. The contributors to the collection have shown a degree of commitment and patience that has been exceptional in its largesse – thank you for being such a delightful group of people to work with.

Finally, an enormous thanks to our respective partners, Tony, John and Sally, for listening, encouraging and helping us in so many ways.

Introduction

Pathways to Reconciliation: Bringing Diverse Voices into Conversation

Paul A. Komesaroff

Discussions of reconciliation often emphasize overcoming conflict, especially through legal, political or diplomatic means. This is partly a result of the work of 'truth and reconciliation' commissions in nearly two-dozen countries, especially South Africa, and the establishment of a high profile international legal structure to deal with allegations of human rights abuse. However, reconciliation encompasses a broader field than conflict resolution alone, extending to the establishment of peace, justice, fairness, healing and forgiveness. It refers to the recovery of cultural identities, building trust and overcoming personal enmities. It includes understanding and responding to relationships within and between communities, the role of cultural, religious and other factors in promoting or obstructing dialogues, and the sensitivity of such dialogues to local variables. It covers a range of social, cultural and legal goals, including human rights, social justice and mutual coexistence.

The broad scope of reconciliation raises the question of whether it is too far-reaching and diffuse to be of practical use. Yet, as recent history has demonstrated, the concept and ideas it commands remain a potent force. One of the objectives of this book is to investigate the vicissitudes of reconciliation, its character and complexity, in order to help refine the issues it is able to address.

The theory of reconciliation spans many disciplines, including theology, philosophy, social theory, law, history and psychology. The word itself in English has a rich cultural history that differs somewhat from that of its correlates in other languages (de Gruchy 2002, 29). While this book largely focuses on Western theories and concepts, all major traditions of thought emphasize a concept of reconciliation. In Arab cultures, for example, there is an ancient structure for resolving conflict (Jabbour 1996; Irani and Funk 1998). Since before Islam, the practice of *sulha* (settlement) was applied to resolve disputes in the absence of a legal system. *Musalaha* (reconciliation) is reached in a step-by-step process emphasizing the links between the psychological and political dimensions of communal life. According to *sharia* law, 'the purpose of the sulha is to end conflict and hostility among Muslims so that they may conduct their relationships in peace and amity ... on both the individual and community levels' (Khadduri 1997). *Sulha* remains widely practised and in some countries is integrated into the judicial system.

In Indian cultures, the earliest theoretical statement on conflict occurs in the *Brihad-Aranyaka Upanishad*. Conflict was seen not as a clash of interests, not as a clash at all, but as a difference in interpretation, arising from an imperfect understanding of the essential oneness of all beings (*Brihad-Aranyaka Upanishad* 2004). Reconciliation, therefore, was a hermeneutical exercise requiring dialogue with the self and the application of interpretative skills through self-purification, abstinence and fasting, meditation and pilgrimages. This approach has been pervasive throughout Indian culture and formed a central part of Mahatma Gandhi's struggle for India's independence (Devy 2004). In Buddhism, the integration of a variety of ideas and concepts through a hermeneutic process of 'reconciliation of doctrinal controversies' is also common, as is the project of reconciliation with community: Through a manner of right-mindedness, 'heart and soul, subjectivity and objectivity, become fused into one whole' (Williams 1989). In this view, all individual entities and things are fundamentally interconnected and interdependent, and the recognition of this is a condition of Enlightenment (Suzuki 1963).

Western concepts of reconciliation derive from a number of sources, which often refer to the idea of 'alienation' and ways to overcome it. These include ancient Greek philosophers, such as Plotinus and other Platonists, Christian thinkers and more recently, those in the Marxist tradition. Plotinus argued that a discrepancy between human thoughts and perceptions and the objective world lead to a duality in human nature which obliged us to regard the known world as essentially different, or alien, from ourselves. This led to a loss of faith in the possibility of paradise and a self-sufficient being representing supreme good (Kolakowski 1978, 16).[1] Similarly, alienation from God and the ensuing project of reconciliation has been a major theme in Christian thought. According to Rowan Williams, every Christian begins 'from the experience of being reconciled, being accepted, being held (however precariously) in the grace of God' (Williams 1990, 2).

John de Gruchy has argued that in Christian doctrine, the word 'reconciliation' is used in two ways. The first is interchangeable with 'salvation', 'redemption' or 'atonement' (de Gruchy 2002, 45). The second is the concept introduced by St Paul, of the human possibility of overcoming alienation from God and achieving a state of grace:

> Created 'in the image of God', all of us share a common humanity and are included in the scope of God's love and purpose... [A]s a result of human disobedience humanity is alienated from God, experiences enmity in its own ranks, and is estranged from nature... God, out of love and grace, freely chooses to overcome this alienation and redeem humanity from its bondage to sin and its consequences (de Gruchy 2002, 48).

This idea of reconciliation refers to the messianic tradition of transcending alienation from God, which belongs to the common heritage of Judeo-Christian belief. It led to four interrelated senses of reconciliation: the theological, the interpersonal, the social and the political (Barth 1981, 440). In all, the path to reconciliation required the development of 'a shared life and language, a public community of

---

1   See also Plato, *Letter* 7, 344a, quoted in (Kolakowski 1978, 16).

men and women, gathering to read certain texts and perform certain acts' (Williams 1990, 2).

Hegel developed a version of this approach in his concept of *Aufhebung*, the overcoming of difference as the transcendence in a unity of opposites (Hardimon 1994). According to this conception, humanity created itself by a process of alienation, alternating with the transcendence of that alienation. Alienation was the alienation of self-consciousness and all objectivity was alienated self-consciousness. The spiritual transcendence of alienation, or reconciliation, occurred when humans re-assimilated their essence and realized their true nature, a process that would come about when the Mind had passed though the travail of history and finally came to assimilate the world as its own truth and to actualize everything in it that was originally only potential (Hegel 1971).

In the 'humanistic' writings of the young Marx this Hegelian idea was applied in a socio-historical context (Marx 1967, 289–90). Marx's point of departure is the eschatological question derived from Hegel of how humans are to be reconciled with themselves and the world (Kolakowski 1978, 177). In place of the Hegelian Spirit, Marx, following Feuerbach, located alienation in the 'earthly reality' of human beings. With the creation of private property and the capitalist mode of production, humans came to be separated from their work, their own products and other people. They were dispersed into solitude, which appeared as an eternal social pathology (Poster 1975, 286). What was left was a denuded, alienated person that had become a mere 'abstraction'.

Marx argued that this distortion of human nature was a direct and inevitable result of capitalist economy and society. Its overcoming required the re-establishment of the 'unity of living and active human beings with the natural, inorganic conditions of their metabolism, with nature, and therefore the appropriation of their nature'. This was to be realized in communist society, which would enable the 'complete return of man to himself as a social (human) being – a return become conscious, and accomplished with the entire wealth of previous development' (Marx 1967, 293–7). Reconciliation through communism was 'not a state to be achieved or a goal to be reached' rather; it was a dynamic, continuing process of healing the breach and reuniting all elements constituting a human being (Marx 1967, 426).

In post-Marxian Western thought, the emphasis shifted from ontology to language. The task of reconciliation became understood as that of overcoming blockages to communication, albeit often still in a schematic and universalistic manner. According to Habermas it is possible to identify and reconstruct the universal conditions of possible understanding, the 'general presuppositions of communicative action' (Habermas 1976). Habermas identified the discrepant dynamics of the large-scale social steering mechanisms, and the local contexts of meaning embedded in the lifeworlds of individuals, as major sources for social and psychological pathologies. Meanings, which arose from individual speech acts, were inherently dependent on the complex horizons of meaning arising within different lifeworlds and remained entwined with the intuitively present background knowledge of participants (Habermas 1987, 350).

The linguistic turn drew attention not only to the link between reconciliation and communication but also to ethics. The problem of reconciliation arose out of, and solutions could only be generated by, the connections established through language, not as an external tool or device but immanently, as the medium of communication itself. In the new formulations language was at once the medium, the mechanism and the embodiment of the struggle for common meaning: it was always already both a trace and infinite self-transcendence (Agamben 1999, 44).[2]

This fluid and dynamic character of language is the basis for all ethical contact. As Levinas has shown, through language a commitment is established between my interlocutor and myself, based not on our participation in a transparent universality but on our proximity and through the act of speaking. Whatever the message transmitted, it is the speaking itself that represents the contact (Levinas 1990, 155). Speech is never a solitary or impersonal exercise of thought: it is an irreducible and primordial part of an ethical interchange. This is not a purely formal or logical process: speech unfolds immanently out of my proximity to the other (Nancy 1991). However, there is always a relationship in speech with a singularity located outside the theme of the speech itself: a singularity that is not thematized by the speech but indirectly approached by it. Accordingly, speech and language are at once the primordial foundation of ethics and society and a great and unlimited creative source of meaning (see Pettigrew this volume).

The link between reconciliation and language raises the question of the possibilities for and limitations of communication across different theoretical and cultural standpoints. This question was central in the twentieth century philosophy of science in terms of incommensurability between theories that stood in the way of mutual forms of intelligibility (Komesaroff 2008, 64–8). The analysis of language, however, has suggested that there are no theories or cultural standpoints that are in principle opaque to each other (Habermas 1976, 116–23). No matter how divergent the theoretical perspective there is always some possibility of translation, of the joint construction and sharing of meaning, even if it remains limited, imperfect and partial. However, these debates highlight the depth of the questions and the complexity of the passage from the inception of the project of modernity.

In the classical project of modernity ushered in by Galileo there was thought to be a single 'book of nature' written, for those who could interpret it, 'in geometrical characters'. This conviction was subsequently challenged by the idea that there was a collection of disconnected regions of knowledge and experience unable to communicate with each other. In the postmodern setting it is accepted that there are differentiated forms of knowledge rooted in culture and language but which are not completely disconnected: a conditional, partial intelligibility cannot be extinguished because it is embedded in the founding ethical bond forged by discourse and language.

Commenting from a contemporary viewpoint on the complexity of the various Western traditions, Habermas refers to an essay by Derrida:

---

2 'Language, which is in the beginning, is the nullification and deferral of itself, and the signifier is none other than the irreducible cipher of this ungroundedness' (Agamben 1999, 44).

There are only books in the plural because the original text has been lost... [Yet] this book written in God's handwriting never existed, but only traces of it, and even they have been obliterated. This awareness has left its imprint on the self-understanding of modernity, at least since the nineteenth century... This lost certainty, this absence of divine writing, that is to say, first of all, the absence of the Jewish God (who himself writes, when necessary), does not solely and vaguely define something like 'modernity'... Modernity is in search of the traces of a writing that no longer holds out the prospect of a meaningful whole as the book of nature or the Holy Scripture had done (Habermas 1987, 164).

The contemporary project of reconciliation is to recognize and honour the complexity of human communication and to preserve the possibility of continuing dialogue. Culture, religion and politics are now understood to be part of a rich palimpsest, subject to ceaseless scrutiny and interpretation. The mediating role that Christianity and Hegel had attributed to God and the Spirit, and which Marxism reserved for social practice, has been enriched by recognition of the intertwining of lifeworld experiences, large-scale social institutions and communicative practice.

The praxis of daily living together rests on a base of common convictions, self-evident cultural truths and reciprocal expectations. Conflicts arise from distortions in communication, from misunderstanding and incomprehension, from insincerity and deception (Habermas 2003, 35). Overcoming difficulties of understanding requires a deliberate and careful process of widening perspectives into a 'fusion of horizons', the development of a common intersubjectivity, a shared horizon of background assumptions and structures of communication that are free from coercion and distortion (Habermas 2003, 37).

This brief review of the history of the concept of reconciliation leads to some broad conclusions. A key feature of reconciliation is that it refers to a process involving communication across the obstacles presented by – among other things – culture, race, religion and politics. Such communication is often difficult, unpredictable, ambiguous and fragile (Habermas 2003, 38). Untrammelled communication may not be possible but some kind of dialogical contact always is, at least where there is a readiness to pass beyond the tyranny of violence and fear.

Reconciliation is a process, not a state to be achieved or a goal to be reached. It can contribute to consolidating peace, breaking a cycle of violence, restoring justice at personal and social levels, bringing about personal healing, reparation for past injustices and building non-violent relationships between individuals and communities. It can help recreate and confirm people's sense of being and belonging (Bloomfield et al. 2003, 77). In the process it can utilize many vehicles, from the arts to economic forms of cooperation. Which objectives are relevant and which practices are likely to be effective depend on local conditions. However, a key question is always how to establish and maintain the process of communication, which may be fraught and requires sensitivity to local possibilities and limitations.

Reconciliation is concerned with dialogue, understood in both a broad and a specific sense. On the one hand, it involves a sharing of meaning-generating perspectives, to use Habermas's expression. As explained by Bohm, it also entails an open, creative process that stimulates 'a stream of meaning ... among and through us and between us ... out of which may emerge some new understanding' (Bohm 1996, 6). On the other hand, this open dialogue occurs between discrepant discourses and the meanings produced are different from the pre-existing meanings within each of them. The process of communication, or dialogical contact, is not one of pure translation, and the result may be novel and fruitful, or partial and unsatisfactory.

Every utterance arises from a particular environment. As language, it is anonymous and social: as an individual utterance, it is simultaneously concrete and filled with specific content (Bakhtin 1992, 272). Communication and dialogue cannot be isolated from the concrete conceptualizations that fill them or the continuous processes of their historical becoming (Bakhtin 1992, 288). Every concrete utterance is irreducibly a social act. Abstracted from their social contexts, words, grammatical forms and sentences, turn into technical signs of meanings that are only possible at a formal level but not individualized historically (Bakhtin 1994, 156). Understanding of any concrete utterance is not possible independently of its values and evaluations in the cultural environment.

Communication across discourses, theories, belief systems and cultures requires a process of translation. It is well recognized that translation involves the production of new meanings rather than a simple transfer of old meanings. The task of the translator is to find an effect upon one's own language that produces in it an echo of the original (Benjamin 1969, 76). Similarly, a person seeking to communicate may introduce into the new discourse a kind of stuttering, which is not simply a stuttering in speech, but a stuttering of the language itself (Deleuze 1997, 107). Reconciliation dialogues are always intractable and obdurate; there is no universal language: in reality, language and communication are the absolute, and maybe the only, presuppositions (Agamben 1999, 43).

There have been many attempts to develop general methodologies of reconciliation or to define common principles. These include formalizing the processes of negotiation or conflict resolution or elaborating techniques for developing 'communicative competence' (see for example: Guliver 1979; Lederach 2005; Agamben 1999, 32–3). As useful as these efforts may be, they are subject to limitations, for the precise reasons that were given above: the practical process of communication is complex and, irreducibly and unpredictably, subject to the local conditions in which it takes place (Komesaroff 2008). There is, and can be, no 'general method' of reconciliation. It is always necessary to embark on a process of negotiation, within which occurs an exchange of information and learning, an exploration of differences and modification of expectations and requirements in the search for mutually satisfactory outcomes (Guliver 1979, xiii).

The experiences of the truth and reconciliation process in South Africa illustrate these points. In addition to the innovative legal framework it introduced, within which both personal experiences and conventional facts were recognized as valid evidence, a distinctive feature was its employment of forgiveness as a key strategy (Tutu 2000). In this setting forgiveness was itself a process to foster dialogue rather than an end in itself: a dynamic mechanism to make it possible for protagonists in a dispute to 'plunge… into the night of the unintelligible and to address not only the malign facts of the operation of state power but also the deep personal pain they engendered (Derrida 2002, 49; 42).[3] Desmond Tutu explains:

---

3   See also: Helmick and Petersen 2001.

[W]e allowed those who came to testify mainly to tell their stories in their own words ... [and discovered that] there were in fact different orders of truth ... There was ... forensic factual truth ... and there was social truth, the truth of experience that is established through interaction, discussion and debate. The personal truth ... was a healing truth... [M]any bore witness to the fact that coming to talk to the commission had had a marked therapeutic effect on them (Tutu 2000, 26–7).

Forgiveness is just one of many strategies which can be used to overcome blockages to communication and the free flow of meaning. Whichever methods are used, like the utterances embedded in language, they are culturally rooted and must be appropriate to the setting. These methods themselves may need to incorporate deliberate steps to undermine cultural stereotypes, including orientalist prejudices and culturally bound assumptions about the nature of truth.

The restorative justice Desmond Tutu proposed for South Africa arises from the traditional African concept, closely linked to forgiveness, referred to as *ubuntu* in the Nguni group of languages or as *botho* in the Sotho languages, according to which one cannot separate one's own self-interest from that of the others in the community (Tutu 2000, 31).[4] A person with *ubuntu* is open to and affirming of others and can act on the basis that he or she is part of a greater whole and is diminished when others are humiliated, oppressed or merely treated with disrespect (Govier 2006):

[T]he central concern is not retribution or punishment [but]... the healing of breaches, the redressing of imbalances, the restoration of broken relationships, a seeking to rehabilitate both the victim and the perpetrator, who should be given the opportunity to be reintegrated into the community he has injured by his offence ... [J]ustice, restorative, is being served when efforts are being made to work for healing, for forgiving, and for reconciliation (Tutu 2000, 54–5).[5]

These examples highlight the theoretical complexity and empirical specificity of the concept of reconciliation and illustrate how it can be associated with many different pathways (see also Deutsch 2006). Pathways already mentioned may aim directly at conflict resolution and peace-building, fostering intra-communal and transcultural dialogues and understanding, developing concepts of justice and fairness, or promoting healing and forgiveness. They include the use of health care, the arts, sport, environmental activism and economic cooperation. There are many others that have been developed with striking effect, for example: aid work, union activities, memorialization, peace activism and empowerment through the provision of micro-credit.

This collection seeks to map some of these pathways through reflecting upon practical instances as well as engaging reconciliation in theoretical terms. It is set out in two parts, which we have entitled 'The Complex Pathways of Reconciliation' and 'Sites of Reconciliation'.

The collection opens with a preface by the prominent Indigenous Australian leader and activist, *Jackie Huggins,* who argues for Indigenous Australia's expectation of

---

4   For an elaboration of Archbishop Tutu's theology of *ubuntu*, see: Battle 1997.

5   It has been widely pointed out that Archbishop Tutu's concept of *ubuntu,* like that of forgiveness, reflects his Christian theology. See: Battle 1997.

equality to be met through the promotion of health, education and quality of life. The first part of the book then addresses current notions of justice, reconciliation and conflict resolution in the work of Derrida, Kant, Nietzsche, Nancy, Ricoeur and others, bringing together established and new voices from the fields of philosophy, ecumenical studies and cultural studies.

Philipa Rothfield's lead essay for this section uses concepts derived from contemporary French philosophy to evaluate reconciliation, arguing that reconciliation will always have an ambivalent character. This is because of a tension between the social and the singular, here enacted between the social goals of reconciliation and the singularity of suffering which provokes it. The interests of the social are inclined to produce normative tendencies, particularly as regards forgiveness. Drawing on a number of authors, including Derrida, Nietzsche and Klossowski, Rothfield seeks to explain the radical difference between corporeal singularity and the interests of the social. *David Pettigrew* also addresses the notion of the singular in a different fashion. He begins by confronting the failure of the *United Nations Declaration of Human Rights* to respond effectively to recent examples of genocide and proceeds by delving into the nature of the human being and his/her relation to justice. He then considers Nancy's thought on human singularity, something which we share but which also separates us from all others, leading to a proposal that textual creations relating to genocide constitute a form of justice, spoken to and offered to the world. *Alfonso Lingis* develops a conception of justice within conflict resolution that integrates reason with emotion as an alternative to revenge and retributive conceptions of justice. He offers a concept of justice that exceeds individualistic notions of responsibility as it creatively refashions our sense of restoration. Lingis looks to our global context in light of this conception of restorative justice, arguing that even the poorest have something to contribute to conflict resolution. *Modjtaba Sadria* does not attempt to rid society of conflict; rather, he looks to the ways in which inequalities of power stand in the way of justice-serving forms of communication. Drawing on post-colonial theory, Sadria argues that listening to the voice of the other rather than the echo of oneself is one of the most demanding yet least obvious conditions for the realization of reconciliation, showing how dominant frameworks of understanding skew the ways in which listening is practised.

Geraldine Smyth argues for an account of the provenance of the notion of forgiveness, tracing its origins in Christian theology. She argues that the theological genealogy of forgiveness needs also to be situated in relation to the socio-political sphere, in part, because reconciliation is relevant to believers and non-believers alike. Smyth's account suggests that forgiveness is self-transcending, bringing about a mutual form of reorientation. *Damian Grenfell* offers an elaboration of Benedict Anderson's influential work on the nation as imagined community, interpreted here in relation to the concrete specificity of reconciliation work in Timor-L'Este as a form of nation building. Grenfell offers an embodied perspective on the practice of nation building by considering the ways in which embodied forms of interaction have played a role in Timor's nationalizing process. Locating her discussion in South Africa, *Kay Schaffer* critically evaluates memorialization projects in post-TRC times, considering how memory is preserved and perpetuated in memorial projects. She also examines the case of a witness to the TRC whose testimony raised questions about modes of listening and an ethics of difference. *Julian Jonker*'s work highlights the limitations and legacy of South Africa's reconciliation processes by reflecting on the problem of memory in relation to sites of burial and reconciliation. The physical and historical past of apartheid are an abiding presence in Cape Town; Jonker shows how economic prosperity is ruptured by the ghosts of the past as excavations unearth a traumatic history, calling for the work of memory and mourning.

The second part of the book offers a selection of reflections and first-hand experiences in relation to different geographical locations. *Paul James'* lead essay introduces this section by addressing the extent to which institutions of international justice are equipped to deal with matters of reconciliation. He reviews the inadequacies of reconciliation practice: its proceduralism, juridical limitations and temporal and financial finitude. Drawing on social theory, he delineates a range of levels of social subjectivity, arguing that reconciliation must take all these levels into account. He proposes an international body charged with sharing, communicating and arbitrating the experience and insights of reconciliation around the globe. *Helena Cobban* situates her discussion in South Africa, Mozambique and Rwanda. She contrasts Western notions of accountability with African responses to conflict and post-conflict reconstruction, which do not always adhere to individualist conceptions of justice. Cobban builds a case for non-Western alternatives to the Nuremberg model of accountability, using the successes of Mozambique as her means of support. *Patrick Burgess* provides an account of the community reconciliation procedures that he participated in designing and implementing in Timor-L'Este from his perspective as Director of the UNTAET Human Rights Unit, charged with leading the United Nations role in establishing a truth and reconciliation commission for a nation emerging from colonialism and conflict. He describes the challenges and rewards of building a reconciliation process relevant to the local context and which built on local skills and traditions. *Vince Gamberale* reflects on how programs of economic development can generate cooperation and provide incentives to overcome ethnic divisions. In his capacity as Country Director for CHF International in Bosnia and Herzegovina (BiH), Gamberale oversaw the implementation of a program designed to improve the economic environment in a number of municipalities in post-war BiH by establishing partnerships between municipal governments, the private sector and civil society. *Daphna Golan-Agnon* presents the search for a future horizon of reconciliation in the Middle East from a present marked by division, conflict and trauma. She looks towards South Africa as a source of insight to resolve the problems that beset Israelis and Palestinians. *Andrew Gunstone* examines why Australia's ten-year reconciliation process failed to meet its goals or its overall aim. His work emphasizes that while governments may establish mechanisms to formally foster reconciliation, any progress will be undermined by a failure to recognize and address indigenous concerns. Finally, *Derick Wilson* shows how community facilitation in conflict resolution and research has promoted citizenship in public institutions in Northern Ireland. He argues that the time is ripe for the lessons of conflict resolution to be incorporated into public bodies and that any legislative goal towards reconciliation will need to be reflected at all levels of state institutions.

This collection examines many examples of effective communication being established across the barriers of narrative voice and lifeworld, philosophical assumptions and epistemological difference, and deep cultural and geographical distance. In each case there is an obvious achievement, although boundaries and limitations remain. None requires or entails the exact transmission of information unchanged between cultural systems of meaning. However, in all there is a common making of sense, of mutually enriching contact, of enhanced respect and understanding, of communication.

These reflections suggest some conclusions, which provide the framework for much of the discussion in this book. First, reconciliation is concerned primarily with the process of restoring fractured communication and enabling dialogue where it has encountered obstacles, where language is difficult or has proved deficient. It seeks to break the silence, to speak the unspeakable. Second, there are no theories or cultural standpoints that are in principle mutually opaque to each other. No matter how divergent the theoretical perspectives, it is always possible to construct some common meaning and sense. Third, the modern theory and practice of reconciliation draws on an extensive tradition, which has addressed ways of dealing with and overcoming past alienation, enmity and pain and of moving forward, personally, socially and spiritually (de Gruchy 2002, 27). Over the years there has been a shift in focus from universalistic formulations, strategies, algorithms and goals to recognition of the singularity of personal experiences and the irreducible complexity of social relationships.

Fourth, the process of reconciliation is effected through the sharing of meaning, by fomenting mutual reflections that generate individual relationships and forms of association that are themselves creative of new meanings. Reconciliation stands in opposition to the installation or enforcement of one dominant discourse in preference to another; it avoids *a priori* commitments to particular goals or end-points, even where they may support beneficent causes such as human rights, social justice or conflict resolution. Fifth, reconciliation dialogues themselves may be complex and span various discourses, and there are no formal rules or algorithms to guide their conduct. There are many modalities of cross-discursive communication and the cultural specificity of any particular experience or utterance is irreducible. This means that understanding may always be imperfect or uncertain or at least subject to limitations.

Finally, reconciliation interventions may occur at the level of civil society and within institutions of power: the two are complementary and interdependent. Institutional change only becomes possible when preconditions are satisfied at the community level. Conversely, to ensure enduring outcomes, community change must ultimately rely on a firm political framework.

As the essays that follow demonstrate, reconciliation does not have a unitary form. It supports – encourages – diverse and at times contrary viewpoints and strategies. The activities and ideas emerging under the banner of reconciliation are not uniform, evolving as they often do from the dissonance of war and conflict in different social and religious settings. At its core, however, there is agreement on a central point: that reconciliation is concerned with bringing diverse voices into conversation with each other and finding a way to balance the perspectives they present.

References

Agamben, G. (1999), *Potentialities* (California: Stanford University Press).

Bakhtin, M. (1992), *The Dialogical Imagination* (Austin: University of Texas Press).

Bakhtin, M. (1994), *The Bakhtin Reader: Selected Writings of Bakhtin, Medvedev and Voloshinov*, P. Morris (ed.) (London: E. Arnold).

Barth, K. (1981), *Ethics* (Edinburgh: T. and T. Clark).

Battle, M.J. (1997), *Reconciliation: The Ubuntu Theology of Desmond Tutu* (Cleveland: The Pilgrim Press).

Benjamin, W. (1969), *Illuminations* (New York: Schocken).

Bloomfield, D. et al. (eds) (2003), *Reconciliation After Violent Conflict: A Handbook* (Stockholm: International Institute for Democracy and Electoral Assistance).

Bohm, D. (1996), *On Dialogue* (London: Routledge).

Brihad-Aranyaka Upanishad, Swami Madhavananda (trans.) (Kolkatta: Advaita Ashram).

de Gruchy, J.W. (2002), *Reconciliation: Restoring Justice* (Minneapolis: Fortress Press).

Deleuze, G. (1997), *Clinical Essays* (Minneapolis: University of Minnesota Press).

Derrida, J. (2002), 'On Forgiveness', in *On Cosmopolitanism and Forgiveness* (London: Routledge).

Deutsch, M. (ed.) (2006), *The Handbook of Conflict Resolution* (Hoboken: John Wiley and Sons, Inc.).

Devy, G. (2004), 'Truth in Indian Traditions' in Tazi, N. (ed.), *Keywords: Truth* (New Delhi: Vistar).

Govier, T. (2006), *Taking Wrongs Seriously* (New York: Humanity Books).

Guliver, P.H. (1979), *Disputes and Negotiations: A Cross-Cultural Perspective* (New York: Academic Press).

Habermas, J. (1976), *Communication and the Evolution of Society* (Boston: Beacon Press).

Habermas, J. (1987), *The Philosophical Discourse of Modernity* (Massachusetts: MIT Press).

Habermas, J. (2003), *Philosophy in a Time of Terror*, Borradori, G. (ed.) (Chicago: University of Chicago Press).

Hardimon, M.O. (1994), *Hegel's Social Philosophy: The Project of Reconciliation* (Cambridge: Cambridge University Press).

Hegel, G.W.F. (1971), *The Phenomenology of Mind*, Part VIII, Baillie, J.R. (trans.) (London: George Allen and Unwin).

Helmick, R.G. and Petersen, R.L. (eds) (2001), *Forgiveness and Reconciliation* (West Conshohocken: Templeton Foundation Press).

Irani, G.E. and Funk, N.C. (1998), 'Rituals of Reconciliation: Arab-Islamic Perspectives', *Arab Studies Quarterly*, Fall, 53–73.

Jabbour, E.J. (1996), *Sulha: Palestinian Traditional Peacemaking Process* (Montreat: North Carolina).

Khadduri, M. (1997) 'Sulh', in Bosworth, C.E. et al., *The Encyclopedia of Islam*, vol. IX (Leiden, Holland: Brill).

Kolakowski, L. (1978), *Main Currents of Marxism*, vol. 1 (Oxford: Oxford University Press).

Komesaroff, P.A. (1986), *Objectivity, Science and Society* (London: Routledge and Kegan Paul).

Komesaroff, P.A. (2008), *Experiments in Love and Death* (Melbourne: Melbourne University Press).

Lederach, J.P. (2005), *The Moral Imagination: The Art and Soul of Building Peace* (Oxford: Oxford University Press).

Levinas, E. (1990), *Philosophical Essays* (The Hague: Martinus Nijhoff).

Marx, K. (1967), *Writings of the Young Marx on Philosophy and Society*, Easton, L.D and Guddat, K.H. (trans.) (eds) (New York: Doubleday Anchor).

Nancy, J.-L. (1991), *The Inoperative Community*, Connor, P. (trans.) (Minneapolis: University of Minnesota Press).

Poster, M. (1975), *Existential Marxism in Post-War France* (Princeton: Princeton University Press).

Suzuki, D.T. (1963), *Outlines of Mahayana Buddhism* (New York: Schocken Books).

Tutu, D. (2000), *No Future without Forgiveness* (New York: Doubleday).

Williams, P. (1989), *Mahayana Buddhism: The Doctrinal Foundations* (New York: Routledge).

Williams, R. (1990), *The Wound of Knowledge* (London: Darton, Longman and Todd).

PART I
The Complex Pathways of Reconciliation

Chapter 1

Lead Essay
Evaluating Reconciliation

Philipa Rothfield

'So let us give voice to this *new demand*: we need a *critique* of moral values, *the value of these values should itself, for once, be examined…*'

(Nietzsche 1994, 3).

We know where Nietzsche went with this thought. That we tame animals, moral inside and out, are nothing if not 'good' people. And yet humans commit the worst atrocities, crimes against humanity amongst them. Reconciliation is one response to this legacy of atrocity. Its impetus is in part to expose – for the record, for history – to make public that which has been committed in the dark. Reconciliation has other motivations, to signal the end of conflict, violence and injustice, as well as to repair, restore and reintegrate. By bearing witness to testimony it gives a voice to the survivors of violence. It is also enacted for the dead. It is an attempt to look evil in the face so that it shall be no more, *nunca más*.

In light of the above, we can only agree with Derrida that 'No one would decently dare object to the imperative of reconciliation' (Derrida 2004, 50). After all, it has so many laudatory, even necessary, aspirations. Yet there is another side, one that bears upon the question and nature of its value. Derrida invokes this other side by addressing the couplet, reconciliation-forgiveness, in the following way:

> I shall risk this proposition: each time forgiveness is at the service of a finality, be it noble and spiritual (atonement or redemption, reconciliation, salvation), each time that it aims to re-establish a normality (social, national, political, psychological) by a work of mourning, by some therapy or ecology of memory, then the 'forgiveness' is not pure – nor is its concept. Forgiveness is not, it *should not be*, normal, normative, normalizing. It *should* remain exceptional and extraordinary, in the face of the impossible: as if it interrupted the ordinary course of historical temporality (Derrida 2004, 32).

Derrida's separation between forgiveness and politics is wide-ranging. If the political realm is to be identified with pragmatic and principled concerns – such as reunification, national recovery and conflict resolution – then forgiveness exists elsewhere, outside calculation, beyond demand, beneath rationality. That is to say, for Derrida, forgiveness 'remains heterogeneous to the order of politics or of the juridical as they are ordinarily understood' (Derrida 2004, 39).

Desmond Tutu, would put the matter otherwise:

When we look around us at some of the conflict areas of the world, it becomes increasingly clear that there is not much of a future for them without forgiveness, without reconciliation. God has blessed us richly so that we might be a blessing to others. Quite improbably, we as South Africans have become a beacon of hope to others locked in deadly conflict, that peace, that a just solution is possible. If it could happen in South Africa, then it could certainly happen anywhere else (Tutu 2003, 2).

For Tutu, South Africa is both a blessing – living proof in the possibility of forgiveness through reconciliation – and 'a national project after all is said and done' (Tutu 2003, 2). By associating forgiveness with reconciliation, Tutu has married what for Derrida remain two distinct orders. Tutu is not alone in adopting such a position. According to Derrida, 'the concept of the "crime against humanity" remains on the horizon of the entire geopolitics of forgiveness' (Derrida 2004, 30). What Derrida draws out, and Tutu illustrates, is the sense in which reconciliation is caught up in a network of confession, repentance and forgiveness: a 'process of Christianisation' that has outstripped Christendom itself (Derrida 2004, 32).

Nietzsche exhibited a similar sensitivity towards the trace of Christianity in secular, humanist morality (Nietzsche 1994). His nostalgia for the Roman age of cruelty shares this with Derrida's account of forgiveness: both are inimical to a social-political order configured in terms of Enlightenment rationality. If Derrida's views thereby appear dangerous – edging towards the irrational – we should remember to whom forgiveness belongs:

> We can imagine, and accept, that someone would never forgive, even after a process of acquittal or amnesty. The secret of this experience remains. It must remain intact, inaccessible to law, to politics, even to morals: absolute... In the radical evil of which we are speaking, and consequently in the enigma of the forgiveness of the unforgivable, there is a sort of 'madness' which the juridical-political cannot approach much less appropriate (Derrida 2004, 55).

Imagine, he says:

> ... a victim of terrorism, a person whose children have been deported or had their throats cut, or another whose family was killed in a death oven. Whether she says 'I forgive' or 'I do not forgive', in either case I am not sure of understanding. I am even sure of not understanding, and in any case I have nothing to say. This zone of experience remains inaccessible, and I must respect its secret (Derrida 2004, 55).

Whilst Derrida does not pretend to understand what it would be like to occupy this position, he defends the right of such a person to decide whether or not to forgive, *without* suffering the judgement of others.

This is a right which Jean Améry, an Auschwitz survivor, felt compelled to defend:

> *I* am burdened with collective guilt, I say; not they. The world, which forgives and forgets, has sentenced me, not those who murdered or allowed the murder to occur. I and others like me are the Shylocks, not only morally condemnable in the eyes of the nations, but already cheated of the pound of flesh too (Améry 1996, 75).

Améry felt betrayed, that his reluctance to forgive was subjected to the tribunal of world opinion. He is not alone in this regard. Consider two recent examples. In 1996, Steve Biko's widow, Ntsiki Biko, challenged South Africa's proposed amnesty process so as to retain her right for prosecution and civil remedy in the courts. South Africa's Constitutional Court held that the TRC's enabling legislation was valid partly because of the Constitution's call for 'national unity and reconciliation' (Hoffman 2004, 10). The Court weighed the nation's interest in truth and reconciliation against Biko's claims, deciding in favour of the nation. Another illustration arose from a conference discussion on reconciliation and the inadequacies of the Dayton Peace Accord's two-state division of Bosnia. Munira Subašić, an activist from Srebrenica, controversially quipped that she would like to see her country divided into two groups – comprising good people and bad people – proposing that she would live with the good ones. Her remark was made in a place that has not yet (and may never) brought its war criminals to justice. For Subašić, who lost 26 members of her family in the Srebrenica massacres, there can be no reconciliation without justice, no (re)integration without accountability.[1]

Biko wanted to resist the exchange of amnesty for truth (or disclosure). The Court's decision could be read as an encroachment upon her prerogative – to pursue justice, to deny forgiveness – all of which is potentially compromised through the provision of amnesty. Subašić spoke against rehabilitation, against living together and amongst unprosecuted war criminals. The force of her remark has the *gravitas* of one who has experienced immeasurable loss.[2] Améry was no less entitled to bestow forgiveness. Yet he experienced such pressure to rehabilitate Nazism that he felt the sting of moral disapproval towards his refusal. If not exclusively about forgiveness, these instances illustrate a certain normativity that underlies the social pressure to reintegrate, reconcile or rehabilitate. This is precisely what Derrida aims to resist and recast.

Derrida has extracted from reconciliation one of its key elements – forgiveness – suggesting that it lies outside the realm of political or moral calculation. This is not to reject it. On the contrary, he aims to preserve its purity from the contamination of exchange. Whilst reconciliation projects may broker certain exchanges – for example, amnesty for full disclosure – forgiveness cannot.[3] His position can be contrasted with utilitarian approaches towards forgiveness, which evaluate its merits through a kind of moral calculus. Moral calculus requires the substitution and exchange of values to determine the morally preferable position. For example, Gerald Scarre contests the idea that the Holocaust should be exempted from moral reasoning (Scarre 2004). His position is that 'the best response to harmful acts is normally to do what we can to

---

1 This is not a rare sentiment but was expressed by numerous signatories to a statement coming out of the conference Subašić attended (*Pathways to Reconciliation and Global Human Rights Conference*, 'Outcomes'; Halilovich et al. 2006, 5).

2 Subašić is the head of the *Movement of Mothers of Srebrenica and Zepa Enclaves*. She is involved in the group burials of identified victims, has established a memorial centre and organizes commemorations of the Srebrenica massacre. She lost her son and husband.

3 This is why he departs from Arendt and Jankélévitch, who believe forgiveness cannot be given unless asked for, that it is responsive rather than autonomous (Derrida 2004, 37).

relieve or repair their bad effects' (Scarre 2004, 187). This may call for punishment or forgiveness or both, depending on the circumstance. Ultimately a balance must be struck between punishment and the utility of forgiveness:

> It would be a poor way of exhibiting one's allegiance to humane and civilized values to press for the punishment of a repentant war criminal, particularly one who, like Paul-Damascus, is not merely sorry for his bad acts but has made considerable amends for them. It would suggest that we did not greatly esteem repentance or care to encourage the alteration of bad dispositions into good ones. Only a very crude utilitarianism would conclude that more could be gained by punishing the repentant Paul-Damascus than by upholding him as an object for praise and emulation. A *more sophisticated theory* would stress the *value of forgiving* the sinner who repents and welcoming him back into the bosom of the community (emphases added) (Scarre 2004, 184).

Scarre treats the evaluative subject – the one who judges, grants or withholds forgiveness – as a single entity. It is 'we' who decide, debate and argue the best approach.[4] By evaluating the Holocaust, and other evils, according to universal wisdom – manifest in the subject who exercises philosophical reason – Scarre effaces the prerogative of those affected by atrocity.

Améry contests the abstracted subjectivity implicit in philosophical reason through exercising this very prerogative:

> Speaking out is a waste of words. The voice grows brittle, must fade and die even before the speaker exits. Nonetheless, the impotent anger is there … Therefore, I will begin by asking permission to speak in the first person. For there is a degree of *personal involvement* that turns every attempt at *detachment* into not only a psychological falsification but a *moral* and *political* one as well (emphases added) (Améry 1984, 71).

Améry disputes the norm of objectivity alongside its attitude of detachment. This is because of the depth of his personal experience of Nazi torture and internment. While Améry personalizes his point of view and its expression, he refuses to give this a merely personal significance. The personal perspective he expresses, in his view, supercedes the purported objectivity of historians. Améry thereby condemns the inauguration of Nazi 'rehabilitation' in the name of 'historical objectivity'; an attitude that he argues is a form of 'indifference' and not neutrality (Améry 1984, 64). By employing the first person, Améry keeps close his experience of torture – how could he do otherwise?[5] His retention of a first person viewpoint challenges

---

4   For example: 'Being too ready to forgive can lead to our being perceived as a soft touch and exploited for our good nature; or as not taking evil sufficiently, seriously or being too ready to condone wrong behaviour. By contrast, being too reluctant to forgive, or too eager to punish, may cause us to be seen (perhaps rightly) as hard-hearted and self-righteous, even as vindictive. For individuals, as for states and other collective agencies, it is important, though not always easy to strike the right balance between punishment and pardon' (Scarre 2004, 187–8).

5   Améry writes: 'What happened, happened. But *that* it happened cannot be so easily accepted. I rebel: against my past, against history, and against a present that places the incomprehensible in the cold storage of history and thus falsifies it in a revolting way. Nothing has healed, and what perhaps was on the point of healing in 1964 is bursting open again as an

the presumptuous neutrality of the philosophical subject from the vantage of a perspective Derrida is at pains to preserve. Améry asserts, 'I am more entitled to judge, not only more than the culprit but also more than society' (Améry 1986, 70). He privileges his own position over and above society's right to judge, resisting its absorption according to some greater interest. As a consequence, he calls into question the status of objective, disinterested approaches.

If moral reasoning leads 'us' to weigh up the pros and cons of forgiveness, political calculation is equally liable to transgress the subjective authority of one such as Améry. This is illustrated in the following analysis of the law underlying South Africa's reconciliation commission:

> The legislation governing the TRC at the same time challenges the nation as a whole (victims, survivors, perpetrators, beneficiaries and bystanders) to transcend resentment, retribution, fear and indifference, as a basis for the creation of a new future... In the pursuit of these ideals, the victim is asked to give priority to his or her obligations as a *citizen* rather than as a *violated person* in the creation of a new and different society – within which the bigger picture of national unity and reconciliation is promoted (Villa-Vicencio 2000, 201).

According to Charles Villa-Vicencio, the TRC legislation required everyone to move beyond their personal experience of apartheid. It asked former victims in particular to make a *choice*; between fealty to their own experience and commitment to the good of the nation. It is the force of the 'rather than' that plays a decisive role here, for people are asked to overcome their differentiated subject positions – as victim, survivor, witness or bereaved. This is expressed as a demand for transcendence (of 'resentment, retribution, fear and indifference') (Meister 2005, 94). By complying, their specific relation to atrocity is thereby undermined.

In both these examples of moral and political calculation, the specificity of the victim-survivor is subsumed by a greater interest – whether the universality of moral reason or the future horizon of national unity. In both cases, a particular relation to trauma or tragedy fades from view. The discussion thus far has traversed a series of palpable differences – between forgiveness and the socially pragmatic; between the experience of atrocity and the national interest; between situated individuality and abstract moral rationality. My impulse to keep both these axes alive, and not collapse one into the other, is an ethical one. It arises through respect for those who have experienced what Derrida calls the 'unforgivable'.[6] Derrida theorized this respect by sheltering forgiveness from social, political and moral agendas, by describing it as 'exceptional' and 'extraordinary'. In doing so, he conjures a radical alterity between forgiveness and its socio-political others. If Villa-Vicencio is right, that reconciliation calls for the violated to transcend their feelings in order to found the new nation, what happens to the heterogeneity of these two orders? Has a boundary been transgressed in exhorting citizens to leave their feelings behind? Has one order

---

infected wound. Emotions? For all I care, yes. Where is it declared that enlightenment must be free of emotion?', (Améry 1986, xi).

6   According to Derrida, the very acts that call for forgiveness are those which are, strictly speaking, unforgiveable. (Derrida 2004, 32).

(the political) asked another (the personal) to undermine its own integrity? Should it?

Although I'm not looking at reconciliation in terms of forgiveness, like Derrida, I strongly believe that those touched by atrocity have every right to form their own opinions, free from any kind of moral pressure. As we will see, when it comes to their passage through the reconciliation process this becomes tricky. It is not always possible to protect victims and survivors from the normative tendencies that constitute the beginning, middle and ends of reconciliation. I will argue that the reasons for this give reconciliation an ambivalent character – in the sense of having more than one value or valency. I will also argue that reconciliation's ambivalence is liable to be felt most strongly by those who have experienced violence and that this derives from a tension between the social and the singular. Derrida expresses this tension in terms of a radical difference between calculable, universalizing forms of justice, politics and morality, and the experiential authority which belongs to the few. I will suggest that it operates at a corporeal level, contrary to the demands and needs of the social.

I proceed firstly by focusing on the social needs of reconciliation as it aspires towards national unity. Robert Meister's work will be cited to show the ways in which reconciliation manages the transitional moments of conflict resolution. This leads to a focus on the consequent fate of the individual: both a member of the social polis and an irreducible singularity. At this point, Nietzsche will be drawn on to elaborate the distinction between the social and the singular. Pierre Klossowski's work on Nietzsche will be cited to suggest that the social and the singular cannot coincide, even though each of us depends upon the social as our means of interaction. As a result, it will be argued that the social sphere can never adequately represent the effervescent specificity of human life, that the views of Améry, Biko and Subašić enact a critical stance towards the sociality of reconciliation on behalf of the singularity of corporeal life.[7]

---

7   Subašić was not the only one to disturb the theatre of rational debate. The *Pathways to Reconciliation and Global Human Rights Conference*, which Subašić attended, was made free to locals, while plenary sessions were translated into English and Bosnian. This meant that many people participated. One person who spoke at length was described by an Australian psychologist as 'thought disordered'. I wish to include such 'disorders' alongside the expressions cited earlier as something to be honored. In reconciliation parlance, bearing witness to another's suffering represents an attempt to ethically honor individual testimony. This essay's attempt to address reconciliation's ambivalence is a manner of bearing witness in theoretical terms to these many expressions of suffering. In my view, Derrida's account of forgiveness is an ethical gesture of respect towards the kinds of experience that produce 'cognitive disorders'. By speaking of forgiveness as a kind of madness, he refuses the hyperrationality of moral approaches that require the lucidity of explanation. In doing so, he suspends the demand put on those who do or do not forgive to justify their own 'position'.

Reconciliation: In the National Interest

Robert Meister looks at reconciliation as a transitional activity which transforms antagonistic differences into social unity for the purposes of conflict resolution. He looks at the way in which reconciliation is able to negotiate a collective attitude towards the past which can serve the future. Meister shows how individuals enter the reconciliation process as victims, survivors, witnesses or perpetrators, to become citizens of the social whole. Such are the transformations of social reconstruction.

Whilst reconciliation identifies the various parties to past conflict, it must also stage a coming together so as to assimilate the citizens of the nation state. Meister offers an interpretation of the aftermath of the United States' Civil War to explain the transitions of unification in the wake of social conflict. The credit for this belongs to Abraham Lincoln whose Gettysburg Address and Second Inaugural Speech appealed to the whole nation as the one entity, rather than as separate warring factions or distinct racial identities:

> Rather than compelling all Americans to acknowledge the pain that slavery inflicted on those whom our nation previously treated as *others*, the figure of Lincoln invites all Americans to identify *themselves* as victims who survived the experience of slavery and Civil War (Meister 1999, 136).

The point of this scenario is to address all citizens in the same way, rather than identify them through their differences. Meister argues that identification of the nation as a whole puts a stop to cycles of revenge. This occurred through Lincoln's 'identifying the Union itself as the victim of slavery', rather than the 'historical victims of human rights abuse' (Meister 1999, 139). If the Union as a whole can become the survivor of slavery (rather than just former slaves), then the victim-perpetrator spiral of violence can be broken because everyone – the nation – has become the (imagined) victim (Meister 1999, 139).

Meister combines moral psychology, political theory and psychoanalysis in order to explain the dynamics of his account. He claims that the achievement of national survivorship involves a 'mechanism of reidentification', whereby differential identification gives way to a collective form of (re)identification (Meister 1999, 139). This begins with perpetrators identifying with victims who are, as a result and in turn, able to identify with perpetrators. Once this has occurred, when '… each successfully internalizes the other, the burden of guilt is shared – or perhaps more accurately, the fantasy of collective guilt is created' (Meister 1999, 139).

This is the final transition, from the original identities of victim and perpetrator, to the one mutual form of identification, where all share a sense of responsibility for past wrongs. Meister suggests that the fantasy of shared guilt allows for the thought that anyone could have been a perpetrator, just as Americans are now survivors of slavery and the war. It represents a political set of identifications that begin in the reality of people's actual relationship to the war, and ends with a collectivized identity formed through fantasy, responsibility and empathic identification (Meister 2005, 85).

The point of these politically contrived identifications is to create a single identity – the nation – which owns past abuse but, importantly, is also able to leave it behind. Wholesale survivorship puts a halt to ongoing cycles of revenge (Meister 1999, 142). It is an alternative to the continuation of distinct and hostile identities. If perpetrators are *unable* to identify with victims, they can only fear and hate them, and may consequently dread retaliation. Belief in retribution fuels ongoing aggression. It signifies the projection of fear and hatred upon possible perpetrators who are then experienced in persecutory terms. The difficulty with ongoing divisions of this sort is that the war can never be over, for retaliation is always around the corner. Mutual identification (where all are survivors) is in the national interest, allowing for joint acknowledgement that victims did suffer abuse or trauma. It is a means by which the nation can take responsibility for past wrongs but also stop them continuing: 'The end of the story is *unity* rather than the autonomy of victims and perpetrators' (Meister 1999, 140).

If collective identity puts a stop to perpetual revenge, it also affects the status of former (actual) victims. Meister claims that the collective subject-position of survivor enjoins '"us" to stop listening to the voice of the victim insofar as this is what it takes to "recover" from a traumatic history and reunite' (Meister 1999, 145). Reunification silences the voice of the (former) victim *qua* victim. This is what 'recovery' means in terms of post-war reconstruction, that the newly formed subject position displaces the antagonism inherent in the old ones (by transforming old identities into new ones). Hence, 'historical victims of abuse' are supposed to be content with peace rather than, for example, demand reparations (Meister 1999, 140). Survivorship therefore inaugurates a new beginning. It puts historical hurts in the past, by foregoing the identifications associated with such hurts.

The same holds for South Africa, though somewhat differently. Rather than the figure of survivorship, Meister analyses South African reconciliation in terms of the reconciled versus the unreconciled victim. He accounts for this in the following way: In order to establish a human rights culture for the future, South Africa *as a whole* needed to recognize apartheid's history of human rights violations. Its TRC progressed towards this acknowledgement through producing a single narrative of apartheid's ills – built upon the testimony of victims, witnesses and the evidence of perpetrators – thereby brokering a national attitude towards the past.

If South Africa were to achieve post-apartheid unity, it needed to find the means whereby the separate parties to conflict could reach some kind of mutual identification in order to forge a new social and political future. Mutual identification is no easy matter, however, for the situation is complicated by the fact that apartheid was politically dismantled but never economically resolved. From a revolutionary point of view, the struggle against apartheid is incomplete. If the victims of apartheid maintain a revolutionary attitude towards apartheid, then mutual identification cannot be obtained. The beneficiaries of apartheid will not identify with its victims because they threaten the beneficiary's economic privilege, whilst victims will refuse to identify with beneficiaries who are – from a revolutionary point of view – liable to become tomorrow's perpetrators (Meister 2005, 84). According to Meister, the reconciliation process needed to persuade victims to abandon the revolutionary position, to trade struggle for a form of victory articulated in moral, though not material, terms. This was achieved in terms of a moral superiority that attaches to the reconciled victim, the one who 'accepts' victory. By accepting moral victory, the reconciled victim relinquishes the desire for ongoing struggle, that is, relinquishes the revolutionary (unreconciled) position.[8] This is the price of peaceful transition, and the condition under which the victim and beneficiary can form, what Meister calls, a 'pact' (Meister 2005, 85). According to this pact, the reconciled victim and beneficiary together put apartheid in the past, keeping beneficiaries safe from reprisal while placing the newly reconciled victim on the winning side.

The reconciled victim stands in marked contrast to the unreconciled victim, for whom the struggle is not yet over. Meister refers to Winnie Mandela as an exemplar of the unreconciled victim in the reconciliation process:

> Time and time again, Archbishop Tutu pleaded with her [Winnie Mandela] to admit her moral damage … The overall effect was to construct her as the very figure that the TRC meant to marginalize. She now represented the implicit antitype of Nelson Mandela, the reconciled and morally undamaged victim who was fit to rule (Meister 2005, 86; See also: Boraine 2000, Ch. 7).

One of the corollaries of attributing moral damage to the revolutionary position was the inclusion of the African National Congress (ANC) in the TRC's report. Not everyone was happy with the alignment of the ANC's struggle with apartheid's crimes.[9] But the morally damaged victim establishes the *bona fides* of the morally undamaged, reconciled victim: an important player in establishing the legitimacy of the new social order.[10] According to Meister, there is widespread agreement that if a new human rights culture is to take hold, '"nonvictims" are the constituency who must be persuaded that the past was evil' (Meister 2005, 91). If the reconciled victim has a sense of winning, of defeating apartheid, he or she can identify with its passive beneficiary, who in turn can identify with the (now) non-threatening victims of apartheid. Acknowledging that human rights violations occurred in the past reassures non-victims that the rule of law will hold in the future. And the past can only be so if victims accept that the struggle is over. This is a crucial feature of the transition to liberalism, for the rule of law individualizes responsibility, thereby obstructing the logic of collective responsibility (and reprisal).

Meister's account raises questions regarding whether this form of reconciliation can offer an equitable resolution for victims of former regimes and conflicts. The problem is that mutual identification requires the dissolution of distinct identities, according to which victims are to be satisfied with the future prospects of the nation

---

8   'For them, moral victory must be victory enough', (Meister 2005, 85).

9   Meister claims that the TRC had the difficult task of legitimating the ANC's right to rule, as morally undamaged leaders; and that it thereby had to allow for a moral equivalence between the ANC's activities and apartheid's wrongs from the point of view of the present ('after the struggle'), whilst averring that they were justified *while* the evil of apartheid reigned (Meister 2005, 90).

10   Meister writes that the new social pact assumes that unreconciled victims have been damaged by the past, and that passive beneficiaries of apartheid would have grounds for hearing that voice as a threat. This contrasts with the non-threatening, reconciled victims, whose moral superiority sets them apart from unreconciled (= damaged) victims (Meister 2005, 85).

as a whole. If in the United States, 'historical victims of abuse are morally expected to dedicate themselves to the "proposition" that peace is victory enough', in South Africa, the victims of apartheid are offered an exchange – relinquish the struggle, reconcile, for moral victory and national recovery (Meister 1999, 140).[11]

Meister's analysis draws attention to the sense in which former victims are both necessary and, at a certain point, surplus to the requirements of reconciliation. Inasmuch as reconciliation aims to unite, it cannot depend upon a divisive social imaginary for fear of promoting a return to conflict. Yet former victims may not feel better for having participated (Henry 2000, 166–173). Nomfundo Walaza, Director of the Trauma Centre for Survivors of Violence and Torture, Cape Town, writes:

> If we are to accept that at the core of the Truth and Reconciliation Commission's (TRC) formation was a national gain (a political settlement and avoidance of bloodshed), then we have to face the unfortunate reality of a conflict between the interests of victims and survivors on the one hand and those of the nation as a whole on the other (Walaza 2000, 250).

Walaza's remarks do not denigrate the achievements of reconciliation, rather, they identify a gap between reconciliation at the national level and the situation of former victims.

Derrida looked at this difference through pitting forgiveness against the social sphere, Meister through mutual identification and national recovery. I would like to conclude this discussion by proposing another basis for the difference identified by Walaza – as a distinction between the social and the singular. My approach grows out of Nietzsche's work on the body's relation to language. For Nietzsche, language can never properly represent the specificity of corporeality. This is because language is oriented to the many. It belongs to the herd. Language consists of values, symbols and ideas that can be exchanged and circulated. By contrast, the singularity of successive bodily states cannot be exchanged.[12] That which is communicable (exchangeable) is inherently at odds with the body (a series of singular states). Pierre Klossowski uses the term 'gregarious' to draw out the inherent sociality of language (Klossowski 1997, Ch. 4). According to Klossowski, the gregarious interests of language, exchange and communication can never serve the particular. The gregarious is about the many, not the one. This is manifest in the following. He asks what is singular and what is gregarious, offering a table of values (Klossowski 1997, 59):

---

11   According to Meister, by giving the reconciled victim a notion of winning, the TRC is further able to portray itself as a form of justice and not merely a compromise with injustice (Meister 2005, 90). This controversial point is important for many of those involved in the politics of reconciliation. Johnny de Lange writes of the need for the TRC to achieve 'both justice and reconciliation' (de Lange 2000, 23).

12   Nietzsche understands the body as a place of change, rather than fixity. He criticizes the idea of a stable, corporeal identity as a distorting perspective of the self, which is, in turn, a distorted interpretation of what is actually a series of changing bodily states. The body, which the self appropriates as an identity is no more than, a 'locus, where a group of individuated impulses confront each other so as to produce this interval that constitutes a human life', (Klossowski 1997, 21).

singular	gregarious
degenerate type	successful type
unexchangeable	exchangeable
unintelligible	comprehensible
muteness	communication
non-language	language

By analysing the difference between these columns as a question of *differential value*, Klossowski brings to light the privilege of gregarious sociality. That which can be exchanged and therefore understood is inevitably valued over the unique instance that remains rooted in unintelligibility. This leads to a distinction which underlies the very basis and operation of 'value'. Only gregarious values – that which can be exchanged, circulated and communicated – can actually *have* value. He asks how 'can the attributes of power, health and sovereignty be restored to the singular, to the unexchangeable, to muteness – since language, communication and exchange have attributed what is healthy, powerful and sovereign to *gregarious conformity*' (Klossowski 1997, 59–60).

The notion of conformity adds a twist to the radical difference between the social (gregarious) and the singular. It reminds us that the singular instance is *expected* to conform. This recalls Derrida's rejection of the 'normal, normative, normalizing' tendencies of the social, political sphere in that Derrida could be seen to be protecting the singular instance of forgiveness from the conforming pressure of the socially pragmatic. But if the singular were to conform to the gregarious, were it to become intelligible, it would no longer be singular.

Here we are returned to the relation between national interest and the individual instance. From the herd's point of view, it is better that the nation comes together. What Klossowski shows is that something of singularity is lost when victims and survivors enter reconciliation. Klossowski is right to signal the normative aspect of 'gregarious conformity', that the herd privileges the communicable over that which is singular. This sheds light on the normalizing dimension of reconciliation, which asks victims to transcend their suffering for the greater good, for the herd attributes to itself all that is 'healthy, powerful and sovereign'. Klossowski's account explains why the normalizing moment of reconciliation pathologizes non-conformity for its mute inexchangeability. This is evident in Améry's lament, and it is why he insisted upon a first person perspective. It also explains the need to construe the unreconciled victim in terms of moral damage – as improperly holding back.

The distinction between the gregarious and the particular suggests a tension between sociality and the corporeal legacy of suffering. This has been alluded to by a number of authors who recognize the difficulties of articulating trauma (Humphrey 1993; Scarry 1985; Das 1996, 67). If the body cannot find an appropriate articulation for its pain, discourses of reconciliation may not be able to properly accommodate its expression (Humphrey 1993, 107). Klossowski's point is that communication is itself inimical to corporeal particularity, a particularity we might (with some license) extend to those subjects whom Derrida depicts. Imagine a victim of terrorism, he says, but then claims that imagination falls short of understanding. This is the dilemma of reconciliation: to work with unspeakable suffering, and to cajole its utterance. To respect the victims and survivors of atrocity, yet broker their participation. National projects of reconciliation are about creating a viable social future out of the horrendous. If they enjoin victims and survivors to participate, and in a sense they must, they are also likely to pathologize resistance, to judge non-conformity, and exert moral pressure to conform. Such is reconciliation's ambivalence.

It's a fine line to tread. If reconciliation projects are inherently ambivalent, it is not that they are misconceived. Reconciliation is incredibly important for countries like Australia, which has just begun to acknowledge past wrongs, and needs to address its continuing legacies of injustice (see Gunstone and Huggins this volume). Rather, it is that national projects cannot incorporate corporeal difference. Améry, Biko and Subašić have, in my view, expressed something of that difference through not conforming to the social flow. These are 'individuals, who form a kind of bridge across the turbulent stream of becoming' (Nietzsche 1997, 111). If they are negatively construed, from a gregarious viewpoint, they can also be seen in creative terms, as enacting a critical stance on behalf of life.

References

Améry, J. (1984), 'The Time of Rehabilitation', in Rosenfeld S. and Rosenfeld, S. (eds) (trans.), *Radical Humanism: Selected Essays* (Bloomington: Indiana University Press).

Améry, J. (1984), 'Wasted Words: Thoughts on Germany since 1945', in Rosenfeld S. and Rosenfeld, S. (eds) (trans.), *Radical Humanism: Selected Essays* (Bloomington: Indiana University Press).

Améry, J. (1986), *At the Mind's Limits: Contemplations by a Survivor on Auschwitz and its Realities*, Rosenfeld, S. and Rosenfeld, S. (trans.) (New York: Schocken Books).

Boraine, A. (2000), *A Country Unmasked: Inside South Africa's TRC* (Cape Town, Oxford: Oxford University Press).

Das, V. (1996), 'Language and the Body, Transactions in the Construction of Pain, Mourning Rituals Conducted by Women in India', *Daedalus*, 125:1, Winter.

Derrida, J. (2004), 'On Forgiveness', in *Cosmopolitanism and Forgiveness* (London and New York: Routledge).

Halilovich, H. et al. (2006), 'Pathways to Reconciliation', *Local Global, Studies in Community Sustainability*, 2.

Henry, Y. (2000), 'Where the Healing Begins", in Villa-Vicencio, C. and Verwoerd, W. (eds).

Hoffman, C. (2004), '"A Grain of Truth": An Appraisal of the TRC's Contribution to the Process of National Reconciliation in South Africa', *BSIS Journal of International Studies*, 1.

Humphrey, M. (1993), *The Politics of Atrocity and Reconciliation: From Terror to Trauma* (London and New York: Tavistock/Routledge).

Klossowski, P. (1997), *Nietzsche and the Vicious Circle* (London: Continuum).

De Lange (2000), 'The Historical Context, Legal Origins and Philosophical Foundation of the South African Truth and Reconciliation Commission', in Villa-Vicencio, C. and Verwoerd, R. (eds), *Looking Back, Reaching Forward, Reflections on the Truth and Reconciliation Commission of South Africa* (London: Zed Books).

Meister, R. (1999), 'Forgiving and Forgetting: Lincoln and the Politics of National Recovery', in Hesse, C. and Post, R. (eds), *Human Rights in Political Transitions* (New York: Zone Press).

Meister, R. (2005), 'Ways of Winning: The Costs of Moral Victory in Transitional Regimes', in Schrift, A.D. (ed.), *Modernity and the Problem of Evil* (Bloomington: Indiana University Press).

Nietzsche, F. (1994), *On the Genealogy of Morality*, Ansell-Pearson, K. (ed.), Diethe, C. (trans.) (Cambridge: Cambridge University Press).

Nietzsche, F. (1997), 'On the Use and Disadvantages of History for Life', in Hollingdale, R.J. (trans.), *Untimely Meditations* (Cambridge: Cambridge University Press).

Pathways to Reconciliation and Global Human Rights Conference, Sarajevo, 16–19 August 2005, 'Outcomes' <http://www.sourcesofinsecurity.org/events/outcomes.html>.

Patterson, D. and Roth, J. (eds) (2004), *After-words: Post-Holocaust Struggles with Forgiveness, Reconciliation and Justice* (Seattle: University of Washington Press).

Scarre, G. (2004), 'Moral Responsibility and the Holocaust', in Scarre, G., *After Evil: Responding to Wrongdoing* (Aldershot: Ashgate).

Scarre, G. (2004), *After Evil: Responding to Wrongdoing* (Aldershot: Ashgate).

Scarry, E. (1985), *The Body in Pain: The Making and Unmaking of the World* (New York: Oxford University Press).

Tutu, D. (2003), 'Forward', *Truth and Reconciliation Commission of South Africa Report*, vol. 6 <http://www.info.gov.za/otherdocs/2003/trc/.>

Villa-Vicencio, C. (2000), 'Restorative Justice: Dealing with the Past Differently', in Villa-Vicencio, C. and Verwoerd, W. (eds), *Looking Back, Reaching Forward, Reflections on the Truth and Reconciliation Commission of South Africa* (London: Zed Books).

Walaza, N. (2000), 'Insufficient Healing and Reparation', in Villa-Vicencio, C. and Verwoerd, W. (eds).

Chapter 2

The Task of Justice

David Pettigrew

Contemporary discourse about human rights makes pragmatic use of the 1948 United Nations *Universal Declaration on Human Rights*, as the Declaration presents a set of guidelines that are based on assumptions about the nature of human beings: their thoughts, ideas, freedom of expression and freedom of association.[1] Article 1 of the Declaration states, for example, that 'All human beings are born free and equal in dignity and rights. They are endowed with reason and conscience and should act towards one another in a spirit of brotherhood.' The document engages the idea of the human being as having rights, regardless of ethnicity or gender. Such rights include life, protection from harm, and access to the latest in scientific technology.[2]

The Declaration is based then, on the idea of the inalienable moral worth and sovereignty of every human being as such. The philosophical basis for such a principle can be found in the ethical theory of Immanuel Kant, who asserts that every rational existence exists as an end in itself: 'Now I say that man, and in general every rational being, exists as an end in himself, *not merely as a means* for arbitrary use by this or that will: he must in all his actions, whether they are directed to himself or to other rational human beings, always be viewed *at the same time as an end*' (Kant 1964, 95). The ethical significance of this formulation for Kant is that one should, 'Act in such a way that you always treat humanity, whether in your own persons or in the person of any other, never simply as a means, but always at the same time as an end' (Kant 1964, 96). Thus it would be my assumption that a document such as the Declaration depends on the Kantian postulation of the absolute and inalienable moral worth and sovereignty of the human being solely on the basis of its rational existence.

Yet, given the increased incidence of dehumanisation, human rights violations and catastrophic violence in the last century, including the all too familiar names of Auschwitz, Hiroshima, Vukovar and Srebrenica, one wonders about the ultimate efficacy of the theoretical framework provided by the Declaration as well as by Kant's ethics. Perhaps Kant's presentation of the idea of the intrinsic worth of each human being – which I uphold – and the ideas contained in the Declaration are overly ideal and abstract and, hence, do not allow for the consideration of the visceral suffering

---

1 The author would like to thank John P. Dudley, of the Philosophy Department of Southern Connecticut State University, for his editorial assistance in the final preparation of this chapter.

2 These ideas are guidelines; ideals to be disseminated and pursued. See, for example, the preamble of the *Universal Declaration*.

and death of the victims of dehumanization and catastrophic violence. Perhaps we need an ethics that could respond to the vulnerability of the singularity of human existences, one that could give thought to the fragility of a community made up of those very singularities. Further, one could speculate that the Declaration, along with Kant's moral theory, is overly static, even a limitation on freedom rather than its reliable guarantor. Kant speaks, for example, of a principle that is 'the *supreme limiting condition* of every man's freedom of action (Kant 1964, 98).

In this respect, in relation to the possible limitations of Kant's moral project, I would like to address the work of French philosopher Jean-Luc Nancy, who offers a framework for giving thought to the singularity of human existence in the contemporary world. For Nancy, beings are 'singular', in their finite being, in the finitude of their existence that is theirs alone. Nancy's thinking of singularity is grounded in Heidegger's ontology and involves a strategic appropriation of Heidegger's notion of the human beings 'ownmost' being-towards-death or finitude.[3] Nancy appropriates this theme and emphasizes that one's being-toward-death cannot be taken over, taken on, or shared by the other.[4] For Nancy, such singularity insures the consequent impossibility of cohering in an absolute community with others. Nancy indeed insists on the danger of the absolute immanence or absolute coherence of community because he associates any such immanence with totalitarianism.[5] The finitude of singularity interrupts any such absolute immanence of community that would stifle freedom or difference.

But, for Nancy, the finite singularity of our 'ownmost' being-toward-death is shared with others in the following paradoxical sense. One shares, precisely, the impossibility of sharing in any traditional sense. We share that which we cannot share: our singular being-toward-death. Nancy expresses this paradoxical sense of sharing with the French term *partager* which can mean both to share and to divide, and has been rendered in English as a 'sharing-out' in an effort to capture each of these nuances. To be singular is always already to be-with other singular beings, or according to Nancy's well-known formulation, it is a 'being singular plural'. He writes, 'Being cannot be anything but being-with-one-another, circulating in the <u>with</u> and as the <u>with</u> of this singularly plural coexistence' (Nancy 2000, 3).

---

3   I refer to this as a strategic appropriation since, in a number of texts, Nancy suggests that Heidegger either did not recognize or did not fully develop the implications of the finitude of Dasein and its being with other Dasein for an ethics. See, for example, Nancy 2008.

4   See, for example, Heidegger 1962, 284–94.

5   Nancy writes: 'Yet it is precisely the immanence of man to man, or it *is* man, taken absolutely, considered as the immanent being par excellence, that constitutes the stumbling block to a thinking of community ... Consequently economic ties, technological operations, and political fusion (into a *body* or under a leader) represent or rather present, expose and realize this essence necessarily in themselves. Essence is set to work in them; through them, it becomes its own work. This is what we have called "totalitarianism." But it might better be called "immanentism," ... ' (Nancy 1991, 3). Further, 'if it [immanence] were to come about [it] would instantly suppress community, or communication, as such ... immanence, communal fusion, contains no other logic than that of the suicide of the community that is governed by it' (Nancy 1991, 12). Nancy equates such immanence with the totalitarian political culture of Nazi Germany.

In his text *The Inoperative Community*, Nancy cautions that such a 'being-with' 'is <u>not</u> a communion... nor even a communication as this is understood to exist between subjects. But these singular beings are themselves constituted by sharing, they are distributed and placed, or rather <u>spaced</u>, by the sharing that makes them <u>others</u>' (Nancy 1991, 25). These singular others communicate by 'not communing' (Nancy 1991, 25). The communication of sharing takes place in this 'very dislocation' (Nancy 1991, 25). Any community would be composed of singular existences that 'share' the exposure of their singularity in their being toward death. What is 'communicated' is nothing other than the exposition of singularity (Nancy 1991, 29). Community means that there is 'no singular being without another singular being' (Nancy 1991, 28).

However, it is crucial to recognize that, for Nancy, singularity is not the same as individuality.[6] He writes: singularity 'is not individuality; it is, each time, the punctuality of a "with" that establishes a certain origin of meaning and connects it to an infinity of other possible origins' (Nancy 2000, 85).[7] Each singular existence, then, in its ex-position, is a source from which the world can be created and recreated. He proposes that, as part of this being singular plural, we are exposed with language through an 'originary sharing of voices' that exposes not the voice or a meaning but 'the world and the being with all beings of the world' (Nancy 2000, 85). This exposure 'makes the world consist in its proper singular plurality' (Nancy 2000, 85). Nancy asserts that: '*The speaker speaks for the world, which means the speaker speaks to it, on behalf of it, and in order to make it a "world"*' (Nancy 2000, 3). This struggle for making or creating a world in its singularity and in finitely finite enactment of possible beginnings is, for Nancy, nothing less than the condition and definition of justice. We read in his recent text, *The Creation of the World* or *Globalization*:

> *To create the world* means: immediately, without delay, reopening each possible struggle for a world, that is, for what must form the contrary of a global injustice against the background of general equivalence. But this means to conduct this struggle precisely in the name of the fact that this *world* is coming out of nothing, that there is nothing before it and that it is without models, without principle and without given end, and that it is precisely *what* forms the justice and the meaning of a world (Nancy 2007, 54–5).

Each 'singularity' makes sense or creates a world in a finite way, in a sense that this making sense happens as a singular event. The finite event of sense making, which leaves room for other events of sense making, is infinite.[8] Nancy thematizes

---

6   Nancy equates the concept of the individual with immanence; an abstract form of atomism: 'it is another, and symmetrical figure of immanence' (Nancy 1991, 3). It is such an immanence that he contrasts with singularity.

7   For Nancy, the term 'punctuality' refers to the discontinuity of the moment, the 'each time' of a 'being-with' that is a singular and unique event of encounter, but as 'being-with' it is always already plural. He writes, '"Each time" implies *at one and the same time* the discreteness of "one by one" *and* the simultaneity of "each one"' (Nancy 2000, 65).

8   Nancy writes: 'To sense oneself making sense, and even more, to sense *oneself as the engenderment of sense* – this is without a doubt the ultimate stake of philosophy...' (Nancy 1997, 162).

a world which is always already under formation and concludes that justice would entail a world that is constituted by this inexhaustible creation of meaning.[9] The prevention of such a creation of meaning, of 'each possible struggle for a world', would be injustice. The work of what he calls 'mondialisation' or 'world-forming' is itself then, the work of justice.[10] The inexhaustible nature of this work does not mean that justice cannot be achieved but that each time it is achieved or enacted as a fact, it still remains to be created, or re-created. Perhaps Nancy's emphasis on beginnings, on the fact that each singular existence can inaugurate a world, is an advance on Kant's thinking of autonomy in the sense that the concept of a sovereign autonomy is rendered more dynamic, particular and more fragile. The 'undecidability', the singularity of each act and its openness to the next, is what preserves 'incompletion', insures 'inoperativity' and what resists totalitarian closure.

Moreover, Nancy's treatment of the finite singularity of the human being, a singularity that is at the same time constitutively ex-posed to and with others, opens to a nuanced thinking of sovereignty. The sovereignty articulated in Nancy's thought is a '*shared sovereignty* shared *between* Daseins', that is, 'between singular existences that are not subjects' (Nancy 1991, 25). With such a paradoxical treatment of sovereignty, Nancy seeks to approach the possibility of a non-substantial place from which another beginning, another creation, another world (or a world anew), could ensue.

In *The Creation of the World* or *Globalization*, Nancy advances upon his proposition in *The Sense of the World* that such a 'being-in-common' can make itself 'sovereign in a new way' Nancy 2007, 91). This 'new way' could be formulated as follows: a sovereignty is based on nothing: 'no finality, no order of production or subjection, whether it concerns the agent or the patient or the cause or the effect. Dependent on nothing, it is entirely delivered over to itself, insofar as precisely, the "itself" neither precedes nor founds it but is the *nothing*, the very thing from which it is suspended' (Nancy 2007, 103). Such a sovereignty, which he contrasts with a sovereignty of autonomy, domination and mastery, calls for a nuanced thinking of an 'anti-sovereignty', a kind of 'negative sovereignty or a 'sovereignty without sovereignty'. That negative sovereignty marks the withdrawal of substantiality and subjectivity. Such a thinking of non-sovereign sovereignty casts his use of the term 'ex-position' in a new light. The singular being is 'sovereign' in its ex-positioning. For Nancy this paradoxical sense of sovereignty plays or opens as the 'origin of the

---

9   Nancy writes: 'What we call a world is nothing more than this dispersal of origins, their dissipation, and their prodigality. Neither an absence of origin... nor an origin compacted in on itself... but the violent irruption of possible origins and of the equally multiple sense of sense. Sense: nothing but sculpted shards of sense' (Nancy 2006, 177).

10   This justice is a justice that is appropriate, a justice that is due. What is appropriate to sovereign singularities in their being? The ultimate measure of appropriateness is the exposure of singularities to one another. Nancy writes: 'But existence is nothing other than being exposed: expulsed from its simple self-identity and from its pure position, exposed to the event, to creation, thus to the outside, to exteriority, to multiplicity, to alterity and to alteration. (In a sense, certainly, this is nothing other than being exposed to being itself, to its own "being" and also consequently, being exposed as being: exposition as the essence of being)' (Nancy 2007, 110).

world', an origin that occurs 'at each moment of the world. It is the each time of Being and its realm is the Being-with. The origin is for and by way of the singular plural of every possible origin' (Nancy 2000, 83). Nancy's articulation of a being-with as a singular ex-position is significant in the context of this paper as a challenge to the sovereign autonomy of the Kantian ethical subject.[11]

I would like to speculate further about the ethical implications of such an exposure, or of an ex-positioning, and of such a paradoxical non-sovereign sovereignty, by drawing on the work of Emmanuel Levinas. For Levinas as well, human beings are singular and irreducible to a whole or to a same. Each singular being that we face remains an irreducible alterity. More importantly, this irreducible alterity demands an ethical response. It is intrinsic to Levinas's thought that we respond to the Other; respond to the face (*le visage*), that is, a singular face. In a 1981 interview (with Richard Kearney), Levinas said that the approach to the face is the most basic mode of responsibility. The face is the other who asks me not to let him or her die alone (Kearney 1995, 189). This face, Levinas writes, speaks (*le visage parle*) (Levinas 1985, 82). The notion of 'speaking' bears particular mention in Levinas's work because he raises a distinction between 'the saying' (*le dire*), and 'the said' (*le dit*). 'Saying' is an event that conveys something such that I respond. Levinas distinguishes this from the predicate content of the said, a statement. In the 1981 interview Levinas stated, 'Saying is ethical sincerity insofar as it is exposition' (Kearney 1995, 193). One could speculate that the event-like exposition of the saying is free of the linguistic content of the statement and as such it allows for a plurality of voices, each one containing a demand for a response. The 'saying' entails an excess that exceeds the semantic or linguistic content of the statement. The excess lies in the very fact of the address of the saying; an address that raises the necessity of response and recognition. For Levinas, the saying means speaking to the other and for the other, it brings about an ethical proximity.

For Levinas this responsibility for the address of the other is the fundamental structure of subjectivity. In his 1968 essay *On Substitution*, he asserts that, 'To be a "self" is to be responsible without having done anything' (Levinas 1996, 94). I am responsible for responsibility itself. We must substitute ourselves for the other and expiate for their transgressions. Our response to the face of the other, however, can never be completely satisfied. The call is infinite. This is a constitutive insufficiency that must be understood in a positive sense. Levinas's ethical thought offers, in this respect, a resource for the interruption of the dehumanization and violence of our age. For Levinas the responsibility to the other, the response to the face of the other, is a significantly non-reciprocal relation. This non-reciprocity begins to intimate the counter-intuitive and seemingly impossible nature of his thought. Levinas is conscious of the radical nature of his thought and of the following formulation:

---

11   In its displacing ex-position, singularity is neither sovereign in the Kantian sense of autonomy nor sovereign in the sense formulated by Carl Schmitt, who claimed that the sovereign 'is he who decides on the exception' (Schmitt 1985, 1). In Schmitt's state of exception the sovereign is above the law. But for Nancy, the non-sovereign sovereignty, conceived in terms of singularity, is exposed both in the sense of being desubstantified and exposed in the sense of 'being with' or plural.

'I employ this extreme formulation. The face orders and ordains me (to serve it)' (Levinas 1985, 97).

What sort of ethical framework could be woven from the work of Nancy and Levinas? With Nancy we have the inoperative community with the exposure of each to all, an inoperative community that recognizes a fundamentally constitutional limit at the heart of its composition. Further, for Nancy, we have the world of singular plural beginnings, each beginning a fact, each beginning a creation of a world. This process is impossible in the sense that it is never complete but always justice in act. With Levinas the face of the other makes an impossible demand. We substitute for the other in a self-effacing expiation. Would such an ethics drawing upon singularity and alterity be an impossible ethics? But could it be that, after Kant and after the Universal Declaration, an impossible ethics – not abstract and ideal, but grounded in singularity and alterity – is precisely what is needed for our time, which in some respects, with genocide and ethnic cleansing, is an impossible time: an impossible ethics for impossible times?

But how would one participate in such an inoperative community comprised of the exposition of each singularity; how would one respond to the impossible demand of the other, and how is one to enact a world? Is such a framework just as theoretical and inaccessible as that of Kant's notion of sovereign self-worth? It is in this context that I would like to identify a genre of literature that has emerged from recent catastrophic events. The texts that I will address provide a possible model for thinking of the exposition and exposure of singularity, for responding to the suffering of the other, and for the creation of the world. Some of the most important texts about the war in Bosnia-Herzegovina, for example, were already published in 1994 and are now either out of print or difficult to obtain. It may be unique to our time that so many accounts of dehumanization and catastrophic violence, from different perspectives and in different styles, have been published and disseminated so quickly. Of course the violence and suffering outpaces the reports, as in the case of Rwanda, where as many as 800,000 were slaughtered in one hundred days, roughly 8,000 per day. It is said that this was at a faster rate than was achieved at Auschwitz (Gourevitch 1998, 3). In other words, as quickly as it comes, the literature comes too late. The publications are not immediately capable of stopping the violence but, insofar as they expose the suffering of the other, they might slow the violence. However, it was too late when Michael Sells wrote that the Yugoslav Army had captured Vukovar and handed over the inhabitants in the hospital to the Chetnik irregulars for interrogation. A mass grave was found at the nearby village of Ovcara (Sells 1998, 185).

While the literature is generally 'too late', in many other crucial respects, the work continues to be indispensable. Comprehensive texts by Michael Sells and Ed Vulliamy, for example, provide important historical, geographical, cultural, linguistic and other forms of information (Vulliamy 1994). The texts weave a historical context in which the people of the region live. In the face of ignorance and dehumanization, the places and the experiences of history are re-humanized. There are details about specific events and the human beings who suffered, endured or perished. There are reports about the destruction of buildings, the shelling of markets and playgrounds, the murder of intellectuals and the effacement of cultural memories and traditions.

Sells asserts that the Serb artillery systematically targeted major libraries, manuscript collections, museums and other cultural institutions for destruction (Sells 1993, 3). When armies were able to get closer the buildings were dynamited. 'In many cases,' Sells writes, 'the mosques have been ploughed over and turned into parking lots or parks; every evidence of their existence has been effaced. Graveyards, birth records, work records and other traces of the Bosnian Muslim people have been eradicated' (Sells 1998, 3).

Vulliamy was one of the first journalists to discover the concentration camps at Omarska and Trnopolje. Following the first rumours of mass killings and the conditions in such camps, he managed to convince Serbian authorities to allow him to visit the sites. In spite of restricted access and close supervision at Omarska, Vulliamy was able to see and report on groups of men:

> ...their heads newly shaven, their clothes baggy over their skeletal bodies. Some are barely able to move ... The men are at various stages of human decay and affliction; the bones of their elbows and wrists protrude like pieces of jagged stone from the pencil thin stalks to which their arms have been reduced. The skin is putrified, the complexions of their faces have been corroded. These humans are alive but decomposed, debased, degraded, and utterly subservient ... (Vulliamy 1994, 102).

Later that day at Trnopolje, Vulliamy encountered another startling sight: thousands of men, women and children surrounded by barbed wire fencing. He writes, 'The men were stripped to the waist, and among them was the young man with the famished torso and xylophone rib-cage who that day became the symbol of the war: Fikret Alic ... Fikret had literally been starved into a dismal, malnourished condition in which we found him, after fifty-two days in Kereterm' (Vulliamy 1994, 104–5).

Vulliamy's text provides remarkable details about both the Serbian guards and the Muslim prisoners behind the wire. The reports from Omarska and Trnopolje brought international outrage and led to further investigations that revealed Omarska, for example, to have been a place of 'savage killing, torture, humiliation, and barbarous cruelty' (Vulliamy 1994, 108).

Chuck Sudetic's book, *Blood and Vengeance: One Family's Story of the War in Bosnia*, is a text that follows a particular family, the Celiks, who endured the Srebrenica siege and massacre that took the lives of more than 8,000 Bosnian Muslims. The book provides remarkably personal details of the Celik family and the community, including the marriage and marriage feast of Huso and Hiba Celik (Sudetic 1999, 50–51). We partake of family travels and travails against the backdrop of the gathering storm. We accompany them on their perilous arrival in Srebrenica on September 19 1992. We are given an intimate glimpse of the Celik family taking shelter in a cramped basement on a night when the shells were falling every two minutes; little Edin, born in 1994, had a stuffy nose and was romping around and getting on everyone's nerves, Mirza, born in 1990, was running a fever and refusing to eat. The adults were trying to console them whilst dreading the days ahead. (Sudetic 1999, 270).[12]

---

12   In addition to the story of the Celiks, we learn of the beating of Muslim men in Bratunac, including the humiliation, beating and murder of Mustafa Mujkanovic (Sudetic 1999, 152–53).

As the Bosnian Serb Army closed in on Srebrenica the residents tried to flee. Men made their way through the woods through shelling and gunfire. In *Srebrenica: Record of a War Crime*, Jan Willem Honig and Norbert Both tell of the fate of a thousand of the men captured and herded to a soccer field in Nova Kasaba:

> Many more of the men from Srebrenica never even made it beyond Nova Kasaba. The Serbs had captured them in the hundreds... They were assembled on the football ground just north of Nova Kasaba. On Thursday, Dutch soldiers spotted an estimated 1,000 squatting on the football pitch (Both and Honig 1997, 59).

A few days later an American U-2 spy plane detected that the field was empty 'but that a nearby field had changed in appearance: it showed signs of recent digging and experts identified what they believed to be three mass graves' (Both and Honig 1997, 59).

In addition to the accounts of the systematic murder of men and boys, there are unbearable accounts of the violence against women during the war in Bosnia, that Sells refers to as 'Gynocide', 'a deliberate attack on women as child-bearers', a strategy of dehumanization and brutalization through organized 'rape centres' (Sells 1998, 21). Vulliamy provides further accounts of this violence against women with names and extensive testimony reporting that 20,000 women had suffered sexual violation (Vulliamy 1994, 195–6). He details organized camps such as Kod Sonje, a motel at Vogosca outside of Sarajevo (Vulliamy 1994, 199).

The range of books that have been published are too numerous to discuss in the context of this paper. However, one other book bears mention in order to clarify the diversity and value of the genre: Clea Koff's *The Bone Woman*. Koff is a forensic anthropologist who worked for 'Physicians for Human Rights', a Boston-based non-governmental organisation that assembled a team of forensic experts to investigate mass graves for the International Criminal Tribunal on Rwanda (ICTR) and the International Criminal Tribunal for the former Yugoslavia (ICTY). Koff's goal was to end human rights abuses by making the 'bones talk' in order to bring the murderers to justice (Koff 2004, 7). Koff's book provides us with a voice that is exemplary of this genre. It is not that of the reporter or analyst, but a very personal voice. The book offers a journal-like account of the exhumation and identification of bones in Kigali, Rwanda, Cerska, Bosnia and Ovcara, Croatia. Koff speaks of the 'power of human remains' (Koff 2004, 177). We learn intimate details about the land, the roads and the mines. We gain a sense of what it is like to arrive in a field, on a hillside that is a mass grave before the exhumation and markings of graves, identification of bullet holes, and the sound of shovels. (Koff 2004, 127–8) We learn something about the victims. In addition, we learn something of the catastrophe. The majority of the dead at Srebrenica were men, unlike the victims in Rwanda, which meant that the surviving women could help with the identification (Koff 2004, 120). We learn of the details of the remains at Ovcara. Allegedly marched to their death from the hospital, some are in hospital garb and their medical records assist in the identification of the bodies (some with casts on their limbs). One man is found buried with x-rays that he tucked in his bathrobe (Koff 2004, 180). Finally, we read of her work in Kosovo:

Then I picked it up and realised it wasn't a bone fragment loose from the trauma; in fact, it was an intact distal epiphyseal cap of the tibia. It had not even begun to fuse with the rest of the tibia, and the superior surface of the epiphysis was billowy with youth. The skeleton was that of a young person (Koff 2004, 226).

Koff had found a child. 'The boy in my grave had a pocket full of marbles, and that told me more about his life than almost anything else could' (Koff 2004, 227).

Perhaps such books respond to singularity as they give voice to the suffering of the other. To some extent they take responsibility for the other and they give the other a voice to which we must respond. By offering this responsibility for the other, perhaps the writers, journalists and intellectuals, engage in what Levinas called 'the authentic relation' (Kearney 1995, 82). The fact that the representation of the loss and the suffering can restore the voice and the humanity to those who have suffered and died recalls Levinas's comment that the other 'asks me not to let him or her die alone' (Kearney 1995, 189).

Both Nancy, with the notion of singularity and ex-position, and Levinas, with his re-articulation of the self that substitutes itself for the other, problematize the egoic conception of the self as an autonomous, isolated or discrete phenomenon. For Levinas, for example, the responsibility for the other occurs in a passion of obsession and passivity, a passion that exceeds consciousness and the identity of the self (Levinas 1996, 82). He writes that the obsession 'strips the Ego of its self-conceit' (Levinas 1996, 88). To be a self is to be responsible for the other and to be delivered over to this responsibility, to be hostage to this responsibility.

The texts cited here, texts that bear witness to the singularity of suffering of the other, would also seem to problematize the position of the self. In many cases the act of bearing witness carried a traumatic personal cost for the authors. Engaged in this 'authentic relation' of bearing witness, the authors were ex-posed from and de-centred from their personal egos or selves. They write openly of the psychological and physical traumas they endured. This trauma becomes part of 'the authentic relation', part of what renders it ethical. Their egos are undone by the act of bearing witness. We are reminded of Levinas' statement in *Otherwise than Being* that, 'One is exposed to the other as a skin is exposed to what wounds it, as a cheek offered to one who strikes it' (Levinas 1998, 49, trans. modified). Anthony Loyd, a photojournalist and reporter in Bosnia, reported some of the worst atrocities of the war and his stories later guided the war crimes investigations. Loyd maintained his composure when on assignment but on return to England he lapsed into alcohol and drug abuse and was unable to sleep. He reports that his own face was ravaged from bearing witness to the suffering. Looking in the mirror he writes, 'The face that looked back at me was haunted and furtive' (Loyd 1999, 262). Bill Carter, an aid worker in Sarajevo during the siege, writes of dodging sniper bullets and mortar shells and of severe weight loss, due to the scarcity of food and water, as well as the stress. Carter writes of the way the stress, fear and adrenalin began to rot the flesh and transform the features: 'premature wrinkles show up and the hair begins to fall out. Teeth rot, skin turns grey and sullen' (Carter 2003, 169). Koff, for example, after hours at exhumation sites and hours in the morgue, writes of nervous exhaustion, nightmares and loss of a sense of self in letters to her family, reporting that she felt 'out of touch, homesick, and cynical about too many things' (Koff 2004, 149–150). Koff wrote in her journal of having 'lost track of who I used to be, because I could barely remember the things I used to like' (Koff 2004, 149–150). A sign of her fragile state, a state that she would normally deny or repress, was that she would burst into tears at the sound of her brother's voice on the phone (Koff 2004, 149–150).

Both in their singularity of style and content, and as a genre, as well as the cost of bearing witness that wears on their flesh, these texts enact an ethos that would be preliminary to any ethics of norms. The authors have attempted to respond to the suffering of the other, to expiate for their pain. They and their texts speak the names and places of those who suffered the violence and who were unable to speak for themselves. In the context of Jean-Luc Nancy's *The Creation of the World* or *Globalization*, the acts of literature discussed here re-humanize those who have been dehumanized and restore, in some sense, worlds that war criminals attempted to erase. In this respect we recall Nancy's assertion that, 'the speaker speaks for the world, which means the speaker speaks to it, on behalf of it, and in order to make it a "world"' (Nancy 2000, 3). I suggest that as these texts respond to the singularity of the suffering of the other, they undertake the task of justice. As multiple restorations and beginnings of worlds, each of the texts is, each time, an act of justice, a fact of justice.

References

Both, N. and Honig, J.W. (1997), *Srebrenica: Record of a War Crime* (New York: Penguin Books).

Carter, B. (2003), *Fools Rush In* (New York: Wenner Books).

Gourevitch, P. (1998), *We Wish To Inform You That Tomorrow We Will Be Killed With Our Families: Stories from Rwanda* (New York: Picador).

Heidegger, M. (1962), *Being and Time*, Macquarrie, J. and Robinson, E. (trans.) (New York: Harper and Row).

Kant, I. (1964), *Groundwork of the Metaphysic of Morals*, Paton, H.J (trans.) (New York: Harper and Row).

Kearney, R. (ed.) (1995), *States of Mind: Dialogues with Contemporary Thinkers* (New York: University Press).

Koff, C. (2004), *The Bone Woman: A Forensic Anthropologist's Search for Truth in the Mass graves of Rwanda, Bosnia, Croatia, and Kosovo* (New York: Random House).

Levinas, E. (1985), *Ethics and Infinity*, Cohen, R. (trans.) (Pittsburgh: Duquesne University Press).

Levinas, E. (1996), 'On Substitution' in Peperzak, A. et al. (eds), *Emmanuel Levinas: Basic Philosophical Writings* (Bloomington: Indiana University Press).

Levinas, E. (1998), *Otherwise Than Being: Or Beyond Essence* (Pittsburgh: Duquesne University Press).

Loyd, A. (1999), *My War Gone By, I Miss It So* (New York: Penguin Books).

Nancy, J.-L. (1991), *The Inoperative Community*, Connor, P. (trans.) (Minneapolis: University of Minnesota Press).

Nancy, J.-L. (1997), *The Sense of the World*, Librett, J.S. (trans.) (Minneapolis: University of Minnesota Press).

Nancy, J.-L. (2000), *Being Singular Plural*, Richardson, R. and O'Byrne, A. (trans.) (Stanford: Stanford University Press).

Nancy, J.-L. (2006), *Multiple Arts: Muses II*, Sparks, S. (trans.) (Stanford, CA: Stanford University Press).

Nancy, J.-L. (2007), *The Creation of the World* or *Globalization*, Raffoul, F. and Pettigrew, D. (trans.) (Albany: The State University of New York Press).

Nancy, J.-L. (2008), 'The Being-With of the Being-There' Raffoul, F. and Pettigrew, D. (trans.) in Raffoul, F. and Nelson, E.S. (eds), *Rethinking Facticity* (Albany: State University of New York Press).

Schmitt, C. (1985), *Political Theology: Four Chapters on the Concept of Sovereignty*, Schwab, G. (trans.) (Cambridge: MIT Press).

Sells, M. (1998), *The Bridge Betrayed: Religion and Genocide in Bosnia* (Berkeley: University of California Press).

Sudetic, C. (1999), *Blood and Vengeance: One Family's Story of the War in Bosnia* (New York: Penguin Books).

Universal Declaration for Human Rights (Office of the United Nations High Commissioner for Human Rights) <http://www.unhchr.ch/udhr/lang/eng.htm.>

Vulliamy, E. (1994), *Seasons in Hell: Understanding Bosnia's War* (New York: St. Martin's Press).

Chapter 3

Conflict Resolution and Reconciliation of Peoples

Alphonso Lingis

Great barbarous empires, world wars massacring millions of people, genocides, and today again wars that flare up every year – we might well think that our capacity to get along with one another is derisible indeed. Today the proclaimed war on terror depicts groups of humanity as mad dogs bent on annihilating civilian populations with no realistic benefits to be gained, and societies as a multiplicity of nations each pursuing its own interest and defence. Terrorists are not to be negotiated with; they must be hunted down and exterminated.

The human species has evolved languages, tool-making abilities and social organization. Should we not assume that the human species has also evolved the capacity to resolve conflict? The fact that, despite all our sanguinary history, we are still around testifies that natural evolution has produced in us a lot of conflict resolution capacity. It is somehow natural that we get along with those of our own kind. Hornets get along with hornets, deer get along with deer, even predator species get along: cheetahs do not prey on other cheetahs, hawks do not prey on their own kind. It is not our nature that man be a wolf to man.

Reason and Justice in Conflict Resolution

Interests involve particular situations, goals and emotional or passionate commitments; they thus produce conflicts. According to our dominant discourse, disputes where conflicting interests are at stake can be resolved by reason, not by the confrontation of emotions. Indeed the mind is taken to be a general-purpose problem solving apparatus. Logic diagrams the forms of valid reasoning.

Modern game theory is the dominant model now used in analyses of conflict resolution. Once the interests and advantages of each player are identified, reasoning can map out all possible moves and obstacles. Part of the calculation of advantage is calculation of cost: one has to calculate what sacrifices to make to acquire what advantages. In a game one makes changes and exchanges: game theory is an economic model of social interaction.

Resolution becomes possible when the players recognize that it is in each one's interest that the conflict ends. Individuals must sacrifice their own interests and advantages for the general interest and advantage of cessation of conflict. This requires that each one disengage his emotional or passionate commitment to the interests and advantages he has pursued hitherto.

Conflict resolution requires that each partner apply reason to the problem, and that reason employ the same logical paradigms and rules. The rational faculty is taken to be universal and unchanging – to be ready-made – rather than a product of natural evolution.

But contemporary cognitive psychology and neuroscience conceive the mind to be composed of a diversity of modular capacities. Attention, perception, long and short term memory, judgement, different kinds of appraisal and reasoning, decision and execution are so many diverse capacities of the mind. Reasoning – assemblage and appraisal of evidence, derivation of conclusions – means different things when it is a matter of mathematics, physics, biology, history, literary criticism, military strategy or automobile mechanics. The mind has many different problem solving mechanisms. Do we not then need to study the kind of reason involved in resolving conflicts among humans as a distinct capacity that is the result of evolution? Emotions are a result of natural evolution, promoting fitness and survival. They are essentially involved in problem solving. Emotions sustain attention. Emotions identify problems and preferences and charge them with meaning. Emotions motivate, direct and accelerate strategic reasoning. Emotions help store and retrieve memories (Long and Brecke 2003, 124).

Justice is fundamental to human society: all human interactions and contracts – and all conflict resolution – invoke the sense of justice. Our dominant concept of 'distributive justice' focuses on individuals or individual parties, and on determining the identities, roles and resources of each. Doing justice involves compensating individuals or individual parties for unjust losses. We can call this 'retributive justice'. Much of the work of justice consists of determining sentences and compensations. The revival of capital punishment in the United States invokes the notion that justice should not only protect society from the wrongdoer and undertake to reform him or her, but also compensate the victim – a death for a death. In our market societies there is a tendency to regard compensation in financial terms. In recent litigation in the United States, large numbers of persons who alleged sexual misconduct on the part of clergy, often years ago in their adolescence, are demanding monetary compensation.

In our dominant discourse, justice is envisioned as a transcendent and universal value. As such it is akin to reason itself, and reason is taken to be internal to justice, such that justice is worked out through the rational calculation of interests, advantages, choices and costs. The work of justice is taken to be dispassionate, requiring a suspension of emotional forces. The concept or ideal of justice then acquires some of the integral and unchanging character of reason: as if it were also ready-made, and not a product of natural evolution.

But is not the sense of justice intrinsically bound to anger? Anger is a force that focuses attention, evaluates and demarcates the limit of the unacceptable, the intolerable. Are not other emotions inevitably involved: fear of being pushed aside or oppressed or of being blocked from the path of one's work and identity; sadness before a situation that is obstructed; joy when not only one's own identity and work are affirmed, but also when the general environment promotes the identity and work of one's neighbours?

Conflict Resolution as Restorative Justice

I would like to introduce a conception of problem solving reason that is integrated with emotion, and a conception of justice that is different from both distributive and retributive justice – the work of justice practised as compensation for losses incurred or harms suffered. To do so, I will invoke an incident from long ago that first made it clear to me.

I live with a number of birds and occasionally I need a male or female partner for a bird I have. In this instance I needed a male Moluccan cockatoo. This was back when it was possible to import birds. I was spending a summer in Indonesia, and came upon, in the Pasar Burung of Jakarta, an old man who spoke English and helped me locate the bird I wanted. I gave him $300 to pay the owner for the bird, and another $300 to pay for the expenses of veterinary certification, export license and shipping that the old man said he would handle. Shortly after, I left the country, realizing that he could well just keep the money, but deciding to trust him. In fact I never received the bird and was neither especially surprised nor upset.

By chance, I passed through Indonesia the next year, and still needing a male Moluccan cockatoo, returned to the Pasar Burung. I was surprised to immediately run into the same man. He was visibly agitated upon seeing me and proposed that we go to the police post. He must have thought I might throttle him. He spoke, in Indonesian, to the police captain, who then invited me to sit down and sent an officer for tea and snacks. Understanding that this was etiquette in Indonesia, and that it would be rude to bluntly state my business, I took a seat. The captain sat down in a wicker armchair next to me and asked what parts of Indonesia I would be visiting, from time to time describing curious places he knew of. Other police officers came, sat down, had tea, chatted and left. Hours passed and the conversation wandered. Eventually, the police captain asked what I would like him to do with the man who had failed to send the bird. I hastened to say that I had no desire to press charges and see him imprisoned. The captain wondered if it would be agreeable to me to pay once again for the bird and the shipping costs, if the man would locate the bird I wanted. Since I still wanted a male Moluccan cockatoo, very hard to locate in Java, I agreed. We all shook hands amicably and the police captain invited us to return two days later. I walked away thinking how unsatisfactory this would have been in terms of the conception of justice dominant in my society. In my country a police captain would have required of me proof that I had indeed paid the old man $600, and had not received the bird. He would have then required of the old man either that he now supply me a bird (but the old man does not have any birds), or return my money (which the old man had long ago spent on his needs and those of his family). Failing both, the old man would have been arrested. And all that would have been settled expeditiously. Here I was going to have to pay again $600 for the bird I had already paid for.

But the police captain in the Pasar Burung had seen the situation differently. Someone had a grievance against someone in his community. The problem was not simply to compensate the aggrieved party, but to heal the ill feeling. Had he simply required of the old man either a bird or the $600, he would have left the old man with bitterness in his heart. Imprisoning the old man could not reform him, and would spread the ill feeling in the community. Asking instead the old man to locate and ship the bird for me, he extended his trust to him, addressing him not as a delinquent but rather as a responsible member of the community. The police captain was also concerned that I not part with contempt for the old man and ill feeling against the community he represented. He had spoken with me long enough to understand that as a foreigner rich enough to come all the way to Indonesia twice, and to have the money to buy an expensive bird, acquiring the bird I had so long wanted would make me forget the loss of $600. I would leave Indonesia pleased that Indonesian justice takes care of foreign visitors.

Can we say that a process of forgiveness was worked out? Forgiveness involves re-framing the other such that one continues to be aware of him as responsible for a misdeed, but in that very sense of the other as a responsible agent, one sees more deeply into his complex motivations, dilemmas and needs: one sees an agent capable of different kinds of actions.

Forgiveness involves a change of heart in oneself: from anger, bitterness and rancour to empathy. From a sense of sadness and fear, a sense of damage to one's self-esteem – from feeling like a victim and a fool – to self-composure and strength. Forgiveness can be difficult because it involves a veritable transformation: one no longer sees oneself simply as a victim and becomes aware of a richer and more complex identity. Forgiveness means forgoing the option of revenge, however natural, desirable or justifiable, and it breaks with the cycle of injury and counter-injury. This is accomplished with some ritual act, which pledges a continued but different relationship between the two parties. A handshake and a smile before witnesses pledges an intention not to simply avoid one another but to maintain a civil relationship and undertake some new actions together (Long and Brecke 2003, 30).

Two days later I returned at nine in the morning to the police station. The police captain again welcomed me cordially and had tea and snacks brought. Again conversation. Again other police officers joined us and left. The morning passed. There was no sign of the old man. The captain invited me to join him and his family for a trip to the mountains over the weekend.

No doubt the old man did not come because he had not succeeded in finding a male Moluccan cockatoo. The policeman did not require that the old man come and know shame for having failed to make good on his promise, for he believed the old man had tried to do so. While the initial solution devised by the police captain had failed, he did not step back from what he saw as his responsibility: now he would personally undertake to heal the grievance. Unable to provide a male Moluccan cockatoo, he would offer me an opportunity – rare for a foreign visitor – to spend a weekend with a family, gain insight into the local culture, and to share with them a deeper understanding of foreigners. When I left Indonesia three months later it was this encounter that remained the deepest and most cherished memory of that trip.

Let us call the police captain's conception of justice 'restorative justice'.

Civil Wars and Reconciliation

The twentieth century saw 430 violent conflicts – civil wars, bloody coups, massacres, democides, riots – in 109 countries. Most of these ended with military defeat and police repression of the insurgents – although the conflicts repeatedly flared up again. William J. Long and Peter Brecke, in their important book *War and Reconciliation*, examine eleven cases of violent and lethal civil conflict that ended with a process of reconciliation (see also: Stedman 2001 in Crocker et al., 737–52). These are the civil wars in Columbia, North Yemen, twice in Chad, Argentina, Uruguay, Chile, El Salvador, Mozambique, South Africa, and Honduras. After reconciliation events, seven of these countries did not experience a return to violent conflict.

Settlement of conflicts by negotiation based on rational choices, the calculation of advantages and costs, is intrinsically difficult in civil wars because each side becomes vulnerable if it lays down its weapons. There is no way to structure an agreement such that it would at worst allow each side to return to the status quo ante should one side decide to cheat. Long and Brecke find that when civil conflicts have come to an end, it was through a process of reconciliation.

Common to the cases of successful reconciliation are:

1. A process of establishing truth: The parties to the conflict must recognize shame and anger and acknowledge the injustice, injury, harm, material and personal destruction that gave rise to these emotions and brought about the violent conflict, and acknowledge the atrocities committed during the conflict. Truth telling entails substantial risks – it may create greater resentment among the parties that had waged civil conflict. The military, judiciary or guerrillas may resort to violence to prevent certain facts from becoming public knowledge (Haynes 1996, 19–30).
2. A redefinition of the identity of the former belligerents: The belligerents must transcend seeing themselves as victims and the opposing party as enemies. Those on one side must cease identifying themselves as representatives of law and order, indeed of civilization itself, and those on the other as subversives and terrorists (O'Donnell and Schmitter 1995, in Kritz, 57–132). The belligerents must acquire new identities as citizens with positive contributions to make to the social order – as social partners. They must begin to interact with mutual respect, realized in concrete social interaction.
3. A call for a new relationship marked by a public and ritualized reconciliation event: The reconciliation event must itself be novel, an invention, displaying a break with the past. Peace accords are signed and embraces exchanged by heads of formerly belligerent groups, legislatures pass solemn resolutions, statues and monuments to the tragedy are erected, textbooks are rewritten (Schmitter 1995 in Kritz 1995, 72). Former marginalized belligerents may be brought into the political process or assigned public funds for social and economic integration. The role of political parties may be determined in new ways. The military may be depoliticized and its impunity removed. Judicial and political reform may be enacted. Institutionalized civilian control over the police and the armed forces may be legislated .

4. A willingness to forgo revenge: There must be a will on both sides to break the cycle of an eye for an eye, a tooth for a tooth. Instead, an impartial tribunal must undertake a partial redressing of wrongs – restoration of the identity and good name of those tortured and disappeared, material compensation for destructions, and exclusion or punishment of perpetrators of war crimes. This must not be undertaken according to the abstract and idealized notion of justice conceived as universal retributive justice that is realized through sanctions and compensation for wrongs suffered. There is no justice in this sense, for three reasons. First, the deaths of so many cannot be compensated for and the museums looted and libraries destroyed cannot simply be replaced. Homes and farms ravaged will generally not be able to be compensated for with the resources of the society now at peace. Second, a process of trying those guilty of war crimes can find only artificial and arbitrary limits: a majority of the population may well have been complicit in the crimes carried out – one of the parties may have long profited from the economic oppression of the other – and the judiciary may have been implicated in abuses and therefore be incapable of impartiality. Third, the process of identifying and bringing to trial those responsible for war crimes and civil war itself may produce a new polarization of the population; those being prosecuted may regroup to defend themselves and even attain legal or violent control of the government (Siegel 1998, 431–54).

Justice may be enacted not through judicial prosecution and incarceration, but through loss of impunity, reputation, moral standing, office or privileges (Siegel 1998). Sometimes partial or full amnesty may be decreed as expedient in view of the risks of judicial prosecution. But it may well also represent an expression of mercy and forgiveness on the part of those who have suffered. Friedrich Nietzsche pointed out that it frequently happens in human history that the victor suddenly turns magnanimous toward the vanquished. He also spoke of the impulse to transcend justice toward mercy on the part of institutions, societies and states: he called it a 'royal prerogative', that of the lion who says: 'What are my parasites to me? May they live and prosper: I am strong enough for that!' But does not the one who has been harmed also become strong through forgiveness? How often in civil disputes does someone who has suffered harm refuse to demand punishment and compensation: feeling himself or herself thereby diminished and brought down to the same level as the one who had done harm to him or her. Forgive and forget: the one who practises it shakes himself free of rancour and turns to the future innocent and strong. Does not a judiciary that requires that all grievances be adjudicated deny the right of citizens to be merciful? The justice at work in reconciliation then is not distributive and retributive, but restorative justice.

Interstate War and Reconciliation

Long and Brecke also examine 53 cases of war between two nations in the course of the last 50 years (Long and Brecke 2003, 163–8). Of the 21 that ended with a negotiated cessation of war and the engagement of more pacific relations, they selected eight that have been extensively studied. These were the conflicts between the Soviet Union and West Germany, between India and China, Egypt and Israel, Vietnam and China, West Germany and Poland, Great Britain and Argentina, Cambodia and Vietnam, and El Salvador and Honduras. Of these eight, three were followed by subsequent outbreaks of armed conflict. Negotiation aimed at an end of the war can be the last resort of belligerents driven by fear, revulsion, loss of control or simple exhaustion. Resolution of these conflicts followed much more closely the rational choice and game theory model. When wars become manifestly too costly to continue, effort at cessation of hostility and negotiated resolution of the conflict over borders, populations or resources becomes possible.

However, negotiations can begin only when one or both parties signal a commitment to a resolution of the issues in dispute. Signals of a will to resolve the conflict are most likely to break conflict patterns when they are dramatic and unexpected. Making non-contingent and irrevocable offers are more likely to initiate negotiated settlement, for example, when there is a unilateral withdrawal that the other country can take advantage of. These signals sent forth by leaders of the belligerent countries are effective when they are militarily or politically costly: costly signals are more reliable determinants of a leader's true intentions. The leaders risk their prestige and power in a public and irrevocable act.

Direct dialogue between senior representatives of the warring countries begins negotiations to establish a cease-fire, establish permanent borders, withdraw troops and end hostile military manoeuvres. Peace treaties are signed and diplomatic relations established. The reconciliation event is enacted before domestic and international audiences and is potentially exploitable by one or even both belligerent parties. Still, this vulnerability is not as extensive as in civil conflicts, where once the insurgents lay down their arms, there is no way to return to the status quo ante should one side decide to cheat. However, the settlement of interstate conflicts has typically not involved a process of establishing the truth. Leaders are unwilling to risk systematic investigations or determinations of culpability for wartime activities. There has been no independent agency set up to establish truth after interstate wars: no independent agency set up to investigate the effects of agent orange on childbirths in Vietnam or the effects of defoliants on the ecology of that land.

Further, in the termination of interstate wars, there are inadequate mechanisms for the redefinition of national identities. The belligerents do not redefine their relationship to one another in new or amended constitutions or construct new roles for themselves in international institutions.

Finally, there are inadequate mechanisms to realize limited justice, the isolation of those responsible and the restoration of the identities and good name of the victims. There has been no agency set up to identify the civilians buried in mass graves after the US bombing of Panama, nor of the estimated 250,000 Iraqis killed in the bombing of the first Gulf War.

Thus we can say that interstate wars typically come to an end through negotiation, and mutually beneficial economic and political relations may follow, without there being a reconciliation of peoples. In fact, only nations with contiguous boundaries with another nation even attempt to reconcile.

Yet from the beginning of empires, all nations in some sense share the same space – that of the continent and the planet. Today even nations that are remote from one another are allied for their defence with other nations whose borders touch possibly belligerent nations and alliances. Today the multiplicity of nations is beginning to share some of the features of individual nations – common rules and common institutions. In the measure that they do, an international society is being constituted. Some of the negotiated settlements of conflicts between nations have issued into the beginnings of what we have identified as the reconciliation process that ends civil wars.

The War on Terror and Reconciliation

Terrorist acts are differentiated from acts of war and from criminal acts in that they are acts of violence unleashed upon populations in view of political goals in the absence or inadequacy of means to directly decimate the opposing armed forces. The agents of terrorism can be nations, as in the German blitz on London, the British firebombing of Dresden and the American thermonuclear destruction of Hiroshima and Nagasaki. They can be nationalist groups opposed to foreign occupation, such as the IRA in Northern Ireland or ETA in Basque country, the French *maquis* during the Second World War, and the Iraqi resistance to the Anglo-American occupation. They can be groups fighting a national social order judged unjust, such as the anarchists and revolutionaries fighting the Tsarist regime at the end of the nineteenth century, leftist commandos in Italy, Germany, Belgium, and France in the 1970s, and Islamist groups today in Saudi Arabia and Algeria. They can also be groups united by religious convictions, such as the Klu Klux Klan and certain militia groups in the United States.

In the First World War, 90 percent of the killed and wounded were soldiers: in the Second World War, but 40 percent. In the wars of the last decade, 90 percent of the killed and wounded have been civilians. In today's civil and guerrilla wars, the civilian population is the principal strategic target. When a hyper-power launches military initiatives in which not one of its own soldiers is in principle to be killed, then the civilian population is likewise the real target. If foot soldiers are not to be risked during an invasion, then the smart military technology must not simply exterminate the enemy troops but destroy the civilian will to resist, inducing them to repudiate their leaders.

The United States has launched what it calls a 'war on terrorism'. The only possible goal, it is stated, is the complete destruction of the national or international organizations called terrorist. It is said that terrorists are not to be negotiated with; they must be hunted down and exterminated.

Combat against terrorist organizations, as against criminal organizations like the Mafia or drug cartels, employs the police of cooperating countries and policing methods – surveillance, infiltration, bribery, assassinations and eventually raids. However, some countries harbour terrorist organizations. Thus the United States has affirmed the necessity to wage punitive war against Afghanistan and preventive war against Iraq.

The United States takes the war on terror as a war legitimated by its own right to sovereignty and self-defence. The United Nations is viewed not as a higher tribunal that invests legitimacy on the foreign initiatives of nations, but as a multiplicity of nations each of which pursues its own interests and acquires its legitimacy only from its own constitution. The United States has withdrawn from all outstanding international treaties: the Kyoto Protocol, the Anti-Ballistic Missile Treaty, the Comprehensive Test Ban Treaty and the Biological Weapons Convention, as well as the Geneva Convention for prisoners taken in the war on terror. This new nationalism counters the movement since the end of the Second World War and of the Cold War to build the international system into an international society, through institutions such as the European Union, the European Parliament, the United Nations and the International Criminal Court.

The security of the United States will require that access to weapons of mass destruction be eliminated from terrorist organizations and all countries potentially hostile to the United States, and this in turn is taken to require that no other country or alliance ever approach the military power of the United States. Because modern market democracies do not wage war on one another, the security of the United States requires active promotion of the establishment of secular market democracies everywhere. The United States sees its security as also requiring control of the petroleum resources that fuel its industrial economy.

Could we envision the war on terror to come to an end not by the simple extermination of terrorist organizations and the implantation of market democracies policed by the American hyper-power, but instead by reconciliation with the peoples from among whom militants are recruited and armed?

In light of our earlier discussion, such an outcome would require:

1. A process for establishing truth: The control of information by the military and of the media by the political and financial powers of the hyper-power has brought about, with the resurgence of nationalism, a resurgence of manufacturing of consent. There must be mechanisms through which parties to a conflict recognize shame and anger and acknowledge the injustice, injury, harm, material and personal destruction that gave rise to these emotions. Official investigations and judicial proceedings must be independent and objective.
2. A redefinition of identity: One party must cease identifying itself as the representative of law and order, indeed as civilization itself, and the other as atavist enemies of freedom. The 'belligerents' must acquire new identities as populations with powers and with positive contributions to make to the world social order. It is not true that the destitute have nothing to contribute. Anger is the source of the sense of justice, and without their anger the sense of justice in the world fades.
3. A new relationship: The ritualized reconciliation event must itself be novel, displaying a break with the past. After the massive bombardment of Afghanistan the United States briefly promised a new Marshall Plan to rebuild the country. Given the global concentration of wealth, if but a fraction of the cost of the war had been spent beforehand on a Marshall Plan for the populations falling

further and further behind, recruitment for desperate terrorist assaults on rich countries would have progressively diminished.

4. A renunciation of revenge and engagement in the partial retribution of wrongs: The massive bombardment of Afghanistan and the torture and indefinite incarceration without trial or legal counsel of prisoners in the Guantánamo Bay prison answered to a natural but also politically manipulated desire for revenge. But the growing concentration of the planet's wealth in the richest countries and the exploitation of the resources of the poorest lands will have to be reversed. With the active promotion of secular democracies with open markets for intrinsically undemocratic multinational corporations, other countries find that they can no longer keep their economies responsive to local employment and consumer needs.

The new nationalism reverses the efforts since the end of the Second World War and the Cold War to build the international system into an international society, invested with the mechanisms that could nurture this fourfold process of reconciliation. A watershed in European and world history was the determination of General de Gaulle and Conrad Adenauer to reconcile their two nations, which had been at the centre of the two World Wars, and to redefine their identities with respect to each other. There have also been beginnings of a truth process: Germany's public acknowledgement and apology to Poland during Willy Brandt's *Ostpolitik* and President Gorbachev's public statement that the Soviet invasion of Afghanistan was illegal and disastrous. Within limits, the International War Crimes Court will function as a truth commission and a mechanism for the partial redressing of wrongs. In the absence of fully working mechanisms – of an international society – for the reconciliation of nations, all we have are individual historians seeking the objective truth of the conflict, non-governmental organizations helping people redefine themselves from victims into partners for a new world order, and political activists working to bring hostile communities into communication. The political will to restore the institutions of a genuine international society depends vitally on their work.

References

Haynes, P. (1996), 'Commissioning the Truth: Further Research Questions', *Third World Quarterly*, 17:1.

Long, W.J. and Brecke, P. (2003), *War and Reconciliation: Reason and Emotion in Conflict Resolution* (Cambridge MA: MIT Press).

O'Donnell, G. and Schmitter, P.C. (1995), 'Transitions from Authoritative Rule: Tentative Conclusions about Uncertain Democracies', in Kritz, N.J (ed.) *Transitional Justice: General Considerations*, vol. 1 (Washington DC: United States Institute for Peace).

Siegel, R.L. (1998), 'Transitional Justice: A Decade of Debate and Experience', *Human Rights Quarterly*, 20.

Stedman, S.J. (2001), 'International Implementation of Peace Agreements in Civil Wars: Findings from a Study of Sixteen Cases', in Crocker, C.A. et al. (eds), *Turbulent Peace: The Challenges of Managing International Conflict* (Washington DC: United States Institute of Peace Press).

Chapter 4

Hegemony, Ethics and Reconciliation

Modjtaba Sadria

Reconciliation is related to conflict. It is borne of conflict situations.[1] At a time when conflicts are motivated by utopian visions of life and society, the wider context in which they occur is particularly important as they have such bearing on global events. If social change could be conceived, organized and conducted in a non-conflictual way, we would all be happier. Yet despite the abundance of managerial, institutionalized approaches to avoiding conflict, we have not yet learned to eliminate it. Thus, in a broad sense we have not yet invented a successful non-conflict-based mechanism for changing and improving peoples' lives. Were conflict to retain its historical function of aiming towards a better future, reconciliation would be an interim process of conflict mediation, negotiation and resolution. Yet it is harder than ever to identify any emacipatory potential in our most destructive contemporary conflicts, which makes the need to resolve them even more pressing.

This paper attempts to look at the difficulties posed by reconciliation from two different angles. The first relates to the ways in which resistance or refusal to reconcile is influenced by perceptions of the context of reconciliation, which is also implicitly related to the goals of reconciliation. The second concerns the problematic of listening, in terms of need and difficulty. These matters must be overcome if we are to realize the possibility of conflict as a tool for change rather than an end in itself, where mutual destruction is the officially declared aim.

The Logic of Silence

Any conflict that aims at social, cultural transformation has its proponents. When these conflicts attain a certain degree of visibility in the public sphere, civil society responds with a proposal for a resolution. I call this form of conflict resolution, 'deliberative reconciliation'. Those deeply involved in the process of social transformation have often argued that deliberative reconciliation, seen in terms of presenting arguments for the cessation of conflict, often tends to favour the most powerful (Young 2001).[2] Unequal power relations underlie certain refusals to

---

1 My heartfelt thanks to Philipa Rothfield and Sikeena Karmali for their generous help in rendering the text readable.

2 'Deliberation sometimes occurs in the real world. Officials and dignitaries meet all the time to hammer out agreements. Their meetings are usually well organized with structured procedures, and those who know the rules are often able to further their objectives through them by presenting proposals and giving reasons for them, which are considered and critically

participate in deliberative forms of reconciliation, for the disempowered may feel unable to properly articulate their concerns. As Iris Young argues: 'Under conditions of structural inequality, normal processes of deliberation often in practice restrict access to agents with greater resources, knowledge, or connections to those with greater control over the forum' (Young 2001, 679).

At stake in this sceptical view of reconciliation and deliberation with regard to conflict is the superior capacity of the established order and its protectors to articulate and present knowledge. The way that 'things are said' by the establishment, with whom advocates of reconciliation are often – willingly or not – identified, becomes the main issue for those who resist dialogue. Hannah Arendt writes:

> And still, it was by no means visible to all, nor was it all easy to perceive it; for, until the very moment when catastrophe overtook everything and everybody, it was covered up not by realities but by the highly efficient talk and double-talk of nearly all official representatives who, without interruption and in many ingenious variations, explained away unpleasant facts and justified concerns. We have to take this camouflage, emanating from and spread by 'the establishment' – or 'the system,' as it was then called – also into account (Arendt 1968).[3]

Those who aspire to empower and improve life for the majority need to address issues concerning the legitimacy of resistance in light of power inequalities, alongside the desire to change realities, which are shaped and framed through power relations. Nevertheless the question remains: what do we want to do with the 'other' side once change has been achieved? And for those who have the will to maintain the status quo, one needs to remember that our particular historical moment has some salient features: first, the discursive means by which others are pressured into accepting the conditions imposed on them has lost efficiency, at least for 'them'; and second, the growing complexity of the hegemonic system brings with it an increase in the capacity to disturb that system, that is, there is an increase in vulnerability in the world.

Thus, not talking and not listening have become more problematic than ever before. The major question has subsequently become: in this shrunken world, this global village, do we want to live together? In order to answer this question, we

---

evaluated by the others, who give their own reasons. Deliberation, the activist says, is an activity of boardrooms and congressional committees and, sometimes, even parliaments. Elites exert their power partly through managing deliberative settings. Among themselves they engage in debate about the policies that will sustain their power and further their collective interests. Entrance into such deliberative settings is usually rather tightly controlled, and the interest of many affected by the decisions made in them often receive no voice or representation' (Young 2001, 677).

3   Arendt pushes the argument further by saying: 'If it is the function of the public realm to throw light on the affairs of men by providing a space of appearances in which they can show in deed and word, for better and worse, who they are and what they can do, then darkness has come when this light is extinguished by "credibility gaps" and "invisible government," by speech that does not disclose what is but sweeps it under the carpet, by exhortations, moral and otherwise, that, under the pretext of upholding old trusts, degrade all truth to meaningless triviality' (Arendt 1968, viii).

may need new frames of thought, or rather, a new social imaginary. Charles Taylor, Michael Warner and Jurgen Habermas, each in his own way, have suggested that the public or public sphere can be thought of as instances of the social imaginary. Social imaginaries are neither strictly ideas nor institutions but the 'ways in which people imagine their social existence, how they fit together with others, how things go on between them and their fellows, the expectations that are normally met, and the deeper normative notions and images that underlie these expectations' (Kelty 2005, 186).

One of the basic and most important challenges linked to this capacity to create or enter into a different social imaginary is the way we do, or do not, listen to the other. In the case of reconciliation, the idea of an 'ethic of listening' becomes key.

Difficulties of Listening

Making generic statements concerning the need to listen in reconciliation, even if good, cannot help much if one does not grasp the difficulties of listening. These difficulties are in part due to the cultural nature of listening. If we accept the social constructivist's position that meaning is not pre-given but is socially constructed, listening cannot be regarded as the transparent reception of information. Rather, listening is part of an active process whereby meaning is constructed and reconstructed. Listening is thus inextricably entwined in power relations.

The question of listening would be less problematic were the speaker and the listener to share a framework that is taken for granted by both parties. However, in the case where such a framework is not shared, and one of the parties is the majority and the other is in the minority, 'listening' to the other can be a means to oppress and exclude. Listening to the other in this sense means to position the speaker in accordance with the audience's framework for seeing the world.[4] It is thus possible for an audience to manipulate the speaker's message into something completely different from that which was intended (Jones 2003, 10).[5] In other words, distortion through listening can and does occur according to dominant frameworks of perception.

The social constructivist notion of meaning also suggests that listening is itself a justice-oriented activity. If, as social constructivists suggest, human beings are part of the process of meaning construction, then humans have the ability to affect the social formation not only through speaking but also listening. If a listener positioned the speaker in a way that was different to how the speaker had been formerly positioned, this might affect social meanings that previously failed to recognize the speaker. Listening can be a way to take unjust relations or silenced voices into consideration,

---

4 According to Kazama, Foucault mentioned this point (Kazama 2002, 354). It is worth noting that the audience does not have complete control over positioning the speaker, because, as Hall observed, there must be '*some* degree of reciprocity between [the] encoding and decoding moment' (Hall 1992,136). Although Hall calls this reciprocity 'preferred meaning', in this paper, it is discussed in terms of 'hegemonic frameworks'.

5 Examples can be found in relation to Gay Studies and relations between western and non-western feminists (See Kazama 2002; Kawaguchi 2000; Oka 2000).

to recognize the other's voice, hitherto discarded as unreasonable, insane or excused, and to reformulate it into something to which attention is due. These activities have the potential to take a more inclusive approach towards the notion of community membership. They are also able to bring moral considerations to bear upon the creation of new forms of social practice, rules or norms which may in turn lead to a less unjust world (Saito 1997, 173).

If one wants to define listening as a normative, moral activity – as an ethical practice – then its epistemological foundations must be clear. This paper aims to explicate the concept of listening as a democratizing force. It will do so by investigating certain modes of listening, with a view to revealing the kinds of epistemological foundation that can create the possibility of listening as a normative action leading towards justice. The conceptual framework of the field of scholarship known as Subaltern Studies will be used to this end.[6]

Listening as Placement

Let us begin with the notion of listening in terms of meaning construction. How has the concept of 'listening' been understood and practiced in conventional terms? In what follows, we will discuss three modes of listening and their limitations in relation to the work of the Subaltern Studies group.

The first mode of listening can be found in the very target that Subaltern Studies has criticized throughout its history of scholarship. Hereafter, this mode of listening is to be called 'Listening as Placement'. According to the Subaltern Studies group, the dominant historiographies of India, which preceded their own work, assumed that the elite exercised the power to dominate in such a way that it 'turned the common people into dupes of their superiors' (Prakash 1994, 1477). The problem with these accounts is that they fail to offer the perspective of a subordinate people exercising any form of agency. In the conventional historiography of modern India, the people are thereby 'positioned' via an elite-centred approach that refuses to attribute any agency to those subordinated by colonialism. Yet, as Partha Chatterjee points out, whilst a people may be materially and economically subordinated to the colonizer, spiritually they are able to achieve a relative autonomy of thought (Chatterjee 1993, 6).

---

6   The term 'Subaltern' derives from the Latin 'Subalternus' (*sub*, under, *alter*, another), and was originally used in military language to refer to the second class: the adjutant (Motohashi 2005, 163). In the twentieth century, the Italian philosopher Antonio Gramsci drew on it to refer to those groups or individuals who are marginalized or subordinated (Kavanagh et al. 2004, 4; Motohashi 2005; Prakash 1994, 1477). In the early 1980s, the Subaltern Studies Group imported Gramsci's use of the term, adapting it to an Indian context where it suggests 'the demographic difference between the total Indian population and all those whom we have described as the "elite"' (Guha 1982, 8). According to Vinayak Chaturvedi, the editor and introducer of *Mapping Subaltern Studies*, the introduction of Gramsci to an Indian context was inspired by Susobhan Sarkar, Ranajit Guha's teacher (Chaturvedi 2000, viii). The term 'subaltern' generally refers to the group 'who are not hegemonic, and means lacking in autonomy, being subjected to the hegemony of another group' (Kavanagh et al. 2004, 5). This is in terms of race, caste, gender or culture. Note, that the way Subalternists use the term differs from Gramsci (Chopra 1982, 57–8).

One might speculate whether this historical construction of subordination as a lack of agency was due to the fact that the non-elite's voice never reached the ears of the elite (a question of 'not' listening). 'The elite perspective', in this analysis, belongs both to the Indian colonizer and to these conventional forms of historiography, for they both share a certain vision of the subordinate other. Here, the elite's inability to listen to the other, grounded in terms of material and social differences, leads to certain presumptions and constructions that manifest as a kind of positioning with respect to listening. This might be plausible in many instances but it cannot cover all elite interpretations of the non-elite.

In an important contribution to Subaltern scholarship entitled, *Chandra's Death*, Ranajit Guha criticized the conventional reception of testimony (Guha 1987). Guha refers to an incident in which an Indian woman from a lower caste, Chandra, died through drug abuse. Although her family gave the drug to her to bring about an abortion, her family was accused of murder. According to Guha, in the judicial discourse, her family's testimonies were recognized and interpreted in terms of, and in relation to, murder: '[I]t is speech prompted by the requirements of an official investigation into what is presumed to be a murder' (Guha 1987, 139). As a result, the family's speech was 'listened' to by officers but manipulated 'in order to conform to the logic of a legal intervention which made the death into murder, a caring sister into a murderess, all the actors in this tragedy into dependants, and what they said in a state of grief into *ekrar*' (Guha 1987, 140–1).

Shahid Amin also shows that there was contact between the elite and the non-elite, but that in this process, although the non-elite's voice reached the ears of the elite, it was manipulated (Amin 1987). Amin considered the discursive construction of the 'insurgent' by analyzing the juridical scene in which the testimony of a political activist, Shikari, is filtered through dominant discourses. According to Amin, Shikari's testimony can only be heard in terms of the interests of the establishment. His account was represented via sporadic and fragmented episodes, where the episodes were understood as parts of an entire, intelligible narrative that pertained to criminal prosecution (Amin 1987, 180–184).

These examples show that rather than being a monolithic society under colonial rule, there was a diversity of perspectives in India at the time. However, they also show that this plurality could not gain recognition because the non-elite's voice was given its position according to the elite's interpretive framework. As such, this mode of listening cannot be recognized as action towards democracy because it denies the agency of the speaker.

Listening as Addendum

The second mode of listening can be called 'Listening as Addendum'. In this mode, the other's voice is 'restored'. The early works of Subaltern Studies focused on this and began to redesign the historiography of India to restore tribes, castes or other such groups to a status of historical beings (Chatterjee 1987, 97; Brydon 2005; Das 2000, 1479; Chaturvedi 2000, vii). The aim was to retrieve subaltern histories and pluralize the understanding of modern India beyond any dominant singularity.

For example, Partha Chatterjee has shown the differences between the modes of power found in state-formation and the peasant insurgency in his paper, 'Agrarian Relations and Communalism in Bengal, 1926–1935' (Chatterjee 1982). According to Chatterjee, in the former mode (state-formation), power is 'characterized fundamentally by sheer superiority of physical force, i.e. a relationship of domination' (Chatterjee 1982, 13). On the contrary, in the latter form (peasant insurgency), political power is organized as the authority of the entire collectivity (Chatterjee 1982, 13). And '[e]ach individual conducts himself only as a link, as a member of the community' (Chatterjee 1982, 12). Chatterjee observed tensions when claims based on the former power were allocated to the subaltern domain, which was under the latter, collective mode of power in the process of state-formation (Chatterjee 1982, 14). He concluded that the subaltern domain was independent of the elite domain by insisting that, '[T]he relatively unorganized world of politics among the people continued to exist, and exist quite autonomously' (Chatterjee 1982, 17)

One might see this mode of listening as better than the first because the second mode seems to allow us to widen the perspective, relativize the hegemonic framework, and pluralize the value system. As Gyanendra Pandy noted, the recovery of history 'allow[s] us the possibility to write a different kind of history' (Pandy 1985, 233). The early works of Subaltern Studies use a history of the other as a means to give voice to the marginalized historical subject. Problems arise, however, if one were to regard this mode of listening as the best way to improve relations between the majority and the minority. In contemporary society the 'diversity of reality and value systems' is taken for granted (Ito 2000, 59). If social diversity has already become a premise of the way in which society is commonly understood, the ability of the subaltern history to relativize the hegemonic framework might correspondingly be weakened. There is a difference between offering an alternative perspective to a monolithic, singular account and offering an alternative to an approach that already acknowledges difference but is equally hegemonic. De-construction of the master narrative may not always be the remedy for an unjust situation.

Listening as Replacement

The third mode of listening, hereafter called 'Listening as Replacement' is found in the work of critics writing in relation to the 'late-period' of Subaltern Studies' scholarship. This mode asks the listeners to revise their own knowledge of the other by listening to the other's voice. Thanks to the impact of postmodernism, especially brought about by Gayatri Spivak, the work of late Subaltern Studies tends to treat the subaltern as a people who cannot speak, though this was not what Spivak intended to say – a point I will return to. This view was rightly seen as too pessimistic (for example, Haynes 2004). And, it provoked counter arguments which asserted that the 'subaltern can speak'. For example, Ramachandra Guha (1995) criticized this tendency and asked subalternists to return to their initial quest of 'the recovery of the voice and memory of the subaltern' (Guha 1995, 2057).

Pier Larson insisted that '[s]tudies of power and knowledge in imperial contexts need to pay greater attention to the basic process of subaltern reception and conversion of European discourse' (Larson 1997, 970). He also insisted that the subaltern has agency even if subordinated by the imperial colonizer. The colonized people could 'understand what was new to them in analogy to what they already knew' (Larson 1997, 970). So in this sense, the subaltern is no mere object of domination. On the contrary, '[b]y filtering European discourses through their own orders of meaning, the "subaltern" limited the potential of those discourses to rule effectively in the service of colonial power' (Larson 1997, 970).

The discovery of the 'real' subaltern who in a certain sense retains their agency appears to exhibit a good manner of listening. However, 'listening as replacement' has three problems. The first is evidential. When one looks at the history of Subaltern Studies, there is a dearth of documentation about the subaltern. According to Bahl, 'Indian workers and peasants did not leave behind any "original authentic" voices' (Bahl 1997, 1334). Even if one could find a document about the subaltern, it would be contaminated by elite perspectives because '[n]arratives ... are necessarily "interested", conditioned by power equations and varied expectations, bound by different kinds of narrative conventions, [and] productive of different kinds of truth-effects' (Pandey 1995, 228). So it will be difficult to replace the old (distorted) notion of the subaltern with an 'authentic' subaltern voice.

Second, this mode of listening resulted in replacing the listener's understanding of the world with that of the speaker, but is it really justice-oriented? The answer is no. This mode forgets the listener's 'positionality' as a matter of convenience. Positionality is a position or point of view which is relative to socio-historical location. To replace one's own understanding with that of the other means to assimilate to oneself the other's identity, or at least to position oneself as being on the side of the speaker. But even if the listener wanted to have the same perspective as the speaker, they would not see the world in the same way the speaker sees it (Bailey 1998, 30). Even worse, the attempt to do so results in 'concealing' the listener's privilege. In other words, the process by which the speaker's position comes to be adopted may consequently efface the listener's privileged origins. According to Mato, whilst information about the subaltern will enhance knowledge of them, at the same time it makes it possible for the hegemonic agent to take advantage of the subaltern yet again (Mato 2002, 4–5).

Third, if one pluralizes the value system, the triumph of the speaker's value system over that of the listener would once again emerge as a further story of domination. (Pandian 2002, 1736). As Beverley argued, '[i]f in order to become hegemonic that which has been subaltern has to become like that which is already hegemonic, then in a sense the dominant culture and the ruling class or classes continue to win, even in defeat' (Beverley 2000, 38).

Epistemological Shift for Listening as Justice-Oriented Action

We have argued that the search for social justice in unequal power relations makes speaking difficult. If this is the case, what is the meaning of listening as a justice-oriented activity? We have discussed three modes of listening in order to show their epistemological premises. While they appear to operate differently, they actually share a common structure: each in its own way represents two tangible perspectives, one belongs to the speaker, the other belongs to the listener, and the critical question is to decide which of the two is right, good and promotes democracy. In 'Listening as Placement', the listener's cognizance won, whereas the third mode 'Listening as Replacement' produced an opposite result. The second mode avoided the notion of replacement by introducing an alternative rather than supplanting one perspective with another. In other words, these understandings of listening reduce the problem at hand to a matter of choice, whether by replacement or the postscript of adding perspectives.

This tangibility of cognizance appears to be acknowledged by some subalternists through mention of the essentialization or reification of subaltern subjects. Sarkar has said that in the earlier works of Subaltern Studies the autonomy of subaltern agency was hailed and the separation of domains emphasized, but there was a tendency to homogenize 'both within their separate domains' (Sarkar 1997, 90). In other words, Subaltern Studies 'emerged towards essentializing the categories of "subaltern" and "autonomy", in the sense of assigning to them more or less absolute, fixed, decontextualized meanings and qualities' (Sarkar 1997, 88). Through reification, the subaltern's identity and opinion emerged as something tangible.

In the antagonistic struggle between tangible and reified opinions, the problem is reduced to a matter of choice, whilst the subject is posited as a self-contained entity. If 'listening as justice-oriented' epistemologically stays at this level, one might perceive the second mode as the best option, though there are problems inasmuch as the acceptance of alternatives could arguably lead to the promotion of indifference or detachment (Bauman 2001,144). After all, if there is no Archimedean point to decide what is good, there are no grounds for critical acceptance or rejection of particular, problematic perspectives: hence, the indifference.

However, the mode of listening inspired by Subaltern Studies has much deeper implications. One can discern the seeds of 'listening as justice-oriented' in late Subaltern Studies. The tendency of Subaltern Studies changed around the late 1980s because of the influence of postmodernists, especially Gayatri Spivak. Spivak gives us an important clue: she urges us to consider the epistemological premises of listening as justice-oriented. Spivak began her discussion by criticizing Michel Foucault and Gilles Deleuze (Spivak 1998). She maintained that Foucault and Deleuze agreed on the potentiality of the oppressed and held that if they were given a place where they could act as subjects, the oppressed would be able to express themselves perfectly (Spivak 1998, 12). However, according to Spivak, even if the oppressed emerged as 'authentic subjects' within the dominant discourse, they would nevertheless be unable to speak (Spivak 1998, 22, 44). Spivak did not deny the importance of supporting or participating in social movements that aim to revise the situation of coloured or oppressed women (Spivak 1998, 73). But she did criticize the idea that this political goal would somehow be achieved by letting the oppressed speak for and by themselves. For Spivak, the subaltern is always the residue that cannot be made visible according to particular formations of discourse.

What does this mean? By referring to the situation of coloured or oppressed women, Spivak seems to acknowledge that there are multiple understandings of the world: 'differing social situations (economic, sexual, cultural etc.) produce differing understandings of the world, differing knowledge of reality' (Bergin 2002, 198). However, humans are positioned in time and space and cannot escape that specificity.

No matter how human beings try to be 'position-free' and neutral, they inevitably 'perceive' the world from their own viewpoint, a viewpoint informed by their social, political and personal interests (Bordo 1991, 116). In short, humans understand the world by selecting points of view relevant to their interests (see Schutz 1971, 60). When a human being constructs a narrative to understand reality, he or she must expel something from the logic of that narrative in order to make it coherent. Discourses always leave 'something' outside of their logic as a form of residue, and it is this residue that Spivak identified and re-named, 'the subaltern'. Consequently every discourse inevitably entails the construction of subalternity as residue. Spivak argues that we cannot meet authentic subalterns: 'When the subaltern appears, their subalternity disappears, while simultaneously, the very discursive formation that allows them to appear paradoxically *constitutes* their subalternity' (Spivak 1999, 81).

It is worth noting the critics who insist on the inappropriateness of this claim. They have pointed out that Subaltern Studies has treated the subaltern only in terms of a certain kind of impossibility (Haynes 2004, 1).[7] In short, these arguments counter that the subaltern can speak (listening as replacement), and that the reason why subalternists highlight the difficulty of listening to their voice is that they have been deprived of their ability to speak by naming them as subaltern. However, the term 'subaltern' always means the 'other' or that which is lost in the process of meaning construction. In the phrase 'the subaltern cannot speak', grammatically the nominative was 'subaltern', but the problem at hand in that phrase was not 'subaltern' but its implied audience. Why is the listener's inability to hear to the voices of the subaltern perceived as being identical with the negation of the agency of the subaltern?

Spivak herself maintained that she was not interested in whether the subaltern can physically speak or not. What she means is that the subaltern cannot emerge as an 'agent' in cases where an exchange between the speaker and the listener is lost (Spivak 1999, 85). In other words, as Beverley argues, when Spivak makes a claim that the subaltern cannot speak, 'she means that the subaltern cannot speak in a way that would carry any sort of authority or meaning for us without altering the relations of power/knowledge that constitute it as subaltern in the first place' (Beverly 1999, 29). Therefore, the phrase 'the subaltern cannot speak' connotes, in a sense, the infinite affirmation of the subjectivity of the subaltern, for no matter how strong and acute the desire to control the oppressed through knowledge, subalternity is, by definition, outside or beyond the hegemony of the particular discursive formation. No matter how hard one tries to describe and represent the subaltern, their

---

7   However, this redefinition was widely accepted by other subalternists. For example, Dipesh Chakrabarty, one of the representatives of Subaltern Studies, also observes the difficulty of listening, maintaining that even when the subaltern's history is represented as part of history, it cannot be listened to, for when the 'lifeworld' of the subaltern is translated into history, subaltern history is banished by the very historicizing process (Chakrabarty 1998). The figure of Europe always functions as a silent referent of the historicizing process: it represents the origin of history and that from which history spreads (Chakrabarty 2000, 7–8, 28). Any activity that cannot fit this referent is marginalized, devalued or ignored. For Chakrabarty, there is no principle that can historicize subaltern history without obeying this Eurocentric principle.

representation is much flimsier than their 'reality' and is thus inherently constrained by the audience's imagination.

In sum, Subaltern Studies have paid great attention to the residues of meaning construction. The 'subaltern' is always beyond the discursive formation that functions as a framework to construct meaning, so they cannot emerge as subjects without altering the framework, which makes them subaltern in the first place.

What are the implications of Spivak's argument? The notion of the relation between language and the subaltern is radically different from the epistemological premises of the three modes of listening. It questions the belief that the other's attitude shows their 'authentic' stance. This questions the framework that allows us to 'listen' to the voice of the other as something that can be positioned as communication or opposite to one's own opinion. If the subaltern can be defined as the residue of dominant discourses, the language that the subaltern uses cannot guarantee them entrance into the general field of human relations. No matter how hard the subaltern tries to speak in a language that is accepted in the public sphere, they cannot speak because the language that circulates is contaminated and constrained by the dominant narrative. In the case of Subaltern Studies, as Chakrabarty observes, in the history of the West and the non-West, 'time' is used as the criterion with which the observer can compare the contents of each history (Chakrabarty 2000). 'Time' as a criterion seems to be neutral, but the relations of dominance have already contaminated it. Chakrabarty calls this 'historicism': that which 'makes modernity or capitalism look not simply global but rather something that became global over time, by originating in one place (Europe) and then spreading outside it' (Chakrabarty 2000, 7). Even if the non-Western historian tries to show that non-Western history is as important as Western history, this cannot be heard in the framework given by 'historicism' (Chakrabarty 2000, 8).

This notion implies and incorporates the idea of the subaltern as residue. By acknowledging the notion of the subaltern as residue, it is necessary to search for or construct new formations for discourses that allow the subaltern to emerge. Such a reformulation is a temporal matter because subaltern identity is itself historical (Mallon 1994, 1511). Yet when a person deconstructs a given discursive formation, what the person faces is yet another limitation – thus to 'de-limit is to delimit'. In other words, 'the Other itself is ungraspable, so even if a category is deconstructed many times, "I" cannot grasp the "Other" fully' (Nakamasa 2003, 27).

This is not a mere theoretical implication. Sexual harassment is one example of reformulating a dominant discursive formation. Before the term historically emerged, a woman who complained in the workplace would most likely have been criticized as 'too emotional'. In this situation, she had two options: to accept the abusive situation, or accept the stigma of emotionality. Those who were not content with that succeeded in partially constructing, and thus reformulating the discourse: through criticizing the social structure of patriarchy.

In this example, 'listening as justice-oriented' involved 're-orienting' dominant frameworks so as to recognize something different about the world. This re-orientation is not what I discussed in the second section of this paper: Placement, Addendum, or Replacement. It does not involve 'exclusion of her', nor 'letting her speak', nor 'acceptance of her opinion unstintingly'. The dominant (patriarchal) perspective sees the other's voice as a form of competition to his own opinion or identity, as something which cannot be incorporated without destabilizing his own framework. Nevertheless, given an epistemology in which 'listening as justice-oriented' has its own basis, the framework itself can be re-oriented to include the other. Here, the other is not necessarily competitive. Once the framework is re-oriented, everyone becomes part of the moral discourse.

Conclusion

The two main arguments of this paper have considered the difficulty of speaking in the context of reducing inequality. Thus we have the process of generating conflict, and paradoxically, the idea of 'listening as justice-oriented', which is epistemologically different from conventional understandings of listening.

Subaltern Studies, and the critics of late Subaltern Studies share in common the treatment of the other as a tangible voice, easy to put into the listener's framework, and competitive with one's own opinion. But the concept of 'listening' derived from late Subaltern Studies requires altering the framework of the listener.

This paper concludes with the meaning of 'justice' in 'listening as justice-oriented'. In the three modes of listening discussed above, the key question is who has the power to narrate? This question is itself based on a notion of distributive justice. As Matsuba Syoji has shown, distributive justice has its basis in the formation of sensibilities which decide who should be counted as a member of society, who can enjoy the distribution of social wealth, and who should be excluded from it. The sense of justice in 'listening as justice-oriented' requires a reformulation of the idea of sensibility to include the subaltern who can not appear without altering the framework that displaces the subaltern in their place. This certainly does not solve all social conflicts, because one should tackle the problem of distribution after rewriting the cognitive paradigm. It can neither prevent 'injustice' from occurring, nor heal the wounds of the subaltern.

However, this perspective will make it impossible to exclude claims of the other by misrepresenting 'injustice' as 'misfortune'. Finally 'listening as justice-oriented' opens the door for an encounter with the person who has been discarded as an illegitimate actor. Ultimately then, this becomes the ethic of reconciliation.

References

Allen, K.R. and Baber, K.M. (1992), 'Ethical and Epistemological Tensions in Applying a Postmodern Perspective to Feminist Research', *Psychology of Women Quarterly*, 16, 1–15.

Amin, S. (1987), 'Approver's Testimony, Judicial Discourse: The Case of Chauri Chaura', in Guha, R. (ed.), *Subaltern Studies V: Writing on South Asian History and Society* (New York: Oxford University Press).

Applebaum, B. (1997), 'Good Intentions are Not Enough! Racism, Intentions and Moral Responsibility', *Journal of Moral Education*, 26: 4, 409–20.

Arendt, H. (1968), *Between Past and Future* (New York: Penguin Books).

Arendt, H. (1968), *Men in Dark Times* (New York: Harcourt, Brace and World Inc.).

Arendt, H. (1982), *Lectures on Kant's Political Philosophy*, Beiner, R. (ed.) (Chicago: University of Chicago Press).

Bahl, V. (1997), 'Relevance (or Irrelevance) of Subaltern Studies' *Economic and Political Weekly*, June 7.

Bailey, A. (1998), 'Locating Traitorous Identities: Toward a View of Privilege-Cognizant White Character', *Hypatia*, 13:3, 27–42.

Bauman, Z. (2001), 'The Great War of Recognition', *Theory, Culture and Society*, 18 (2–3), 137–50.

Bergin, L.A. (2002), 'Testimony, Epistemic Difference and Privilege: How Feminist Epistemology Can Improve Our Understanding of the Communication of Knowledge', *Social Epistemology*, 16:13.

Beverley, J. (1999), 'Writing in Reverse: The Subaltern and the Limits of Academic Knowledge', in Beverley, J., *Subalternity and Representation* (Durham and London: Duke University Press).

Beverley, J. (2000), 'The Dilemma of Subaltern Studies at Duke', *Nepantla: Views from South*, 1:1.

Bordo, S. (1991), 'Docile Bodies, Rebellious Bodies: Foucauldian Perspectives on Female Psychopathology', in Silverman, H. (ed.), *Writing the Politics of Difference* (New York: SUNY Press).

Brydon, D. (2005), 'Postcolonial Cultural Studies 2: 1990 and After', in Groden, M. et al. (eds), *Johns Hopkins Guide to Literary Criticism and Theory*, 2nd edn, (Baltimore: Johns Hopkins University Press).

Chakrabarty, A. (1995), 'Writing History', *Economic and Political Weekly*, December 23.

Chakrabarty, D. (1993), 'Marx after Marxism: A Subaltern Historian's Perspective', *Economic and Political Weekly*, 28:22.

Chakrabarty, D. (1998), 'Minority Histories, Subaltern Pasts', *Economic and Political Weekly*, 33:9, 28 February.

Chakrabarty, D. (2000), *Provincializing Europe* (Princeton: Princeton University Press).

Chatterjee, P. (1982), 'Agrarian Relations and Communalism in Bengal, 1926-1935', in Guha, R. (ed.), *Subaltern Studies I* (Delhi: Oxford University Studies Press).

Chatterjee, P. (1993), *The Nation and its Fragments: Colonial Postcolonial History* (Princeton: Princeton University Press).

Chaturvedi, V. (2000), 'Introduction', in Chaturverdi, V. (ed.), *Mapping Subaltern Studies and the Postcolonial* (London: Verso).

Chopra, S. (1982), 'Missing Correct Perspective', *Social Scientist*, 10:8.

Comack, E. (1999), 'Producing Feminist Knowledge: Lessons from Women in Trouble', *Theoretical Criminology*, 3:3.

Das, V. (2000), 'Subaltern Studies as Perspective', in Guha, R. (ed.), *Subaltern Studies VI*, (Oxford: Oxford University Press).

Guha, R. (1982), 'On Some Aspects of the Historiography of Colonial India', in Guha, R. (ed.), *Subaltern Studies I* (Oxford: Oxford University Press).

Guha, R. (1987), 'Chandra's Death', in Guha, R. (ed.), *Subaltern Studies V: Writing on South Asian History and Society* (Oxford: Oxford University Press).

Guha, R. (1995), 'Subaltern and Bhadralok Studies', *Economic and Political Weekly*, 19 August.

Guha, R. and Spivak, G.C. (eds) (1998), *Selected Subaltern Studies* (Oxford: Oxford University Press).

Hall, S. (1992), 'Encode/Decode' in Hall, S. et al. (eds), *Culture, Media, Language* (London: Routledge).

Hayashida Y. (2005) 'About Place for Those Excluded from the Political Process' in Nakamasa, M. (ed.) (2004).

Haynes, C.L. (2004), 'Subaltern Challenges to the Authority of the Colonial Subject within One Jamaica Gal and A Study in Colour', <http://www.sg.inter.edu/revista-ciscla/volume31/haynes/pdf>.

Ito, K. (2000), 'Composition of Back Rush in Relativization and Self-Centered Society', *Impaction*, 117, 53–61 (in Japanese).

Jones, M. (2003), 'Un-Writing the "Authentic" Subaltern: Testimonio, Autobiography and the Possibility of Global Hybridity in Knowledge Production', <http://www. washington.edu/research/urp/sinst/pubs/2003/Un-Writing%20the%20Authentic %20Subaltern_Jones_03.pdf>.

Kavanagh, D. et al. (2004), 'Stories of the Subaltern', <http://www.ex.ac.uk/sobe/ Research/DiscussionPapersMan/Man2002/Man0210.pdf>.

Kawaguchi, K. (2000), 'Politics in Personal Things', *Impaction*, 117, 35–7 (in Japanese).

Kelty, C. (2005), 'Geeks, Social Imaginaries, and Recursive Publics', *Cultural Anthropology*, 20:2.

Kikuchi N. (2003), 'From Sexual Violence and Prostitution: The Problem of the Politics of Representation of Comfort Women', in Nakamasa, M. (ed.) (2003).

Larson, P.M. (1997), 'Capacities and Modes of Thinking: Intellectual Engagements and Subaltern Hegemony in the Early History of Malagasy Christianity', *American Historical Review*, 102:4.

Mallon, F.E. (1994), 'The Promise and Dilemma of Subaltern Studies: Perspectives from Latin American History', *The American Historical Review*, 99:5.

Mato, D. (2002), 'Not "Studying the Subaltern," But Studying With "Subaltern" Social Groups, or At Least, Studying The Hegemonic Articulations of Powers', *Nepantla: Views from South*, 3:3.

Mizudome, M. (2000), 'How Subaltern could have Solidarity?: Morisaki Kazue's Essay, "Third Sexuality"', *Jyoukyou*, 11:5, 92–115 (in Japanese).

Motohashi, T. (2005), *Postcolonialism* (Tokyo: Iwanami Shoten) (in Japanese).

Mouffe, C. (1999), 'Deliberative Democracy or Agonistic Pluralism', *Social Research*, 66:3, 745–58.

Moynagh, P. (1997), 'A Politics of Enlarged Mentality: Hannah Arendt, Citizenship Responsibility, and Feminism', *Hypatia*, 12:4, 27–53.

Nakamasa, M. (ed.) (2003), *The Politics of Deconstruction* (Tokyo: Ochanom-izushobo) (in Japanese).

Nakamasa, M. (ed.) (2004), *Community and Justice* (Tokyo: Ochanomizushobo) (in Japanese).

Ohba, K. (1994), 'The Context of Universalism', in *Iwanami Lecture Series: Contemporary Thoughts 14 – Modern/Antimodern* (Tokyo: Iwanami Shoten) (in Japanese).

Ohkawa, M. (1998), 'The Difficulties of Sharing and Knowing Each Other', *Mirai*, 2:376, 18–25 (in Japanese).

Ohsugi, T. (1999), *Idle Creole* (Tokyo: Iwanami Shoten) (in Japanese).

Oka, M. (2000), *What is Her 'Right' Name?* (Tokyo: Seidoshya) (in Japanese).

Okano, Y. (2002), 'To do Justice: What does it mean?', *Jyoukyou*, 3:7, 34–53 (in Japanese).

Pandey, G. (1995), 'Voices from the Edge: The Struggle to Write Subaltern Histories', *Ethonos*, 60, 2–3, 223–42.

Pandian M.S.S. (2002), 'One Step Outside Modernity: Caste, Identity Politics and Public Sphere', *Economic and Political Weekly*, 4 May .

Pels, D. (1996), 'Strange Standpoints: Or, How to Define the Situation for Situated Knowledge', *Telos*, 108, 65–91.

Prakash, G. (1994), 'Subaltern Studies as Postcolonial Criticism', *The American Historical Review*, 99:5.

Saito, J. (1997), 'Politics of Representation/Politics of Appearance', *Gendaishisou*, 25:8, 158–77 (in Japanese).

Sakiyama, M. (2001), '"Style" which Resists Style', in Sakiyama M. (ed.), *Subaltern and History* (Tokyo: Seidosya) (in Japanese).

Sarkar, S. (1997), 'The Decline of the Subaltern in Subaltern Studies' in Sarkar, S., *Writing Social History* (Oxford: Oxford University Press).

Schutz, A. (1971), *Reflections on the Problem of Relevance* (New Haven: Yale University Press).

Shimabukuro, M. (2002), 'Hybrid Politics and Mixed Blood', *Emancipation Sociology Study*, 16, 16–51 (in Japanese).

Spivak, G.C. (1990), 'An Interview with Gayatri Spivak on the Politics of the Subaltern', Interview by Howard Winant, *Socialist Review*, 3.

Spivak, G.C. (1999), *A Critique of Postcolonial Reason: Toward a History of the Vanishing Present* (Cambridge: Harvard University Press).

Squires, C.R. (2002), 'Rethinking the Black Public Sphere: An Alternative Vocabulary for Multiple Public Spheres', *Communication Theory*, 12:4, 446–68.

Yack, B. (1999), 'Putting Injustice First: An Alternative Approach to Liberal Pluralism' *Social Research*, 99:4, 1103–120.

Young, I.M. (2001), 'Activist Challenges to Deliberative Democracy', *Political Theory*, 29:5, 670–90.

Yun, K. (2001), '"Postmodern" and State in Modern Japan', *Kan*, 15, 139–52 (in Japanese).

Chapter 5

Telling a Different Story: Hope for Forgiveness and Reconciliation in Northern Ireland

Geraldine Smyth O.P.

Now I could tell my story.
　It was different
　　　　　from the story they told about me.
And now also
　it was spring.
I could see the wound in the land I had left
in the land by leaving it.
　　　I travelled west.
　　　　　　　Once there
I looked with so much love
　　　　　at every field
as it unfolded
　　　its rusted wheel and its pram chassis
　　　　　　　　and at the gorse-
bright distances
　　I had been
　　　　that they misunderstood me.
　　　　Come back to us
they said.
　　Trust me I whispered.

(Boland 1998, 42–43)

Ezra Pound described poets as 'the antennae of the race'. When we contemplate such realities as forgiveness and healing and the shifting contours between their personal and cultural landscapes, it is perhaps the poet's vision then that sensitizes our perspective on the complexity and mystery involved. In the search for understanding of forgiveness and reconciliation in such post-conflict situations as Ireland, a poet like Eavan Boland offers insight, at once reliable and elusive, not least on the resonance between the personal and public discourses of forgiveness and healing.

Forgiveness and reconciliation, more readily associated with the interpersonal domain, have found fresh expressions in politics and international relations. Looking back in the direction of the Hebrew Prophets, ancient Greek tragedy or the parables of Jesus, one discerns a clear interplay between the personal, political and religious understanding of these themes. While in recent centuries in the West, the prevailing Christian focus of forgiveness and reconciliation has been linked to the private, religious sphere, this has also begun to change: political leaders and popes alike have re-inscribed its public significance. (Jones 1995, 73–118; Minow 1998).[1] The emergence of truth and reconciliation commissions, from Africa to Latin America, has lent a new formality to such discourse, with the intent of enabling former enemies to come to terms with the past in a way that makes a different future possible. Interestingly, the Truth and Reconciliation Commission (TRC) in South Africa included explicitly religious and inter-religious dimensions.

Recognizing this double edge, Michael Hurley (founder of the Irish School of Ecumenics) comments on the contemporary 'secularization of reconciliation'. He suggests that the secular ethic of reconciliation concentrates on the reconciling of 'differing positions', and is based on justice and redress. By contrast, the religious understanding is more personal, encouraging a change of heart animated by charity and the superhuman act of forgiveness (Hurley 1994, 4). Doubtless, some problems arise in thus introducing Christian theology into this renewed public discourse (not least because churches, until the 1960s, had neglected the sociopolitical scope of these topics and relevant insights from other faiths) (Daye 2004, 19–22). But, a degree of theological precision is needed if there is to be a mutually fruitful encounter between a sociopolitical approach and that of Christian faith.

This chapter continues in two parts: The first will explore the inter-generative meanings and provenance of forgiveness and reconciliation within the Christian tradition, stressing the importance of recognizing these in any public debate. In underlining the importance of not suppressing the transcendent dimension, I imply the relevance of an intrinsic as well as an extrinsic hermeneutic. This is doubly relevant when the field of reference embraces a society divided along politico-religious lines. Attention to the dominant but divergent theologies illuminates how faith and politics continue to intersect in specific and dialectical ways within and between the secular and religious domains.

The second part of the chapter will explore the topic of forgiveness and reconciliation with reference to Northern Ireland as it emerges from more than three decades of conflict, and will discuss whether a truth and reconciliation process would help establish peace on a firmer footing. Specifically, I will propose the inherent value of a public forum in which victim-survivors are enabled to speak and be heard.[2] This will be grounded theoretically in Paul Ricoeur's account of the healing power of narrative remembering, as significant for secular and religious spheres alike.

Forgiveness and Reconciliation in Public Life and Public Theology

Interestingly, it was Hannah Arendt, secular Jewish philosopher, who proposed that the 'discoverer of the role of forgiveness in the realm of human affairs was Jesus of

---

1   See also: Accattoli 1998; R.C. International Theological Commission Report 2000, par 5.1.

2   One must use the word 'victims' circumspectly. They are also survivors and sustainers of life, and often prefer alternative self-descriptions.

Nazareth', observing that the fact 'that he made this discovery in a religious context and articulated it in religious language, [w]as no reason to take any less account of it in a strictly secular sense' with reference to socio-political transformation (Arendt 1958, 1959, 238–9). In short, 'forgiveness' and 'reconciliation' are terms that can be advanced within the secular discourse of conflict transformation and peace-building. However, it must also be remembered that moral philosophy has afforded scarcely any real attention to the conceptuality of forgiveness (MacKintosh 1954, 187). Yet, it has been saturated by religious experience and history and sustained by theological reflection (Ricoeur 1967). Therefore, while theology cannot lay exclusive claims, it would be myopic for political thinkers to enter the field without attempting to acknowledge the theological horizon of forgiveness and reconciliation and their history of effects.

In recent decades, the church has sought to re-intensify the consciousness of sin as social and structural, and *ipso facto*, a corresponding understanding of grace. This is exemplified in the retrieval of such biblical symbols with their sociopolitical implications, as, 'Covenant' and 'Jubilee'.[3] This shift calls Christians to an intentional practice of sociopolitical virtues as a necessary corrective to the privatization of sin and grace in the preceding era. The diminished popularity in the Catholic Church of private, auricular confession, signals a cultural discomfort with the Irish penitential tradition. Although such practices were repudiated by the Reformers, privatized conceptions persisted in both Catholic and Reformed churches. But by the mid 20th century, many Western churches had begun to reassert the connection between forgiveness and justice, de-emphasizing forensic understandings of wrongdoing as individual moral delinquency, positing a more complex moral framework with greater priority assigned to collective responsibility and social justice.

This then is the outer rationale for attending, within the theological remit of this reflection on forgiveness and reconciliation, to the socio-political sphere, as well as to a limited religious sense and theological purpose. Theology provides a legitimate syntax and medium whereby church members can contribute to public discourse. As well as providing believers with an inspiring internal narrative, theology, if it is to be pertinent to Christians' struggle to live compassionate, socially responsible lives must also be able to communicate its message in ways comprehensible to those who live by other narratives and ideologies. There is also an intrinsic theological necessity for keeping 'forgiveness' and 'reconciliation' anchored between the religious and secular spheres. This derives from the nature of biblical revelation itself in its disclosure and exploration of the interrelationship between God, humanity and the world.

---

3   In a New Year Message, John Paul II avowed: 'Only forgiveness can quench the thirst for revenge and open the heart of a real and lasting reconciliation between peoples' (*Irish Times*, 1 January 2002). In a New Year message addressing the Presbyterian Church across Ireland, Alistair Dunlop likewise linked gospel forgiveness with the current sociopolitical challenges to create an inclusive and respectful society (*The Irish News*, 4 January 2002).

Forgiveness and Reconciliation: Clarifying Meanings and Ambiguities

Even secular definitions of forgiveness disclose theological traces of the relational and transcendent aspects of forgiveness. According to the Chambers Dictionary (1998 edition), forgiveness derives from the Old English *'for-giefan'* – to give away; also implying to overlook, to pardon a debt or offence, to give up, to show mercy or compassion. The range of meanings assigned to the Old English prefix, 'for-' suggests 'thoroughly or utterly (intensive)', as in words derived from Old English to form adjectives 'with superlative force'. Clearly, there are possibilities of anchoring certain theses about forgiveness within the socio-theological context: A relational context to forgiveness is implicit, with overtones of prior hurt or fault (sin) and harmed relationships. One discernible Christian aspect in the secular dictionary suggests forgiveness as a free gift – beyond desert, an alternative to revenge. Existentially, it is a giving away of oneself to another – a self-transcending action, likely to create a supreme impression. Also, forgiveness implies a certain mutual re-orientation. In short, there is evident basis for a theological anthropology of forgiveness.

Further theological implications can be inferred. Forgiveness finds its point of reference within the theology of salvation, or soteriology. Gabriel Daly distinguishes forgiveness and reconciliation. He asserts that 'reconciliation' is arguably the most generic term in the vocabulary of soteriology, and that while the scope of reconciliation is larger, forgiveness is reconciliation's most personally significant core (Daly 1998).[4] More will be said of this, but suffice to underscore two points: first, Daly's insistence on the symbolic nature of such theological language; and second, the requirement of a plurality of models and metaphors in theological discourse.

Paradox in Practice: Forgiveness as Gift, and Invitation to Reconciliation

In Christian theology, forgiveness should not therefore be functionalized as a staging post to reconciliation. One way to confront this issue is by adverting to the vexed relationship between forgiveness and repentance. A paradoxical stance is indispensable in asserting that repentance is not a prior requirement for forgiveness.[5] To insist otherwise is to relativize the theological fundamentals of divine freedom and the universal scope of salvation. Challenging the tendency to conflate cause and effect in respect of forgiveness and repentance, Paul Ricoeur goes to the heart of the matter.[6]

---

4   Reconciliation is one of the classically preferred ways of describing the reality of salvation. Redemption, justification, atonement, and sanctification are others, each with a specific resonance. Most critically, such attributes as forgiveness and mercy are ascribed to God only by analogy.

5   Jones argues (against Swinburne) that repentance is not a prerequisite for forgiveness (Jones 1995, 135–62). See also Smyth 2001, 329–59.

6   Ricoeur demonstrates that the self-consistency of the concept of forgiveness in respect of repentance demands its unconditionality, qua gift. Forgiveness remains. Thus too, forgiveness, not tied to an instant, is 'the meaning of a whole life with its ups and downs, its crises but also its quiet display' (Ricoeur 2004, 13).

A Two-fold Grace

Christian forgiveness implies a turning away from sin, but also, a turning towards relationship – with God and others. Without demand for prior repentance, forgiveness invites a new orientation to life with others as an enabling gift, recognizing the disposition of human frailty and flourishing in relationship rather than isolation. Also denoted is the possibility of 'participative sharing' in the transcendent nature of forgiveness (Ricoeur 2004, 13). Both forgiveness and repentance are implied in the Matthean injunction (5:21), 'Leave your offering there before the altar and go and be reconciled with your brother, and then come back and present your offering'[7] But here, Jesus is demonstrating the inclusiveness of mercy, exhorting his disciples that just as God's compassion is unbounded so should be theirs.

Furthermore, Jesus taught that our forgiveness by God is implicated in our extending forgiveness to others (Matthew 6:12). Accordingly, we are to show mercy as God shows mercy (Luke. 6:36-37). Forgiveness opens the door to a fullness of life, healed relationships and the inclusion within one community of sinner and sinned against, symbolized in the eschatological meal of God's reign (Matthew 22:10), in which just and unjust distinctions are overcome and moral opposites reconciled.

For Christians, the other great exponent of forgiveness and reconciliation is St. Paul, whose teaching is shaped by his experience of the sudden grace of forgiveness, at the very times when he (as Saul) was zealously persecuting the early church. In the narrative of his conversion, the two-fold pattern is visible: the first moment describes how, in one blinding flash, without any inner commitment to change, he experiences Christ's forgiveness. The second movement of repentance followed that experience (Acts 9: 3-30). The first singular dramatic event is one moment within a larger sequence involving the wider community. Ananias, a member of that community, in a pre-vision of the event, is given a mandate to welcome his enemy. Here we witness Saul's experience of the moment in which he is struck down, blinded and forgiven. His experience finds fulfilment in the welcome into Ananias's house. Reconciliation is the graced context of forgiveness. Paul's conversion finds its radical starting point in his experience of forgiveness, but from thence, it opens out into the fullness of reconciliation, with worldwide and cosmic implications. Christ is at its heart.

Keeping Both Sides in View: Theology's Need for Bi-Focal Vision

Problems beset the church whenever forgiveness and reconciliation become dislodged from this inherently inter-relational context. Here we should note the dominance of a certain legal model of redemption theology (soteriology), associated with Tertullian and Augustine and informed by metaphors of the law court – punishment, contrition and restitution (Daly 1988, 184–6). In another tradition, the Eastern Fathers, notably Irenaeus, offer a model of salvation more intrinsically relational, with allusions to sin as sickness, and construing salvation in metaphors of healing and restoration of

---

7   This resonates with the Jewish prophets' recurring insistence on the integral link between worship and justice (Amos 5; Isaiah 1; Jeremiah 6).

the body to wholeness (Irenaeus, xxxviii.3; Lossky 1985, 97–110). Interestingly, one finds an analogous understanding among indigenous peoples in many places. One thinks of the liturgical incorporation by Native American Christians of their ancient sweat lodge as a ritual structure for cleansing and renewal. Similarly, at the World Council of Churches Seventh Assembly in Canberra in 1991, the opening worship included the Aborigine ritual of burning eucalyptus leaves, with participants passing through the pungent smoke, betokening openness to purification and transformation (Smyth 1995, 110, note 102).

There are implications here for Christianity to desist from superimposing exclusively European suppositions. Eastern Orthodox theologian, Harakas, prefers integration of these contrasting emphases (Harakas 2001, 51–78). Alongside such indigenous and Orthodox insights, feminist and eco-feminist theology offers a rich vein for correlational approaches to soteriology and to ethics (McFague 1993, 133; Frank Parsons 2002). Ecumenical theology too asserts this 'both-and' approach to identity and relationship, in its concern to connect truth and reconciliation without coercion, and to encourage interchurch cooperation on the healing of memories (Daly 1998, 11–13).

On the Way to Reconciliation: Forgiveness and Healing in Northern Ireland

I have sought to demonstrate that Christian forgiveness is predicated on the acceptance that human beings are constituted by and for relationship. When relations break down, forgiveness offers restoration, not to the status quo ante, but to a new condition with transformed possibilities and responsibilities. The more impossible forgiveness seems the more necessary it is. Without it, both 'victim' and 'perpetrator' become entrapped in cycles of retaliation: 'Without being forgiven, released from the consequences of what we have done,' avows Hannah Arendt, 'we would remain the victims of its consequences forever' (Arendt 1958, 1959, 237). The reciprocity is ineluctable. Forgiveness can neither be merited nor demanded, is both free and costly. Yet, the 'stubborn historicity' constantly enmeshes human capability: limits, resistance, the ubiquity of hurt and resentment, the pervasiveness of prejudice and, for some, the overwhelming scale of evil. And so, I return to Northern Ireland, where the search for reconciliation dramatizes the struggle with that stubborn historicity at every level of life but also the graced moments of breakthrough and learning through dialogue across the historic divide, or through engagement with groups from other places of conflict, in collaborative projects towards overcoming violence and building peace.

Since the 'Early Release' in 2000, in accordance with the terms of the Good Friday Agreement (1998), debates on dealing with the past have intensified. Contesting opinions turn upon the tension between justice and reconciliation and ambivalent views as to whether forgiving means forgetting.[8] This bears out what Martha Minow

---

8 On different ways of remembering, see: Smyth 1997, 59–76, particularly regarding the Jewish tradition of the Sabbath of Remembrance (Shabbat Zachor); Interchurch Group on Faith and Politics 1998.

describes as the typical double concern to avoid 'too much memory or not enough' (Minow 1998, 2).

Paul Ricoeur warns that 'the duty to remember' can be a wheel of no release. 'Within memory lies the most secret resistance to forgiveness.' He prefers therefore to speak of 'the work of memory', of mourning both the loss and the idea of loss – even to letting go any 'claim to construct a story of our life without lacks or gaps …our claim to repair all wounds' (Ricoeur 2004, 15). Some remark that only God can forgive. This need not forever preclude forgiveness but may intimate (as proposed above), that such persons cannot yet face a relationship with the perpetrator, thus emphasising also that human forgiveness partakes in a quality of transcendence.

This has a bearing on current public debate on the workability of a truth and reconciliation commission for Northern Ireland.[9] Many consider it premature or pointless, since prisoners have already been released without requirement of truth or disclosure. Certainly, there must be no question of managed forgiveness. If a full-scale commission is to be convened, concern for victims-survivors should be its priority through the structuring of a public space in which people so long overlooked can speak and be heard. Consensus and clarity would be necessary as to the purpose of a commission (the encouragement of truth-telling, apology, reconciliation, a forum for victims-survivors, the establishment of terms of reparation); the form it would take (juridical or non-juridical; immunity from prosecution (amnesty in exchange for truth-telling – as in South Africa, for example); the authority behind it (judicial, state-sponsored, civic, independent); the range of inclusiveness – victims, non-combatants, combatants, for example. Underlying such questions is the matter of truth and its ambivalent meanings. Here, the TRC helpfully distinguishes four different types of truth: 1) factual or forensic; 2) personal or narrative; 3) social; 4) healing or restorative. Re 2), 3) and 4) the significant work of a number of independent civic groups cannot be overstated. Foremost among these is the 'Healing Through Remembering Project' that has commissioned research and convened cross-community dialogue and public events on healing the past.[10]

Clearly painful memories must be more judiciously addressed, if society is also able to move on. Wounds heal slowly where old resentments are easily re-inflamed by politicization. Too, there are difficulties inherent in bypassing systems of strict legal justice. Furthermore, doubt lingers about paramilitaries' freedom or willingness to tell the truth. Many others distrust any state-sponsored system, with ongoing evidence emerging of state collusion and cover-up. Nevertheless, people's experience of profound loss cries out for appropriate acknowledgement.

---

9   A Commission for Victim-Survivors has been established and four commissioners appointed (beginning in June 2008) though with an unsettled remit. Some churches seem open, if not to a full-scale Truth and Reconciliation Commission, to the idea of a Victims' Forum. Also a Consultative Group on Dealing with the Past is currently sitting, chaired by Archbishop Robin Eames and Denis Bradley, charged with drawing up recommendations to government on acceptable ways forward.

10   This project followed from the report written by South African Methodist minister, Alex Boraine (Boraine 2000), on his invitation visit to N.I. See: McEvoy 2006.

A Forum of Hearing and Healing: Toward Recognition, Acknowledgement and Transformation

Within this discussion I now offer a reflection on one strand in what remains a larger, complex process, which I believe is capable of eliciting support across cultural boundaries, and could generate consensus on further stages of forgiveness and reconciliation. This would take the form of a forum of listening and healing. The space would be open for sharing the uniquely personal memories of those who have come through traumatic bereavement, the impact of the loss on self and family and how far state and society have responded – whether in judicial, moral, civic or restitutional terms. Three interrelated moves can be identified, which, whatever the accompanying obstacles, open a path towards the rediscovery of truth and recognition, healing and forgiveness, and empowerment for reconciliation.

In regard to the search for truth, there is the intrinsic problem that any historical reconstruction is liable to ideological dissimulation, memory distortion and cultural entrapment. While there can be no future without remembering, the kind of remembering must be educative – capable of expanding the collective awareness, moving beyond ingrained preconceptions into a vision that is closer to faith. The second move – towards healing and forgiveness is a move of hope, since it involves the opening of new spaces for public acknowledgement of pain and loss, with opportunities for narrative, symbolic mourning and reintegration, rather than perpetuating sectarian grievances. This acknowledgement enables a third move, for it has the potential to release the transforming power of love, in energy for restorative justice and social reconciliation. In an effort to deepen and broaden the reflection on these inter-related dimensions, the insights of Ricoeur on 'Time and Narrative' will be adduced (Ricoeur 1988).

Memory and Narrative: Giving Truth a Meaning

There is a difficulty in finding a balanced engagement between remembering and forgetting; and for establishing the truth of what happened amid a conflict of interpretations (Interchurch Group on Faith and Politics 1998). In a forum in which victims and survivors would be the protagonists, the aim is not to try to wrest total clarity from past events. Here we touch on the different nature and truth-value of narrative, distinct from that determined by forensic 'facts'.

Ricoeur indicates two approaches to history: the idea of history as past, definitive and objectively retrievable in the form of data; and history viewed in terms of the 'trace' left by those who have passed through it. This second perspective is more open and accessible in every renewed act of remembering. A forum, unlike a law court, would resolutely aim to reconcile these notions of time and history.

Acknowledging Losses and Wounds: the Beginning of Healing

I have underlined that forgiveness and reconciliation are achieved neither by forgetting nor managed closure (Schreiter 1992, 18–27). Schreiter, speaks of 'a spirituality of reconciliation', proposing the paradox that 'wounds [are] a source for a spirituality of reconciliation'. Negatively, if left to fester, wounds do not heal. If attended with care they can become a source of healing for both sufferer and carer. While avoiding the temptation to, in Boland's words, 'make pain a souvenir', re-living memory offers a hope that those grieving can find ways of reconnecting to themselves and to their agency within society (Boland 1998, 21). In an ethos of empathy, they can find voice for what has not yet been said about their lost loved ones and about their own lives beyond the label 'victim'. Thus, narrative identity is shaped by a subjective relationship to one's whole life story – with its hope of overcoming fate and of entering into the flow of self-realization and transcendence (Smyth 2003, 111–2).

This narrative authority of the victim-survivor also allows the living witness the opportunity to 'stand in' for the dead, mediating their story. This is a movement of hope through which such persons can find a way, beyond the sealed-in experience of the catastrophic event that once 'made the clocks stop' on the loss of loved ones or shattering the hope of community (Ricoeur 1998, 184). The public dialogical context is critical to the healing process. Standing in as witness, the bereaved create a place in history for those who died, and find their own identity renewed, as they re-enliven the common memory. Thus, speaker and listener discharge their 'debt to the past, a debt of recognition to the dead' (Ricoeur 1998, 143, 152).

Reconciliation: as Re-Configuring and Transforming the Future

Reconciliation and restorative justice constitute the third move in consideration of a forum for victims and survivors. This is allied to the need to exceed legal categories of guilt and punishment, and to explore possibilities of atonement through reconnecting justice and reconciliation. There has been some laudable experiment in the juridical arena on alternative choices for victim and perpetrator. Within the purpose of collective responsibility and social freedom, a transformed future can be imagined, where space is made for 'the Other' – for victim and perpetrator both as distinct persons and as within every person. Thus, hostility can be reconfigured as hospitality and through restorative justice, love finds its way back to the public domain (Zehr 2001, 330–5; Zehr 2002; de Gruchy 2002, 181–213; Consedine 1995).

It is important to keep this sense of mutuality in clear view in terms of an ethical field structured by the encounter of self and other, and by the reading of the past from the perspective of the victims. Through a reconciling of different readings of the past, the old self-referential cycle is interrupted by a rhetoric that gives imagination its range and encourages a 're-configuration' of the future.

Ricoeur's insights on re-figuring the texts of the past have already been illuminating. But his examination of truth and memory goes further, couching the relationship of speaker and hearer in explicitly ethical terms, in the need to give the Other space, and opening to possibilities of a new story. As people read the texts of the past anew, there is a moral imperative 'to make changes, to participate actively in social transformation' (Ricoeur 1998, 157–8). This puts a value on the witness of testimony, as the most apt discourse within the forum under discussion – narrative, memory, disclosure, ritual – whereby narrators and listeners participate in a process that both reveals and transforms. It is also transforming 'in the sense that a life examined in this way is a changed life, another life' (Ricoeur 1998, 158). Here, the reality of the Other comes into view bearing a demand for change. Many (whatever the testimony of the victims), still fail to acknowledge the need for transformation, for it implies a conversion – the willingness to stand in the place of the Other, to look from a different stance, with ears open to that 'other' reading – and to take on the demands of a re-configured relationship.

Clearing the Way Ahead

While the time may not yet be ripe for a truth and reconciliation commission, it is important to clear the ground and open the soil. Where relationships have been skewed by sectarianism, reconciliation cannot be rushed. Contested interpretations of the past and of the basis and pace of change challenge churches and political leaders to transcend sectarian attitudes and practice, and to find ways of exercising a mediating role that envisages gestures of mutual forgiveness and reconciliation within and across their deeply confessionalistic communities. Comments made above about the direct influence of theology on the politics of forgiveness here reassume sharp moral relevance.

Because inter-community hostility is systemically embedded, institutions as well as individuals need to assume this obligation. In such a context, it is salutary to remember the necessity of transcending the exaggerated Protestant-Catholic polarization of theological perspectives on conversion, seeking instead to hold together visions of conversion as a dramatic event of breaking grace, and as the call to move into the grace of reconciliation in the struggle to restore right relationship.[11] I would therefore argue the need for the respective Protestant-Unionist and Catholic-Nationalist communities to listen and learn from the other's theological text. On all sides there is also a need to abandon the logic of guarantee and embrace the logic of forgiveness, which is rooted in trust and nourished by risk. Political and religious leaders are well placed to give a visible lead.

The religious and specifically Christian narrative of re-configured identity can be discerned in stories and lived examples of mediation and atonement.[12] Many have found it in themselves to forgive those who killed their loved ones. There are places too, imbued with the spirit of wisdom, friendship and care – houses of peace, meeting points for ecumenical conversation, projects of reconciling action. One thinks of

---

11   Schimmel indicates the range of distinctive identifications - from utter dependence on God's grace to human renewal and good works, within Jewish, Catholic and Protestant traditions (Schimmel 2002, 158–9).

12   Some former paramilitaries have established niches of power within their communities, continuing to foment sectarian fear and dependency. There are, however, many notable exceptions. One thinks of recently deceased, Billy Mitchell, former Loyalist paramilitary prisoner, who spoke tentatively about his conversion in terms of Christian faith and expressed in the shaping of a new, inclusive society. See: Fearon 2004. The across the board tributes to David Ervine (leader of the Progressive Unionist Party) following his untimely death in 2007, bear similar testimony to another paramilitary-turned-political peace-builder. Examples from the republican tradition could also be cited.

Corrymeela Community of Reconciliation, the Irish School of Ecumenics and local inter-congregational prayer times or social activities. In such spaces, stories are shared, losses acknowledged and integrated, healing begun. These are seedbeds that will lend sustenance to a fuller-scale public forum.

Already in such settings forgiveness and reconciliation are a constant hope that is sometimes fulfilled. Eavan Boland hints of the way grace does break through in a lost land, in the irreducible capacity for love across 'gorse-bright distances', softening ancient hatred and misunderstanding (Boland 1998, 42–3). In this mysterious, delicate task, we keep listening for reconciling voices, ready to reach out in welcome, patiently accepting of any lingering hesitation:

> *Come back to us*
> they said.
> *Trust me* I whispered.

References

Accattoli, L. (1998), *When a Pope Asks Forgiveness: The Mea Culpas of John Paul II*, Aumann, J. (trans.) (New York: Society of St Paul).

Arendt, H. (1958, 1959), *The Human Condition: A Study of the Central Conditions Facing Modern Man* (Chicago: Chicago University Press).

Boland, E. (1998), *The Lost Land: Poems* (New York and London: W.W. Norton Company).

Boraine, A. (2000), *All Truth is Bitter* (Belfast: NIACRO and Victim Support Unit).

Consedine, J. (1995), *Restorative Justice: Healing the Effects of Crime* (Lyttelton, NZ: Ploughshares Publications).

Daly, G. (1988), 'Forgiveness and Community', in Falconer, A.D. and Liechty, J. (eds), *Reconciling Memories* (Dublin: Columba Press).

Daly, G. (1998), 'One Church: Two Indispensable Values: Protestant Principle and Catholic Substance', *Irish School of Ecumenics Occasional Papers*, 4 (Dublin: Dominican Publications).

Daly, G. (1998), *Creation and Redemption* (Dublin: Gill and Macmillan).

Daye, R. (2004), *Political Forgiveness: Lessons from South Africa* (New York: Orbis Books).

Fearon, K. (2004), *The Conflict's Fifth Business: A Brief Biography of Billy Mitchell* (Belfast: LINC Resource Centre) <http://www.linc-ncm.org/No.2.PDF>.

Frank Parsons, S. (ed.) (2002), *The Cambridge Companion to Feminist Theology* (Cambridge: Cambridge University Press).

de Gruchy, J. (2002), *Reconciliation: Restoring Justice* (Minneapolis: Fortress Press).

Harakas, S.S. (2001), 'Forgiveness and Reconciliation', in Helmick, R.G. and Petersen, R.L. (eds), *Forgiveness and Reconciliation: Religion, Public Policy and Conflict Transformation* (Philadelphia: Templeton Press).

Hurley, M. (1994), *Reconciliation in Religion and Society* (Belfast: Institute of Irish Studies).

Interchurch Group on Faith and Politics (1998), *Remembrance and Forgetting: Building a Future in Northern Ireland* (Belfast: The Faith and Politics Group).

Irenaeus, *Against the Heresies*, IV.

Jones, G. (1995), *Embodying Forgiveness: A Theological Analysis* (Grand Rapids: Eerdmans).

Lossky, V. (1985), *In the Image and Likeness of God*, Erickson, J. and Bird, T. (eds) (New York: SVS Press).

MacKintosh, H.R. (1954), *Christian Experience of Forgiveness* (London: Nisbet and Company).

McEvoy, K. (2006), *Healing Through Remembering Report: Making Peace with the Past* (Belfast: HTR) <http://www.healingthroughremembering.org>.

McFague, S. (1993), *The Body of God: An Ecological Theology* (London: S.C.M. Press).

Minow, M. (1998), *Between Vengeance and Forgiveness: Facing History after Genocide and Mass Violence* (Boston: Beacon Press).

R.C. International Theological Commission Report (2000), 'Memory and Reconciliation: The Church and the Faults of the Past', *Origins*, 48, 16 March.

Ricoeur, P. (1967), *The Symbolism of Evil* (Boston: Beacon Press).

Ricoeur, P. (1998), *Time and Narrative*, vol. 3, Blamey, K. and Pellauer, D. (trans.) (Chicago: Chicago University Press).

Ricoeur, P. (2004), 'The Difficulty to Forgive, in Junker-Kenny, M. and Kenny, P. (eds), *Memory, Narrativity, Self and the Challenge to Think God*, (Münster: LIT Verlag).

Schimmel, S. (2002), *Wounds Not Healed by Time: The Power of Repentance and Forgiveness* (Oxford: Oxford University Press).

Schreiter, R.J. (1992), *Reconciliation: Mission and Ministry in a Changing Social Order* (New York: Orbis Books).

Smyth, G. (1995), *A Way of Transformation: a Theological Evaluation of the Conciliar Process of Mutual Commitment to Justice, Peace and the Integrity of Creation, World Council of Churches, 1983-1991* (Berne: Peter Lang).

Smyth, G. (1997), 'Sabbath and Jubilee', in Ucko, H. (ed.), *The Jubilee Challenge: Utopia or Possibility* (Geneva: WCC).

Smyth, G. (2001), 'Brokenness, Forgiveness, Healing and Peace in Ireland', in Helmick, R.G. and Petersen, R.L. (eds).

Smyth, G. (2003), 'Endangered Identity and Ecumenical Risk', in Pierce, A. and Smyth, G. (eds), *The Critical Spirit: Theology at the Crossroads of Faith and Culture* (Dublin: Columba Press).

Zehr, H. (2001), 'Restorative Justice', in Reychler, L. and Paffenholz, T. (eds), *Peace-Building: A Field Guide* (Boulder and London: Lynne Rienner).

Zehr, H. (2002), *The Little Book of Restorative Justice* (Pennsylvania: Good Books).

Chapter 6

Truth, Reconciliation and Nation Formation in 'Our Land' of Timor-L'Este

Damian Grenfell

In November 2004 community members gathered under a banyan tree in the port village of Hera on the north coast of Timor-L'Este. They had come to participate in the Community Reconciliation Program organized by the Commission for Reception, Truth and Reconciliation of East Timor, commonly known as CAVR.[1] The hearing was an attempt to reintegrate former East Timorese militia who were involved in violence during the withdrawal of Indonesian military and pro-integration militias in 1999.

The hearing was facilitated by a panel comprised of representatives from local church, youth and women's organizations, and was chaired by CAVR's Dili District Commissioner. To the right of the panel were 15 former members of the notorious Aitarak militia. To the left was a victim of their violence.[2] Sitting front and centre were a group of *lia nain*, traditional elders from the community who lent authority to the hearing.[3] Three CAVR administrators ensured that written records of the day were kept, legal processes were adhered to and that the statements of those involved corresponded with pre-hearing testimony.

CAVR procedures and mandates were publicly read, community members asked former militia to clarify their roles in the violence, and testimony from the former militia and the victim was given. The two day hearing was marked by different social and ceremonial acts, such as the reading of CAVR's mandate, a community lunch, the unfurling of the national flag and the testimony from those involved in the violence. Finally, in an act of community-mediated reconciliation, each perpetrator embraced the victim and received from the *lia nain* a red smear of betel nut to their forehead.

---

1   The acronym CAVR is from the Portuguese name *Comissão de Acolhimento, Verdade e Reconciliacão de Timor-L'Este*, though it became used across different languages.

2   *Aitarak* means thorn and was one of the most powerful militias established prior to the vote in 1999.

3   The literal translation of the Tetun term 'lia nain' is the 'keeper of the word'. It describes men who hold spiritual and customary knowledge and are often central to ceremonial activities in Timor-L'Este.

As with other hearings held across the new nation between 2003 and 2005, a banner was suspended above the Hera proceedings that read '*Ho Rekonsiliasaun ita hametin unidade iha ita rain*' ('With Reconciliation we can strengthen unity in our land.) The inferred link between reconciliation and the 'making of the nation' is common throughout CAVR's work, as it is more generally with truth and reconciliation commissions elsewhere.

This chapter aims to explore the link between truth and reconciliation processes and national unity, beginning with an examination of CAVR's community reconciliation and truth-seeking programs. It will be argued that, while such programs have a concern for justice, they remain underpinned by a nationalist logic where peace is sought as a means of guarding the nation. To situate an analysis only within the logic of CAVR's programs would be to miss the subtle yet powerful ways such a body intersects with the more general process of nation formation. Hence, in the second section, the work of Benedict Anderson will be cited to argue that the textual material produced through the truth and reconciliation process worked to integrate people temporally across an abstract territorial space. The third section will extend Anderson's connection between the temporal and the textual so as to argue that, in a post-conflict and agriculturally dominant society, a sense of the nation can be carried significantly through embodied forms of interaction. Taken together, these arguments support the link between reconciliation and the nation as typified by the rhetoric in the banner hung at the proceedings in Hera, Timor-L'Este. They also show that the truth and reconciliation process has effects that extend beyond its immediate intent or the logic of specific programs.

CAVR and the National Future

Born in 'flames and blood' like so many nations before it, on 30 August 1999 the East Timorese voted overwhelmingly against the option of autonomy within Indonesia. This set the stage for a national independence that came on the back of social and material devastation caused by the looting and destruction carried out by pro-Indonesian supporters and the Indonesian military. Much of the country's infrastructure was devastated, approximately 1,500 people were killed and a third of the population was forcibly deported to Indonesia.[4]

The level of destruction in 1999, combined with the effects of Portuguese colonialism and Indonesian occupation, meant that while Timor-L'Este existed on the world map there were none of the usual means to sustain the new nation from within. A plethora of institutions led by the United Nations began the slow and uneven process of nation formation – establishing the mechanisms for directly or indirectly carrying and propagating the idea of the new nation. Resources went into forming a centralized state, a market codified in relation to the national territorial form and the means to carry the idea of the nation (especially through symbols). The means were being built so as to carry the day-to-day reminders, from bank notes to

---

4   This violence came at the bloody end of a conflict that has been estimated to cost more than 180,000 lives.

the time on the clock, that both territory and sovereignty had been brought into a sustainable unison.[5]

As part of this process, enormous efforts went into preventing renewed violence. First, the International Force for East Timor (INTERFET) and then the United Nations Transitional Authority in East Timor (UNTAET) were responsible for a large contingent of foreign troops who were sent to secure Timor-L'Este from continued militia and military activities from across the West-Timor border. However, the question of how to secure the nation from within remained, not least because so many of its citizens had sided with the Indonesian occupiers. To meet this need, a number of institutions were formed over the period of United Nations mandated rule, with CAVR being one of the key post-occupation peace-building institutions. Taking form over 2002, and commencing its public activities in 2003, CAVR focused its activities on two mandates. First, to reintegrate into the community former perpetrators of certain 'less serious' human rights crimes through the Community Reconciliation Program (CRP), and second, through truth-seeking, to determine a factual basis regarding human rights abuses from April 1974 until October 1999 (Pigou 2004; Kent 2005). Both programs can be seen as underpinned by a concern, not just for human rights, but for securing the new nation more generally from renewed conflict and cycles of violence.[6]

While the CRP process was seen as providing a form of justice when virtually no formal legal infrastructure was available, it was also an important step in attempting to secure the nation from cycles of retributive violence. By drawing the perpetrator, victim and community together, an attempt was made to bind those once violently opposed to one another into a peaceful coexistence.

The logic of such a process is that the victim's claims are clearly recognized and recorded with the hope that this will be enough to end ongoing enmity with former militia who live in the same community. Participating in a CRP also gave a perpetrator state-sanctioned security within the new political structures, serving to negate the sense of living in opposition to the new state and nation and perhaps mitigating future possibilities for re-mobilization. As long as the admission of guilt is not disproved by new evidence in the future, former militia members received a guarantee never to be prosecuted by the state for their crime.

'Truth-seeking', the second key program of CAVR, can be construed as a means to establish a human rights culture but it also operates as the condition of the new nation as a whole. As an early CAVR pamphlet suggests:

> We need to build a solid foundation for our new nation. If we ignore the suffering and violations of our past, we run the risk that they will continue to have a damaging effect on our community and nation. The first ingredient of this foundation must be facing the truth – as individuals, communities and as a nation. To acknowledge what has happened

---

5   The influence here is from Gellner 1983.

6   Such sentiments can be found in the earliest calls for a Truth and Reconciliation Commission, for 'political stability', 'national unity' and 'reconstructing and generating peace within the society'. *Outcomes of the CNRT National Congress: 21–30 August 2000*, Dili, 2000, 15.

in our country is the first step to ensuring that such violations are never repeated (CAVR Pamphlet May 2002 (English and Portuguese version)).

Establishing the truth in such situations can limit the potential for violence in various ways. First, the construction of a 'truth' contributes to the public clarification of guilt through hearings or publications. In turn, this can prevent false accusations and community reprisals, creating a sense of justice by publicly identifying a perpetrator and recording their deeds. Second, the establishment of a formalized and circulated truth can consolidate the new nation by creating a clear historical break with the past. The effect of CAVR's program similarly delineated the past – notably the period of its review of April 1974 until October 1999 – marking the present as a distinctly separate and historical phase.

The third way that a truth-seeking program is used to break cycles of violence comes with the circulation of that 'truth' in the new society. CAVR's final report, *Chega*, is full of narratives that convey the impact that violence has on people's lives. By drawing on the testimony of victims, material produced through truth-seeking mechanisms can be used in an attempt to change cultures that may see violence as an appropriate form of conflict resolution. For instance, following a split in the military in early-2006, which led to a complete breakdown of security in Dili, the then President and Prime Minister, both former critics of *Chega*, implored the public to learn from its findings (Gusmão 2006; Ramos-Horta 2006).

'Truth-Seeking' and 'Community Reconciliation' programs feed into the general process of nation formation by reducing the possibility of instability or conflict. This is to consider their work on their own terms however. It is also possible to extend the analysis so as to consider the ways in which CAVR brought together a war torn society. This latter argument will explore how nation formation has been theorized – with emphasis on the work of Benedict Anderson – and how nation formation has occurred in practice in Timor-L'Este.

Building a National Discourse

To use the work of Benedict Anderson to understand the impact of truth and reconciliation commissions on nation formation is to choose one of a possible number of key 'modernist' theorists. While drawing almost singularly from his influential *Imagined Communities*, the arguments in the remainder of this chapter also aim to modify Anderson's modernist tendency towards an abstract account of nationhood.

According to Anderson, ontological shifts across early modernity – new discoveries both social and scientific – stimulated social changes that made possible new forms of community, including the nation (Anderson 1991). Anderson notes a shift away from how time is understood in pre-modern societies, namely as a 'simultaneity along time, where the past and future are bound to an instantaneous present, marked by prefiguring and fulfilment' (which he calls Messianic time). Changes across early modernity result in 'homogenous, empty time', marked by temporal coincidence and measured by the clock and calendar (Anderson 1991, 24). For Anderson, this change in temporal perception towards homogeneity enabled people to imagine themselves as living alongside other people simultaneously.

Although nationalists subjectively call upon less abstract forms of social integration – for example, through the embodied connection of blood and belonging –the nation nevertheless remains understood as a bounded community of strangers moving simultaneously across time. While Timor-L'Este is a world away from the nations that Benedict Anderson wrote of in *Imagined Communities*, his comprehension of the importance of print and also temporality allow for some of his ideas to be carried forward into a contemporary example of nation formation.

To begin with the question of print, it is worth returning to the banner at Hera that proclaimed 'with reconciliation we can strengthen unity in our land'. This banner was similar to a range of other textual materials produced by CAVR whereby the nation was presented as none other than a *fait accompli*. Unlike any other number of possible subjects that could invoke a sense of simultaneity, the content of the material carries information that is explicitly about the nation. Maps, lists of commissioners, laws, mandates, programmatic structures and explanations are all presented graphically or literally within the legal-territorial logic of Timor-L'Este.

The repetitive use of 'we' and 'our' in CAVR pamphlets indicates the way in which readers are not simply presented with the nation as an object but are drawn into it. For example, in the CAVR booklet *Hear Our Voices* people are extracted from their immediate modes of existence and situated within the nation:

> In public hearings in villages and sub-district towns across the country, and at the national hearings, the CAVR placed victims of violations at the centre of the national story of Timor-L'Este. The voice of our sisters and brothers who suffered, and who were silenced for so many years, is a vital voice which must be heard in independent Timor-L'Este. We believe that only through understanding and appreciating the impact of violence upon people's lives we as individuals and as a nation remain vigilant to ensure that this behaviour is never repeated in our land (Guterres 2005).

This is to consider the effect of the text on the reader. Of equal importance is the form of the objects circulated, in this instance, identical, mass-produced, distributed and printed texts. For Anderson, 'print capitalism' played a key role in the emergence of the nation. According to this process, the intersection between modes of communication (mass print) and production (capitalism in search of new markets) gave rise to print languages that were below the elite use of Latin and above the multiple day-to-day vernaculars. These new markets acted as a kind of disembodied field of exchange in which the reader was linked across a territory with countless unknown others.[7]

> Speakers of the huge variety of 'Frenches, Englishes, or Spanishes', who might find it difficult or even impossible to understand one another in conversation, became capable of comprehending one another via print and paper. In the process, they gradually became aware of the hundreds of thousands, even millions, of people in their particular language-field, and at the same time that only those hundreds of thousands, or millions, so belong.

---

7 The notion of disembodiment is used to counter a limitation of the term 'imagined', which does not allow enough of a sense of how abstract processes return to re-frame and shape people's activities. 'The imagined' runs the risk of being seen only as enacted in the mind. See: James 1996.

These fellow-readers, to whom they were connected through print, formed, in their secular, particular, visible invisibility, the embryo of the nationally imagined community.

People were connected not just by the understanding that a common language was being shared, but also by the act of reading the material which linked people according to a sense of horizontal simultaneity, through reading 'at the same time'.

At first glance the applicability of Anderson's ideas to contemporary Timor-L'Este may appear limited, not least because access to mass-communication systems remain limited. Moreover, literacy is extremely low and the majority of people live in agricultural conditions where printed materials, such as newspapers, are rare. In the absence of such infrastructure, CAVR has an important role to play in nation formation, being one of the few organizations able to distribute identical materials, with an explicitly national content, across the country.

One or all of the four constitutionally designated languages of Timor-L'Este wer used in the materials circulated by CAVR; Portuguese and Tetun are the two official national languages, English and Indonesian are working languages. While there was a narrow plurality in the languages used, a sense of language fixity was created. The establishment of these official languages limited the use of other vernaculars and languages to their specific regions. Moreover, whichever language is used still provides a sense of differentiation from a colonial past; Tetun is not spoken in Portugal and Portuguese is not spoken in Indonesia. This meant that the circulation of textual objects – posters, pamphlets, banners and booklets – created an opportunity for a subjective recognition of living simultaneously with a distinct number of strangers within a defined territory.

The sense of simultaneity that Anderson argues is created through the consumption of replicable objects is of course not confined to printed matter. While there was a reliance on textual production in Timor-L'Este following independence, CAVR also employed radio to create a sense of the nation. As a CAVR staff member describes:

> … the whole purpose of our program was to foster this notion of, this is the whole country doing this. So Los Palos listening to Suai, Manufahi listening to Dili, Liquica listening to Viqueque and Oecussi listening to Ermera, and so people can say, particularly around the CRP process, we're all part of this, this is bigger than the single community … At the local level, and at the national level, and at how the two mix through the sharing of experiences through people being brought from all different villages and regions to the national level … And that was our design, that people would feel that in doing this local thing they were part of the national process (Interview with Participant 13, CAVR 2004).

This quote represents the arguments made thus far. In the first instance people learn about a national program and the nation itself, identifying those different places within the territorial confines of the new nation—'Liquica listening to Viqueque and Oecussi listening to Ermera'. But here we also see an oral equivalent to Anderson's notion of the impact of print languages: a radio program held together by the one language of the broadcaster to which all the people are 'listening', simultaneously undertaking one activity and comprehending the same material with a set of strangers in a distinct territory. For all its importance though, mass mediated information is only one way in which the idea of a nation was invoked through the practices of

CAVR. To this must be added a sense of the corporeal: the bodies that carry the nation into being.

Embodying the Nation

The level of violent division within the state apparatus and the emergence of ethnically framed bloodshed across Timor-L'Este during 2006 could prompt the question of national failure.[8] However, this was a conflict triggered from within the state, fuelled by rivalries about how and by whom the country was run. Changing the territorial domain of Timor-L'Este never surfaced as a question through the crisis. Given that this discussion is concerned with the relationship between truth and reconciliation commissions and the processes of nation formation, it is equally reasonable to ask why Timor-L'Este did not collapse in 2006, either as an idea or in practice?

To answer, it is worth returning to the CRP hearing in Hera and the remarkable resemblance between it and several hundred other hearings held around the country. In other sites, the same banner hung, the same procedures were read, participants typically sat in the same formation, the same documentation ensued and the same legal framework supported the process. The pro-forma character of the hearings shows how a body such as CAVR can play an important institutional role in the process of nation formation, suggesting that Benedict Anderson's analysis needs to be tempered and extended.

In a short article written well before the tumultuous events of 1999, Anderson put forward arguments as to why Indonesia's attempt to absorb East Timor had failed. As part of his answer, he argued that from 1975 East Timorese nationalism grew for two reasons. First, a 'profound sense of commonality emerged from the gaze of the colonial state. Indonesian power is infinitely more penetrating, infinitely more widespread, than Portuguese colonial power ever was' (Anderson 1993, 25). In tandem with this was the ability to form a common opposition via the practice of the Catholic faith, at once permissible under the Indonesian regime of Pancasilia while simultaneously in opposition to Islam as the dominant faith of the oppressor.

> The Catholic commonality in some sense substitutes for the kind of nationalism I have talked about elsewhere, which comes from print capitalism. Moreover, the decision of the Catholic hierarchy in East Timor to use Tetun, not Indonesian, as the language of the Church has had profoundly nationalizing effects. It has raised Tetun from being a local language or lingua franca in parts of East Timor to becoming, for the first time, the language of 'East Timorese' religion and identity. (Anderson 1993, 26).

If we accept that East Timorese nationalism grew in part out of the coercive effect of the Indonesian state then it is possible for a sense of modern simultaneity to be freed from the focus that Anderson gives to language alone. What is important is not the cultural artefact in itself – for instance a prayer book – but the subjective response to it; a silent acknowledgment that thousands of others are participating in

---

8   See for instance the Report of the United Nations Independent Special Commission of Inquiry for Timor-L'Este, Geneva, 2 October 2006; Trindade and Castro 2007.

the same process. The idea of a 'Sunday Mass' is a good example. People may never need to enter a different church to receive communion but they know how to do so. A secularized equivalent is the Independence Day ceremony, where people across the country stop at the same time and participate through ceremonial processes in almost identical activities. The spread of an institutional presence over a specified domain carries with it the possibility of people undertaking a range of activities that give rise to a sense of co-presence, of people linked by the likeness and purpose of their activities with unknown others. Hence at the Hera hearing, the use of the phrase 'our land' would have been an absurdity had people not simply assumed that it was a reference to Timor-L'Este as a whole.

The emphasis given by Anderson and other modernist thinkers to the abstract character of the nation, necessary for the sense of co-presence and shared temporal and spatial relations with others, allows us to understand a key process in how nations are formed and sustained. Yet nations cannot simply be understood if they are left at the level of the imaginary, as if taking place only in the 'lair of the skull' (Anderson 1991, 35). For all the emphasis given to the disembodied, via epitaphs such as 'imagined', 'industrial', 'mass', 'modern' and 'abstract', social relations that are constituted face-to-face remain crucial to understanding nation formation.[9] Face-to-face, or embodied-extended relations, are those forms of social relations that are integrated by regular, meaning-generating contact conducted in person. While it is understood that even in Anderson's terms a book is read by a person in an embodied sense, the emphasis here is on concrete forms of interchange between people (James 1996, 23–5).

The notion of corporeality is significant to our discussion in two ways. First, there is the sense of the embodiment of simultaneous activity, for instance the choice of participating in a reconciliation hearing not for the sake of spectacle alone but because the event is seen to be important to a broader society. This then extends the importance of the ceremonial beyond its own immediate logic by giving corporeal significance to an act that is felt beyond rather than within a particular place. In this way, we enter a kind of reciprocal movement between the corporeal and the nation, where on the one hand activities such as a CRP hearing help bring the nation into being, at the same time as the nation bears back upon the physical body of its participants and activities are re-defined as being 'national'.

Second, a sense of the corporeal is important when considering how information was transmitted across territory. With a lack of mass-communication systems, CAVR operations were centred in the capital, which in turn coordinated regional offices and then sub district teams. These teams were to carry CAVR programs to the most localized levels (Interview with Participant 11, CAVR 2003). In such instances people come to be informed about the nation in which they live via the transmission of knowledge by embodied others who make 'speeches'. In this sense the nation is formed through the innumerable tracks across the land that connect otherwise isolated communities with the nation as a whole. As one CAVR worker explained,

---

9   This list could be more extensive, though I am drawing not just on Anderson but the work of Ernest Gellner, Paul James and Tom Nairn.

the embodied character of such relations was crucial to the establishment of lines of communication that enabled the national program:

> Up until the end of the commission we did not have phone lines to these people. ... So people had to come once a week, people from the regional offices and the district team coordinators came to Dili, and the week after that the regional coordination unit from Dili went to the regional offices. ... That is how we communicated...we physically had to do our communication face-to-face, like the rest of Timor-L'Este (Interview with Participant 16, CAVR 2006).

These processes, both embodied and disembodied, transmit notions of nationhood to a multiplicity within the nation, embedding, shaping and further consolidating a conscious sense of integration. In the case of CAVR speeches about the institution's mandate, members of the community hear an embodied voice conveying information but the information itself is authored and authorized from afar. This is one way in which a kind of mutual dependence can be understood to occur between the corporeal ushers of the nation and the disembodied forms of mass organization and communication.

This brings us back to 2006 and to the question of why the national form had not more obviously been brought into question by the violence and collapse of key aspects of the state. While a violent and politically driven competition over resources was occurring within the nation, identification with the nation as a legitimate and assumed territorial domain did not shift. This was in part due to the role CAVR had played in the post-independence era as one of the few institutional means by which people were drawn together and incorporated within the nation. The nation was not simply brought into being in the capital alone. Rather, the new nation is carried by people travelling across territory and creating an exchange of information between a political centre and local communities. As a result, the nation has come to be the logical ground for life, including the enactment of violence.

Other processes can be understood as producing a sense of simultaneity through like activity, for example, the consolidation of the education system and the curriculum, coordinating laws, policing and citizenship, the development of codified and organized production (including state, state-regulated and capitalist driven) and the implementation of taxation. While a complex system of production might be mapped onto a national territorial form, for instance a coffee industry, the intent of such an activity remains the private appropriation of profits. A body such as CAVR may similarly be organized across a territorial domain. However its orientation towards the sustainability of the nation made it a key element of nation formation in Timor-L'Este. While the 2006 crisis may indicate that East Timorese were not willing to see all of their fellow citizens as equals, especially in relation to who could lay claim to forging the nation, Timor-L'Este remained a legitimate point of identification. That alternative national formats – such as further division of the country or a re-integration with Indonesia – did not surface as part of the 'crisis narrative', suggests that East Timorese have, to some degree, come to see the nation as a natural and assumed domain.

Conclusion

Caught between processes of European decolonization and Indonesian power, the high price for Timor-L'Este's independence has been the effort required to buttress the nation against innumerable pressures. The violence across 2006 and 2007 may give the impression of failure, both of bodies such as CAVR and of the process of nation formation as a whole. While the presence of CAVR did not eradicate either a culture of impunity or the use of violence for political ends, it is noteworthy that there was no real discourse that linked previous opponents of Timor-L'Este's independence to the current violence. Integrative processes such as those undertaken by CAVR are just one means toward nationhood. However, with both its aims and organizational domain effectively national, CAVR has been able to temporally draw people together through embodied and disembodied practices in ways that integrate them into new national forms, in effect fulfilling the claim that with 'reconciliation we can strengthen unity in our land'.

References

Anderson, B. (1991), *Imagined Communities: Reflections on the Origin and Spread of Nationalism*, 2nd edn, (London and New York: Verso).

Anderson, B. (1993), 'Imagining East Timor', *Arena Magazine*, 4, April–May.

Gellner, E. (1983), *Nations and Nationalism* (Oxford: Basil Blackwell).

Gusmão, X. (2006), 'Unofficial translation of President Gusmão's televised speech on 22 June 2006', East Timor Action Network Website <http://www.etan.org/et2006/june/30/22xana.htm>.

Guterres, I. (2005), 'Preface', in *Comissão de Acolhimento, Verdade e Reconciliação de Timor-L'Este, Rona Ami-nia Lia* (Dili: CAVR).

James, P. (1996), *Nation Formation: Towards a Theory of Abstract Community* (London: Sage).

Kent, L. (2005), 'Community Views of Justice and Reconciliation in Timor-L'Este', *Development Bulletin*, 68, 62–5.

Pigou, P. (2004), *The Community Reconciliation Process of the Commission for Reception, Truth and Reconciliation* (Dili: UNDP Timor-L'Este).

Ramos-Horta, J. (2006), 'Address by Dr José Ramos-Horta', República Democrática De Timor-L'Este Gabinete Do Primeiro-Ministro' (Cabinet Office of the Minister for Foreign Affairs and Cooperation), 10 July.

Trindade, J. and Castro, B. (2007), *Rethinking Timorese Identity as a Peacebuilding Strategy: The Lorosa'e – Loromonu Conflict from a Traditional Perspective*, (Dili, 6 June).

Chapter 7

Testimony, Nation Building and the Ethics of Witnessing: After the Truth and Reconciliation Commission in South Africa

Kay Schaffer

The Truth and Reconciliation Commission (TRC) hearings in South Africa initiated a project of reconciliation, nation building, and healing through a process of truth telling and forgiveness. Witness testimony provided the nation with a harrowing historical archive that somehow had to be incorporated into the weft and warp of a fractured and deeply divided society. In the decade since the hearings closed, the country has witnessed many acts of remembrance that have been woven into the 'rainbow nation', some with deft stitches to reveal the strength of its diversity, others darned and roughly patched to conceal its gaping divisions. This paper looks at two such initiatives. One concerns large memorial projects initiated by the government to commemorate the Struggle against apartheid, honour its victims and provide unifying myths of nationhood. The other relates to a small project of listening instigated by a trio of researchers concerned to honour the testimony of one TRC witness in order to assist her journey towards recovery. The former relies on a 'top-down' politics of reconstruction for the nation that is often pragmatic in intention and hegemonic in effect. The latter relies on an interpersonal ethic of listening, hospitality and openness to the other that is just in intention and singular in effect. Although both can be redemptive, one encourages a politics of sameness, while the other promotes an ethics of difference.

The first volume of the TRC Report seeds an argument for both sorts of memorial projects. In regard to its mission of reconciliation within the nation, the report insists on a process that depends, firstly, upon the testimony of victims and perpetrators to uncover the 'truth' about the past, in order to provide a path to healing for the nation and, secondly, upon the ethical reception of that testimony by listeners engaged in an ongoing intersubjective dialogue. Archbishop Tutu, the Chairperson of the Commission, repeatedly enacted an ethics of listening and recognition for victims during the hearings. For him the telling and listening process held out a promise of healing and closure for the nation:

> However painful the experience, the wounds of the past must not be allowed to fester. They must be opened. They must be cleansed. And a balm must be poured on them so they

can heal. This is not to be obsessed with the past. It is to take care that the past is properly dealt with for the sake of the future (SAPA News 1997, 1–2).

Exceeding the mandates of truth commissions which had preceded it, the TRC 'explicitly recognized the healing potential of telling stories', thus emphasizing the pre-eminent significance of storytelling in redressing the past, building a new memory archive for the nation, and restoring dignity to its previously disenfranchised citizens (TRC of South Africa Report 2003, 1:1, 112).[1] It also acknowledged multiple traditions within the nation and sought to incorporate Eurocentric and Afrocentric concepts into its processes of healing through forgiveness, including Christianity, psychoanalysis, and the traditional concept of ubuntu, in order to link them to the imperatives of nation building.

The TRC has been hailed as a 'miracle' in its mission of restorative rather than retributive justice. While it avoided outright civil war and modelled reconciliation through forgiveness, the TRC also had its shortcomings. In establishing 'truth-telling' as a condition for amnesty, it could not guarantee that perpetrators would fully disclose the 'truth', nor that reconciliation through forgiveness would occur between perpetrators and victims. In limiting testimony to politically motivated crimes, it could not address broader structural issues of systemic oppression, thus occluding social and economic inequalities and sidelining the suffering of secondary witnesses, particularly women, except as the mothers and wives of male victims of violence.[2] In mandating recognition of the equal status of all citizens in 'a shared, non-ethnically marked nation,' it required the presumption of a common citizenry, thus moderating an appreciation of different experiences, customs and traditions (Posel and Simpson 2002, 10). The TRC itself lacked the resources to provide adequate investigative research, counselling facilities or reparations to witnesses and their families, many of whom were re-traumatized by the process. In reporting to government as a quasi-judicial institution with no ultimate political authority, it had to rely upon the will of Parliament to accept and act on its recommendations.[3] And finally, although the TRC report promoted a process of ethical listening, it stopped short of demanding that white beneficiaries of apartheid take responsibility for change, leaving much of the work of reconciliation to black and coloured individuals and communities. Ten years on, much of the business of the TRC is unfinished and South Africa remains a divided society. The rifts and inequalities within and between individuals and racially

---

1   For a discussion of the significance of this mandate for South Africa in the context of the 1990s, the decade of reconciliation around the globe, see: Schaffer and Smith 2004, 53–84.

2   In particular, see: Ross 2003; Goldblatt and Meintjes 1996.

3   In contradistinction to other commentators who support the TRC's mandate for reconciliation, Antjie Krog contends that the role of the TRC, as mandated by the interim constitution, was a pragmatic one: to grant amnesty to perpetrators. The focus on victims and their testimony was due to pressure from some legislators, combined with the moral guidance and charismatic leadership of Nelson Mandela and Archbishop Tutu. Further, the TRC's mission of reconciliation was eroded by the government's attempts to prevent the release of the TRC report and reluctance in addressing its recommendations. (Personal correspondence, 26 March 2008).

marked communities continue to trouble the nation with the effects of trauma and anger being passed on to the country's black youth.

The concept of reconciliation adopted by the government in the wake of the TRC hearings implied a belief in closure, the possibility of emancipation from an oppressive past and a resolution of conflict through acts of confession, amnesty, and forgiveness. This pathway to reconciliation, defined as a process of negotiation aimed at peaceful coexistence within a culture of human rights, relies on what Dirk Klopper describes as a straightforward trust in a redemptive, liberal humanist mission of healing through the enlightenment ideal of 'liberating reason' (Klopper 2004, 203). A number of commentators have pointed out the difficulties inherent in such a process. [4] Especially when what is 'proper' to the healing of the nation fails to register the divisions that continue to adhere to the social fabric, the different values, customs and traditions of peoples within the nation, the asymmetries of power and privilege between them and the 'improper' affective residues of trauma and pain that the TRC could not address. [5] They believe that ways must be found to keep the stories, counter-narratives and contestations open, to foster a multiplicity of perspectives and critical reappraisals of the past.

This – more difficult but increasingly unavoidable – pathway to reconciliation acknowledges the unequal terrain on which divided communities live and the ambiguities, disjunctive temporalities, and 'hetero-logics' that exist between participants involved in a continuing process of dealing with anger, pain, loss and the residues of the past. [6] Many survivors of apartheid live with daily reminders of the tensions between black and white South Africans that were literally 'written in blood' (Ratele 2003, 200). The dominant framework for reconciliation set up by the TRC, and modified by successive ANC governments, actually undermines those shaping experiences and perspectives, and represses that which remains contested, unarticulated, chaotic and unresolved. These tensions, profoundly felt in practical, material, experiential, symbolic and theoretical terms, are perhaps most apparent in the contestations around memorial projects and memory sites.

Memory Projects and Memory Sites

Within the post-TRC climate of dissent and affirmation and in the name of 'transformation', the government instituted extensive policy units and invested hefty sums in highly visible commemorative projects. Foremost sites include the

---

4   See, for example, Grunebaum-Ralph 2001, 198–213; Posel and Simpson (eds) 2002; Ross 2003, 143–59; Villa-Vicencio and Doxtader (eds) 2003; Wilson 2001.

5   Grunebaum-Ralph adopts Kristeva's notions of the 'proper' and 'improper' body to tease out some of the 'improper' aspects of abjection and loathing that are cast out, dispelled or rejected by the social order in order to stabilize the 'proper' narratives that sanitize and settle the messiness of the past.

6   Derived from Michel de Certeau's notion of heterology, or the logic of otherness, hetero-logics is a postmodern term to designate incommensurable differences, or the lack of correspondence between cultures and belief systems, that exist within and between diverse social groups. See de Certeau 1985.

District Six Museum in Cape Town and Robben Island; the Apartheid Museum and the Women's Gaol, both in Johannesburg; and the Hector Pieterson Memorial Museum in Soweto. Other projects include the creation of 'hero' statues dedicated to inspirational leaders like Nelson Mandela, Steve Biko and Mahatma Ghandi, as well as monuments to comrade-victims like the Guguletu Seven and the Cradock Four and numerous community memorials, some the source of local pride, others publicly disputed.[7] These sites carry on the 'reconciliation through truth' project initiated by the TRC, which sought to acknowledge the struggle and suffering of the past through the creation of a common history intended to rectify divisions, unify the nation and effect closure.[8] They commemorate the Struggle, pay tribute to its heroes, reference and transform sites of suffering and resistance, and cultivate a common national memory archive to signal the politics of the new nation. In articulating hitherto untold stories, museums and memorial sites embed the historical experience of a previously excluded citizenry into new narratives of nation.[9] They have a redemptive mission aimed at closing off the past for the sake of national unity. Driven by political necessities, the new sites of memorialization highlight some features of the Struggle, while occluding others, to homogenize a heterogeneous past and support new ideologies and political hierarchies. These projects can be fraught with difficulties. When developed through a 'top-down' approach to carry out an ideological agenda, they can undermine peace-building initiatives 'at the risk of further marginalizing already vulnerable groups' (Naidu 2006, 2). In choosing who will be remembered and who forgotten, they 'sanitize' history and create a new national consciousness, while also establishing personality cults through a new genealogy of heroes that can function to reduce a complex historical experience (Marschall 2006, 176–93).

When Things Go Wrong …

Memorial sites located in communities that were themselves sites of violent struggle highlight some of the dilemmas about what stories to tell and how to represent them. During the construction phase, there is the question of how to consult with stakeholders who may be divided in their relationship to the past. Once constructed,

---

7   The Center for the Study of Violence and Reconciliation (CSVR) in conjunction with the Khulumani Support Group has conducted case studies of several disaffected communities in which monuments have been erected including Thokoza, Katlehong, Tembisa, Wilgespruit, Vaal, Kagiso and Mamelodi. See: <http://www.csvr.org.za/papers>, under the headings: Living Memory and Memorialization / Southern African Reconciliation Projects.

8   Others include a memorial in Grahamstown to commemorate the victory of Xhosa battles against the British in 1819; Freedom Park in Pretoria, a landscape of remembrance to the Struggle; the Slave Lodge in Cape Town; The Walter Sisulu Square of Dedication in Kliptown; and the Freedom Tower in Port Elizabeth. For a discussion of the projects and the issues of representability they raise. See: Gubeni, Z. et al. 2003, in Villa-Vicencio and Doxtader (eds) 2003, 25–36.

9   This reference invokes Homi K. Bhabha's notion of the nation not as a political entity but as a discourse, a cultural production of language and rhetoric, a 'field of meanings and symbols associated with national life' (Bhabha 1990, 3).

there is the matter of how to encourage communities to 'own' and manage the sites, how to maintain dialogue about the inconsistencies and tensions of the past as they impact upon the present. Sometimes the very places of commemoration lead to bitter disputes within the 'host' community. In such instances, the process of reconciliation is liable to backfire, with damaging and demoralizing consequences for the communities they were meant to 'heal'. This was the fate of memorial projects at Thokoza and Sharpeville, largely due to a lack of prior consultation by the government and the political imperatives and pragmatic intentions that fuelled these initiatives.

Despite these difficulties, it is possible for sites of memory to foster reconciliation in ways that can exceed the institutional, political and ideological mandates of government. Even when driven from the 'top-down', they can invite (or at least tolerate) grass root interventions and involvements that allow for the presentation of multiple perspectives and incite critical and counter-narratives that unsettle unifying representations of the apartheid past.

Guided Cultural Tours

The political mandate of memorial sites, like the internationally renowned Apartheid Museum and the Hector Pieterson Memorial Museum, enjoins the institution to (re-) order the past into a coherent narrative out of experiences that were ambiguous, inchoate, traumatic and inherently unspeakable. Typically, memorial museums select and interpret significant markers of the past by recreating aspects of individual stories that stand in for more complex events. In the translation of personal lives into a collective and shared history, some part of the compromised and ambiguous experience of struggle is concealed so that the symbolic processes of forgiveness and reconciliation can proceed. Government sponsored memory projects also construct a genealogy of 'heroes', often focusing on individual victimization and survival rather than communal aspects of struggle, inevitably re-constituting a masculinist and individualist historical archive (Marschall 2006, 183–6). Conversely, grass root interventions at memorial sites can promote a critical engagement with history, especially when the actual female and male survivors of that history conduct guided tours for visitors.

Active interventions made possible by survivor-initiated action groups, like WECAT (Western Cape Action Tours), sponsored by the Direct Action Centre for Peace and Memory in Cape Town, and the Khulumani Support Group, a national grass root action organization, offer alternative avenues for storytelling that keep alive the memories, the denied or unreconciled fragments of lives and the heterological histories contained within the fractured spaces of nationhood.[10] Typically, guides accompany visitors on trips to museums and memory sites, or host visits to exhibitions, offering their own account of the histories, experiences and narratives represented therein. Often, the guides were former prisoners of the

---

10 I recount my experience with Khulumani guides in 'Memory Work and Memorialisation in the New South Africa' in Gobodo-Madikezela and van der Mewre (eds) forthcoming.

State, persecuted and labelled 'terrorists' for attempting to advance their struggle towards freedom and democracy. The stories they tell interrupt the narrative flow of events depicted or commemorated by the memory site. These active interventions by apartheid survivors address the otherwise occluded performance space of testimony, enlivening it again and in new contexts, providing evidence of ongoing struggle, resilience and survival. Their stories invite visitors into an intersubjective encounter that promotes ethical listening, reciprocity between guest and host and openness to the incommensurable experiences of others.

Remembering Mrs. Konile

The two-fold mission of the TRC involved not only the uncovering of the 'truth' of the past but also the ethical reception of testimony by listeners. Memory sites and grass root interventions address the first goal. These activities are mainly political in motivation. The second goal of ethical witnessing, especially by white listeners, is perhaps the more difficult to achieve. It requires an individual ethic of care, beyond the realm of politics. Briefly made possible by the guides who work in the cultural sphere, it has taken more concrete shape in the research modelled by three academics from the University of the Western Cape, Antjie Krog, Kopano Ratele and Nosisi Mpolweni-Zantsi. Their transcultural memory project addresses the testimony of TRC witness, Mrs. Notrose Nobomvo Konile.[11] Their work, in a different and perhaps more focused way, models an ethics of listening, intersubjective dialogue and reciprocity across cultures of difference.

Antjie Krog, a journalist, poet and writer of the internationally acclaimed account of the TRC, *Country of My Skull*, worked for the South African Broadcasting Company as a journalist during the TRC hearings. She did not, however, report on Mrs. Konile's testimony, which she heard in translation during the hearings. In the absence of the structure or organization of other testimonies, it appeared to lack sense. Krog feared that any commentary she might make would reflect badly on the witness, a dilemma that played upon her conscience for many years. Recently, in a determined attempt to recover this testimony, she enlisted the help of her colleagues, Kopano Ratele, a critical discursive African psychologist, and Nosisi Mpolweni-Zantsi, a translator and teacher of Xhosa language and literature. Together they began an extraordinary recovery project that models not a politics of remembrance but an ethics of listening. Their collective work pursues the second goal of the TRC, namely the ethical reception of testimony to enable the recognition of victims and acknowledgement of their suffering so that they might begin to heal. In its methodological approach, their project bears witness to a Derridian concept of hospitality, a 'welcoming of the other', that engages in 'an art and a poetics' that exceeds even as it depends upon the political (Derrida cited in Naas 2005, 10).

---

11   The trio have given seminars and conference papers and completed two articles and a monograph based on this research, some of which has yet to be published. See Ratele et al. 2007, 188–204; Krog et al. 2008; and Ratele et al. forthcoming. I thank the authors for making the unpublished manuscripts available to me and giving me permission to quote from them.

The TRC was a political process that promoted but could not guarantee an ethics of listening. It also modelled a form of storytelling that initiated a dominant narrative for the new nation. If witnesses varied from the expected 'script', their testimony ran the danger of being misunderstood or not properly acknowledged. This is what happened to Mrs. Konile, whose testimony deviated from the more typical story of violence, victimization, stoic struggle and resistance, resilience and triumph over evil (Ratele et al. forthcoming, 36). Sidonie Smith and I refer to this normative, testimonial form as an 'ur' narrative, 'a common story [that] emerges out of the accumulation of voices telling stories that conform to a similar structure, thematically organized to invoke similar histories of abuse, violence, or degradation, and utilizing similar modes of address that make an emotive appeal' (Schaffer and Smith 2004, 45). Those stories, when incorporated into new national histories, present a template for the nation, what Geoffrey Bennington calls a 'narration at the centre of the nation: stories of national origins, myths of founding fathers, genealogies of heroes', that provide the nation with 'a history, a boundary, a name'.[12] They seed mythologies and genealogies that structure a redemptive narrative trajectory evident in the design of monuments and memorials like the Apartheid Museum, the Hector Pieterson Museum, the 'hero statues' and other commemorative sites.

When victim testimony fails to deliver the expected narrative, its teller can become invisible. This was the case with Mrs. Notrose Nobomvo Konile, the mother of Zabonke Konile, one of the youths murdered in what has come to be called the Guguletu Seven incident.[13] Mrs. Konile provided a seemingly incoherent story when she appeared before the TRC in April 1996, and it was largely overlooked. Her presence before the TRC, her testimony and its history contain many irregularities: she was presented simply as 'Mrs. Konile', without a first name; her name does not appear in the official TRC website index; when mentioned in the TRC report of the 'Guguletu 7', her surname is misspelled as 'Mrs. Khonele,' as it appears in the English translation of her testimony from the original Xhosa. Even, as the research team would later discover, her official identity papers misspell her middle name as Nobovu, not Nobomvo. Thus, the most minimal requirement of hospitality, that begins with a host asking for and receiving a visitor's name, seems to have failed to eventuate in this instance.

The substance of Mrs. Konile's testimony also presented difficulties. It confused and confounded listeners, drifting between the acknowledgement of her son Zabonke's death and seemingly disconnected details of her own suffering. Lacking a temporal or logical sequence, it made references to visions of a goat, of not knowing Cape Town or the ANC. Mrs. Konile seemed full of abnegation: ' I gave up ... I am no-one. I am nothing'. Her story lacked both a 'plot' (the *ur* narrative) and a core central moment (typically for the other grieving mothers, the last time they saw

---

12   Ratele et al. cite Bennington and discuss the relevance of his perspective. See: Ratele et al. 2007, 192.

13   The Guguletu Seven youth were enlisted into the Umkhonto weSizwe military wing of the ANC to be trained as soldiers inside the country by a former liberation youth comrade who, unknown to them, actually worked for the police. The boys were armed, ambushed, and killed by the Security Police in March 1986 as they attempted to surrender.

their murdered sons alive). As such it was not properly received or understood; it failed the expectations of its context. Unable to comprehend the testimony, Krog feared that any commentary or attempt at interpretation might lead to Mrs. Konile being ridiculed or stereotyped in the eyes of her white audience, and labelled as a superstitious, dull-witted black woman. This concern led Krog to question how a white person 'hears' the testimony of a black person. Believing that one can only know oneself and others through narrative, Krog feared that Mrs. Konile's narrative would estrange listeners and that she would not be/had not been afforded the dignity her testimony demanded.

These doubts, and her own ethical commitments as a white person seeking belonging in the new South Africa, led Krog to engage with Mpolweni-Zantsi and Ratele in a project of recovery. Together they listened to the original tapes of the dreamlike, seemingly senseless and incomprehensible narrative in which, as they attempted to re-transcribe and re-translate, they discovered many errors and mistakes. There were other surprises. First, they realized that Mrs. Konile introduced herself as coming not from Cape Town but from Indwe, a former mining region and a remote village in the Eastern Cape. She would not have known the city, nor was she likely to be politically aware of the activities of the ANC. Then they registered that her testimony was punctuated by many deep sighs, cries and pauses. She was a nervous and grieving witness. Mpolweni-Zantsi and Ratele attempted to interpret her testimony through their knowledge of African practices, values and beliefs. As a widow, the loss of her only son meant that she had lost her house and the little income he could provide for her. His death rendered her destitute. Adding to the pain, he had been buried in Cape Town, against her wishes, not at home where the deceased might connect with the ancestors and offer her protection. They speculated that her testimony concerning the goat might have referred to a dream or a foreboding premonition in which the ancestors spoke to Mrs. Konile. Unable to convince the police to permit her to return her son's body to Indwe, she 'gave up'; her son's death created an unbridgeable rupture in her life, rendering her a 'no-body'. As the research team worked closely together, they combined their transcultural knowledge of Western and African cultural, philosophical and psychological perspectives. They re-evaluated the testimony in the light of the specific cultural and communal Xhosa contexts of her life. As a result they listened to and 'read' the testimony differently, 'allowing a new form of story to emerge, registering its culturally-embedded meanings, its poetic richness, its rootedness in the traditions of Mrs. Konile's remote and rural Xhosa community and her personal experience of grief and loss' (Schaffer 2006).

After working together for two years, the colleagues visited Mrs. Konile. Their interview further clarified a number of contexts pertaining to her son's death. At the time of her testimony before the TRC, she had not seen the TV coverage of her son's murder nor had she attended the inquest. She identified her son's body in a mortuary some time later. The image, captured, created and circulated by the media, of Zabonke running towards his attackers, arms raised in a gesture of supplication, seeking forgiveness, remained imprinted in her memory, forestalling her ability to forgive his murderer, Constable Thapelo Mbelo.[14] Her testimony was borne out of this grief, loss and deprivation. She reported that later she took some comfort in the fact that Zabonke's remains eventually had been returned and buried with his ancestors and that the newly commissioned Guguletu Seven monument acknowledged his heroism. These acts of recognition had also helped her to reconnect to community and to establish some sense of control over her life. Through their research, Krog, Ratele and Mpolweni-Zantsi were able to reinterpret Mrs. Konile's testimony and restore 'sense' to the narrative with reference to African critical narrative paradigms. Through their interview with her they effected an ethical listening that had not been possible at the time of her testimony. After their visit to Indwe in 2008, they relate that they could trace a healing movement in her life, perhaps not from trauma to forgiveness, but from debilitating victim hood to some sense of agency, control and community interconnectedness (Ratele et al. forthcoming, 156).

Of Hospitality

The importance of this project might best be understood with reference to Derrida's concept of hospitality. Concerned with questions of justice, Derrida considers the difficulties of restoring 'peace' after times of conflict (Derrida 1999, 49; Derrida 2000). He suggests that something beyond, or more fundamental than, politics is necessary to effect justice for individuals and between conflicting groups. Considering what he calls 'the implacable law of hospitality,' he revisits and destabilizes the terms 'host' and 'guest', reversing the two French meanings of *hôte* and suggesting that one is never truly or completely 'at home' in one's own homeland (Derrida 1999, 37). As Carroll explains, '[t]he law of hospitality is rooted in this original displacement or deferment of the 'natural right' to possess and along with it the right to sovereignty – over either oneself or others' (Carroll 2007, 918). The TRC, as proxy witness for the state, acted (imperfectly) as host to Mrs. Konile at the hearings.[15] It invited her in but it also had to be invited by her; it received her testimony but also had to be received by her. Without that reciprocity, Mrs. Konile remained a foreigner. The TRC, as a state sponsored political process, was unable to address her, to welcome her with the reciprocity demanded of hospitality. She had no 'proper' name, no voice, and no context in which to express her difference from the expected and anticipated protocols of the hearings. Her 'excessive' testimony was provocative in relation to its terms of reference. As a result, she did not receive the recognition or respect owing her. Nor could she, without undermining the TRC processes and the (imperfect) sovereignty of the state and its pragmatic political intentions. What Krog, Ratele, and Mpolweni-Zantsi were able to do approaches what Derrida calls

---

14   The documentary *Long Night's Journey into Day* (2000), directed by Frances Reid and Deborah Hoffmann, documents four events through TRC testimony and subsequent witness interviews, including Guguletu Seven. In it, Mrs. Konile and other mothers confront their sons' murderer, who seeks their forgiveness. Mrs. Konile appears distressed and angry. Unlike the other mothers, she is unable to grant her forgiveness.

15   In this regard, Carroll argues that 'absolute hospitality demands that the sovereignty of the host, no matter how generous, be undermined' (Carroll 2007, 921).

'absolute hospitality', an act of total generosity that is unrealizable in political terms but not beyond the reach of ethics.[16] They gave themselves over to Mrs. Konile, acknowledging her as an unknown, possibly unknowable, other. They opened themselves to her unconditionally, listening and receiving her testimony and positing provisional, non-definitive interpretations. Over the two-year life of the project, the team addressed each 'event' – the tapes, the written testimony in Xhosa and English, the various translations and transcriptions, the visit and interview, considering each one in its unique context and singularity.

While working together, the research team evolved a new model of transcultural research and a new mode of reception, making itself into something more than the sum of its parts.

After visiting Mrs. Konile and preparing the manuscript that details their journey together, the researchers composed a letter to Mrs. Konile that appears on the last page of their book. In it they acknowledge her and people like her as 'people who live good lives beyond the theories and knowledge of the world' (Ratele et al. forthcoming, 166). The openness, reciprocity, and receptivity that the three practice in their dialogues with each other, as well as in their encounter with Mrs. Konile, models an ethic of hospitality that 'makes demands on the political from an extra-political space' (Carroll 2007, 920).[17] Aided by their openness to other ways of knowing and their belief in the interconnectedness of beings, the conduct of their research also enacts something akin to the African understanding of ubuntu, acknowledging that a person is made a person through others.

Conclusion

The testimony taken before the TRC, and reported by the South African and international media, created an archive of memory for the nation. In our book, *Human Rights and Narrated Lives*, Sidonie Smith and I survey the considerable achievements of the TRC while also noting that the processes of reconciliation it instigated were (could only have been) fraught with contradictions, contestations and discontinuities. In reflecting on some of these contradictions, held in a precarious balance by the TRC, we cite 'the different imperatives of African customary traditions and Western law, the different usages of testimony, the deep historical divisions of the past, and the gaps and fissures of memory' (Schaffer and Smith 2004, 70).

This paper extends that argument in order to highlight the difficult challenges of reconciliation and nation building as different survivors of apartheid find distinct pathways to reconciliation. In a country in which museums, monuments and memorials have long made claims on the landscape and marked relations of power and belonging

16   Michael Naas contends that 'hospitality to the event is what was always at the heart of Derrida's thought' (Naas 2005, 12).

17   Carroll continues: 'Absolute hospitality is not an Idea in the Kantian sense but more of an unrealizable possibility, an act of total generosity, a giving over of oneself and an opening of one's "home"—that is, domicile, community, state, or nation—to an unknown and ultimately unknowable other. An "absolute other" who remains other and foreign, perhaps even threatening, as he/she is welcomed and received in one's home(land).'

in the nation's history, new memorial projects assume added importance as the state endeavours to link the national heritage with the history of black struggle, prompting new beginnings. They also generate a range of diverse critical engagements with the past as former victims of apartheid take up different positions of power and privilege that connect them differently, and sometimes ambivalently, to the state's nation-building aspirations. State sponsored memorial projects attempt to enhance political unity by supporting the evolution of common histories and memories for the nation as a whole; contrapuntally, grass root community organizations resist the imposition of new histories and offer alternative models intended to grapple with the residues of intercultural violence, the ambiguities of victim and perpetrator stances, ongoing community conflicts and the pain carried by tens of thousands of individuals.

Sometimes commemorative projects can go wrong, increasing tensions rather than promoting reconciliation, as they did at Thokoza and Sharpeville. This is most likely to happen when the projects efface difference in their attempt to shape and contain complex and ambiguous histories. More often, these projects can foster reconciliation, especially when they invite interventions from grass root survivor action groups and afford first person accounts that provide multiple perspectives on the past. In offering guided cultural tours, grass root initiatives and organizations, like those promoted by WECAT and Khulumani, maintain an openness to a contested past, effect new relations of reciprocity through interpersonal dialogue and testify to the unfinished business of the TRC as the nation faces an uncertain future.

Transcultural projects like that of Krog, Ratele, and Mpolweni-Zantsi carry out the unfinished business of the TRC in another way. Returning to the testimony itself, they enact a process of ethical listening and reception that affords a long overdue dignity to Mrs. Konile's testimony and grants others access to new interpretative frameworks of understanding. The project also acknowledges Mrs. Konile in her unique singularity and enables her to continue a process of healing. Along with the more structured 'ur' narrative of mothers who lost their sons to apartheid violence, this recovery work allows listeners to register a multiplicity of approaches and cultural experiences within the country and move beyond racialized stereotypes of the past. Acting through a series of ethical engagements entailing a Derridian form of hospitality, reciprocity and openness to difference, the transcultural research team offers another pathway to reconciliation through the secondary witnessing to and participation in acts of restorative justice beyond the political arena.

Testimony given before the TRC continues to be an ongoing source of contestation, recovery, forgiveness and healing in the new South Africa. Although its reception varies, and its efficacy has had only limited purchase in a nation still beset with overwhelming structural oppressions and inequalities, its circulation in varied venues has changed forever the face of the nation. Memorial sites carry forward the work of the commission, commemorating the dead, honouring heroes, and creating new mythologies of nation. Testimony, recovered in different contexts, can exacerbate deep divisions or foster interconnectedness. As this paper suggests, the tapestry of the 'rainbow nation' can look very different depending on where one stands and how one views its complex weft and warp. Still, acts of remembrance model to the nation and the world South Africa's difficult, challenging and courageous journey towards new democracy and freedom.

References

Bhabha, H.K. (1990), 'Introduction', in Bhabha, H.K. (ed.), *Nation and Narration*, (London: Routledge).

Carroll, D. (2007) '"Remains" of Algeria: Justice, Hospitality, Politics', in *Modern Language Notes*, 122:4.

de Certeau, M. (1985), *Heterologies: Discourse on the Other*, Massumi, B. (trans.) (Minneapolis: University of Minnesota Press).

Derrida, J. (1999), *Adieu to Emmannuel Levinas*, Brault, P.A. and Naas, M. (trans.) (Stanford: Stanford University Press).

Derrida, J. (2000), *Of Hospitality: Anne Dufourmantelle Invites Jacques Derrida to Respond*, Bowlby, R. (trans.) (Stanford: Stanford University Press).

Gobodo-Madikezela, P. and van der Mewre, C. (eds) (forthcoming), *Memory, Narrative, and Forgiveness: Perspectives on the Unfinished Journeys of the Past* (Cambridge: Cambridge Scholars Publishers).

Goldblatt, B. and Meintjes, S. (1996), 'Gender and the Truth Reconciliation Commission: A Submission to the Truth and Reconciliation Commission.' <http://www.org.za/submit/gender.htm>.

Grunebaum-Ralph, H. (2001), 'Re-Placing Pasts, Forgetting Presents: Narrative, Place, and Memory in the Time of the Truth and Reconciliation Commission', *Research in African Literatures*, 32:3.

Gubeni, Z. et al. (2003), 'Memory and Memorialization', in Villa-Vicencio, C. and Doxtader, E. (eds).

Klopper, D. (2004), 'Narrative Time and Space of the Image: The Truth of the Lie in Winnie Madikizela-Mandela's Testimony before the Truth and Reconciliation Commission', in de Kock, L. et al. (eds), *South Africa in the Global Imaginary* (Pietermartizburg: University of South Africa Press).

Krog, A. et al. (2008), 'The South African Truth and Reconciliation Commission (TRC): Ways of Knowing Mrs. Konile', in Denzin, N.K. et al. (eds), *Handbook of Critical and Indigenous Methodologies* (London: Sage Publications).

Marschall, S. (2006), 'Commemorating "Struggle Heroes": Constructing a Genealogy for the New South Africa', *International Journal of Heritage Studies*, 12:2.

Naas, M. (2005), '"Alors, qui êtes-vous?": Jacques Derrida and the Question of Hospitality', *SubStance*, 106, 34:1.

Naidu, E. (2006), *The Ties that Bind: Strengthening the Links between Memorialisation and Transitional Justice* (Cape Town: The Center for the Study of Violence and Reconciliation).

Posel, D. and Simpson, G. (2002), 'Introduction', in Posel, D. and Simpson, G. (eds), *Commissioning the Past: Understanding South Africa's Truth and Reconciliation Commission* (Johannesburg: Witwatersrand University Press).

Ratele, K. (2003), 'We Black Men', *International Journal of Intercultural Relations*, 27:2.

Ratele, K. et al. (2007), 'Ndabethwa lilitye: Assumption, Translation and Culture in the Testimony of One Person before the South African Truth and Reconciliation Commission', *Tydskrif vir letterkunde,* 44:2.

Ratele, K. et al. (forthcoming), *There was this Goat: Investigating Notrose Nobomvu Konile's Truth Commission Testimony* (working title) (Scottsville: University of KwaZulu-Natal Press).

Ross, F.C. (2003), *Bearing Witness: Women and the Truth and Reconciliation Commission in South Africa* (London: Pluto).

SAPA News (1997), 'TRC Hears About Torture of Former MK Operative by ANC', published online on an unofficial website (now inactive) of the TRC process established by the Former TRC Webmaster, Steve Crawford <http://www.struth.org.za/>.

Schaffer, K. and Smith, S. (2004), *Human Rights and Narrated Lives* (New York and London: Palgrave).

Schaffer, K. (2006), 'Memory, Narrative and Forgiveness: Reflecting on Ten Years of South Africa's Truth and Reconciliation Commission', *Borderlands ejournal*, 5:3.

Truth and Reconciliation Commission of South Africa (2003), *Report*, published online <http://www.info.gov.za/otherdocs/2003/trc/>.

Villa-Vicencio, C. and Doxtader, E. (eds) (2003), *The Provocations of Amnesty: Memory, Justice and Impunity* (Claremont, South Africa: Institute for Justice and Reconciliation).

Wilson, R. (2001), *Reconciliation and Revenge in Post-Apartheid South Africa: Rethinking Legal Pluralism and Human Rights* (Cambridge and New York: Cambridge University Press).

Chapter 8

Reconciliation with the Dead, and Other Unfamiliar Pathways

Julian Jonker

Broken Strings

We live as if to mourn. We can neither forgive nor forget on behalf of those who have preceded us. Their sorrows are already written in our bones, encoded everywhere in the material of the present. We are left with these remains of history, silent ghosts and memorials that go unnoticed by the living.

On a visit to Australia in 2004, everyone was interested in the Truth and Reconciliation Commission (TRC). Later, I hear someone call it 'South Africa's primary export', this heady mixture of confession, forgiveness and optimism about the future. In the discussions about transitional justice taking place around the world, the TRC is often treated as a role model, especially in light of South Africa's successful transition from apartheid to constitutional democracy. For the Australians I meet, the TRC is a desirable import, one that should be studied and possibly emulated.

Yet in South Africa, our relief at having made it to 'transition' has given way to disgruntlement, as we realize that it is not quite the same as achieving transitional justice. Many commentators had once proclaimed the TRC a bad deal and now, as South Africa deals with continued black poverty and anxiety about the role of race and racism, their voices resonate loudly. The transition to democracy was based on a negotiated compromise between the apartheid state and the agents of liberation, and the TRC was marked by that compromise. Some wished that apartheid perpetrators would be met with justice rather than forgiveness. Others remarked that the problem with the TRC was its attention to a narrow class of apartheid officials, rather than the many white beneficiaries of its systematized inequality. Now, ten years later, victims of apartheid still question whether more substantive reparations should have been forthcoming. Prosecutions of those who failed to gain amnesty have been felt not to be swift enough. And perhaps the TRC has not achieved reconciliation: one survey shows that racial relations have become worse since the Commission started its hearings (Dispatch, February 1998).[1]

But Australia looks forward to Reconciliation. This Reconciliation, with its capital R, seems to involve a lot of walking. In 2000, many Australians walk across

---

1 Also see: Gibson 2004 who uses a social scientific methodology to argue that the TRC did further reconciliation in South Africa.

Sydney's Harbour Bridge, as if by walking they might cross the cleft that history has struck between settler and Aboriginal.[2] Other walks have been less fruitful. In 2004, Michael Long walked for ten days from Melbourne to Canberra to address Prime Minister John Howard about the Aboriginal plight, only securing a meeting on his arrival.[3] As if to further spite Long's tired feet, the government went on to dissolve the Indigenous representative body the Aboriginal and Torres Straight Islander Commission (ATSIC).

Yet Australians remain interested in Reconciliation, as if there is some undiscovered pathway that will take tired feet to this restful place. At a conference in Melbourne entitled, *Dialogues Across Culture*, everyone is interested when I talk about South Africa's Truth and Reconciliation Commission. Earlier in the conference another speaker advocates the TRC's model as a positive one for coming to terms with Australia's traumatic history. On the other hand, I have come so far across the world only to share a more ambivalent viewpoint, one informed by the ghosts that still haunt our transition. I share my puzzlement and wonder at how history and the memory of trauma seem to exceed even the generosity of our particular model of transitional justice.

Later, I have time to contemplate Michael Long's tireless journey, roadside walks that end in brutality, my own journey across the Indian Ocean with my ambiguous and haunted stories. I wonder about all these pathways, how they waver and fail to meet.

High up at the top of the Sheraton Hotel, with its riverside view of the city, the conference is opened by a Wurundjeri elder, who prepares gum tree branches and declares us welcome. I feel somewhat assured by this acknowledgement of invisible authorities. Is this reconciliation? A nod, a proud intent, even while staring out at the city, resigned to the present?

As the conference unfolds, I note also how most local speakers preface their presentations with an acknowledgement of these authorities: 'I would like to acknowledge', they obediently repeat, 'the traditional custodians of this land, the Kulin Nation.' Sometimes they acknowledge the Wurundjeri, a subset of the Kulin. Sometimes they play it safe and name them 'the traditional custodians'. Sometimes, more boldly, they pronounce them the 'traditional owners'. The ancestors are silent; they do not contradict any of this. There is instead an intimate and secretive conjunction of the intangible ancestral spirits that crowd unseen around our little conference and the tangible hotel real estate in which we take comfort. For long afterwards, I wonder what sort of reconciliation might be possible between these worlds of the living and the dead.

The ancient art of this place narrates the land. This visual language of lines and dots are not of an abstract nature but plot the comings and goings of ancestral spirits, the lines of force that animate creation and life. They are literal even; a literacy of the land. The dot of white paint marks the sanctity of the site – each dot is a sacred and secret place, as each line is the trace left by an ancient being, manifested equally in the physical landscape. These lines and their perforations trace histories of form

---

2   The People's Walk for Reconciliation, Sydney Harbour Bridge, 28 May 2000.

3   See: <http://www.thelongwalk.com.au/>.

and essence. They tell the story of the formation of the land as well as the ongoing dynamics of its being.

The paintings can be read as maps, just as the land itself can be read as a narrative of the to-ing and fro-ing of Dreamtime ancestors. These beings, which gave rise to all things, formed the land by their roaming. The land is conspicuously inscribed with the stories of its creation and of the Dreamings responsible for it. Paintings transmit these stories. The songlines – equally maps, myths, ciphers, pathways – describe the dynamics and history of power in the land. This art is sacred even as it represents the sacred.

Where I come from, there is another story of the songline: the line is a vibrating string, as if the music of sub-atomic physics and the bloody history of land and country were compatible. Diä!kwain was one of the Xam Bushmen, a people who lived and hunted near Cape Town a hundred thousand years before European trade routes intersected with their country and brought with them history. The Xam language and culture were extinct by the end of the 19th century. Diä!kwain, one of the last of his people, sang: 'because they've broken the string, I no longer hear the ringing sound through the sky'.

I read about an Australian woman who travels through country and writes back that the trails of trauma now recreate the songlines. This delicate web of lines, a map made of genealogies and ancestral stories, frontiers and forced migrations, runs right through the history of the world. I imagine these lines as a kind of skeletal history of the world, the remains of trauma and memory that plot out the topography of our human relations. They give the present its shape and also predict where it might break and fragment.

Roadmaps, Remains, and other Pathways of the Dead

I spend a day with Tony, who works as a custodian of heritage sites in Australia, and is on a brief visit to Cape Town. I've been showing him the city and now we stand in an alleyway leading off Buitenkant Street, towards the District Six Museum. Outside, the street bustles. But behind closed wooden doors, this alleyway is cool, softly aglow with the magic of the late afternoon sun. Whitewash and plaster crumble off the wall's undercoat of rust bricks. In a previous lifetime, this area adjoined District Six, a vibrant inner city area from which black people were forcibly removed under apartheid's segregation laws. In a previous lifetime, this laneway in which we stand was part of a city with a different roadmap.

From here, if you were to step outside into the sunlight and look down Buitenkant, your view would stumble upon successive accumulations of the city's boundaries, as if peering into history. First is Van Riebeeck's star-shaped castle, an enigmatic memorial to colonial might, that overlooks the Parade with its hawkers and statues of foreign royalty and pigeon shit everywhere and lewd-mouthed men selling stolen watches. Beyond the Castle runs Strand Street, which once marked the boundary between the colonial settlement and the ocean from which it was born. And beyond that, the beginnings of the N2 highway and the railway lines, momentarily overlapping before they spread out to connect and divide the far reaches of the modern metropole.

'I like this place', I murmur, meaning the secluded alley; bracing at the thought of entering the turbulence and brightness of Buitenkant Street. 'It reminds me of Beijing,' says Tony, 'There are a lot of walls in both places. If there's one impression I take with me from Cape Town, it's of walls.'

'Really?' I am thinking of the soft white sand of the Atlantic seaboard, of the woolly cloud that bubbles up and over the ridge of the mountain when the weather changes.

'Yes, walls. Walls and barbed wire.' We exit into the street.

A little later, Tony revises this, as the sun sinks into the city's languid rush hour daze. 'My lasting impression of Cape Town,' he says, 'is walls and memory. Why does everyone talk so insistently of memory here?'

It seems that memory is the subject of conversation all over this nation in transition. Weeks after Tony's visit, my editor calls: 'I'm thinking of what Achille Mbembe has written about Johannesburg' - his pronunciation is francophone, so Johannesburg becomes *Jo'annesbourg*; a spontaneous renaming without asking permission. But my editor is more concerned with our own city. 'The comparison with Johannesburg is irrelevant', he says, 'that's perhaps what needs to be said about Cape Town.'

I'm scribbling down notes while he talks but while doing so get lost in my own thoughts of seas and mountains. I pick up his drift again. 'So the cliché of Cape Town being in the shadow of Table Mountain, you can't get away from it! It's the quasi-permanence of this construction project – I mean there are unfinished bridges, for God's sake! We are building monuments; we are building on history. It doesn't have the superficiality of Johannesburg. Things are very fixed.'

Later, I look up Mbembe's essay. It is part of a collection of essays on Johannesburg. In their introduction, Achille Mbembe and Sarah Nuttal pin down their subject with the leisurely interest of entomologists: they wonder about Charles van Onselen's description of the metropolis as a 'concrete encrustation on a set of rocky ridges' lacking 'the landscape of affection or mystery easily appropriated by myth-makers and nation-builders' (Mbembe and Nuttal 2004, 354; van Onselen 2001). Johannesburg, Mbembe decides, suffers from the architecture of hysteria: 'specific historical objects are ripped out of their contexts even as the state busily tries to memorialise and museumize' (Mbembe 2004, 404).

Meanwhile walls are erected across the Golden City, dividing, for example, wealthy Dainskloof from the informal settlement of Diepsloot. 'South Africa right now is not much interested in history; all the talk is of the "new"', writes Christopher Hope, after wandering upon Diepsloot undertakers digging for lost ancestors near the fortress-like walls of the neighbouring gated community. But: '[h]istory goes on being terrifyingly interested in South Africa. Close the door on the past and the ghosts come through the window.' As Hope discovers, there is even a court case: the people of Diepsloot suspect that some of their ancestors lie buried beneath the wealthy suburb's 'Italian tiles and parquet floors' (Hope 2005). Cape Town is even less immune from the ghosts of its past. Traditionally the most liberal of South Africa's apartheid cities, it sits poised between the construction of a new urban future and the presence of a monumental past. Buoyed by a ceaseless property market boom, the cranes and scaffolding of property developers have become fixed features of its humble skyline. Amidst this, a highway that was started decades ago still juts out, unfinished, over the city centre, suspended in a phantasm of grand urban planning. Construction haunts the city. This perpetual incompleteness of the built environment props itself up against the fixed and permanent: Table Mountain and the Atlantic Ocean, the two natural features which have shaped the geography and history of the city. Cape Town's past is always present, at least partly because of its monumental setting amidst rock and water.

The concrete and asphalt of colonial and apartheid urban planning construct spatial segregation in wordless conspiracy with this natural topography. The mountain divides poor areas from wealthy, a complicity of architecture and nature that continues to reflect and effect the racial segregation that was strictly legislated until the early 1990s. To think about reconciliation in Cape Town today is thus to think about space and memory. We remain divided in space, as surely as this was the primary strategy of apart-heid. The network of roads and suburbs that map out the city remain like the skeletal outline of a grand spatial engineering. Roadmaps are monuments to apartheid's fantasy of apart-ness. In navigating them we activate their memory, without remembering, in the same way that habit allows the body to both re-enact and forget. So we take our habitual roads to work, and back home, and memorialize our divided selves.

The visitor who arrives at Cape Town International Airport must travel a national highway called the N2. For many Cape Town residents, the N2 is a part of their daily commute, as much a symbol of this city as the flat topped mountain that is visible from any of its quarters. For visitors, it is a useful introduction to the lay of the land, marking out some of the major divides inherited from the apartheid past. As blacks were removed from the city, first by economics and the colonial administration's orders, and then forcibly by apartheid's segregation laws, they ended up further and further away along this road: Ndabeni, Langa, Athlone, Manenberg, Khayelitsha. Now the highway is lined also by communities made up primarily of migrants from rural areas, lured by the promise of jobs. They live in informal settlements named 'squatter camps'.

The journey along the N2 is a tour through the remnants of apartheid, a reminder of its legacy of brutal segregation and underdevelopment, one that persists more than a decade after political democracy.

While the geometry of greater Cape Town follows the vision of early 20th century social engineering and apartheid's mid-to-late 20th century segregation, the roadmap of the city centre traces even older colonial demarcations. The first boundaries of the colony are still clearly named: Strand Street (Beach Street) recollects where the ocean-bound edge of the city once was. Parallel to it is Waterkant Street (Water's Edge), which ran alongside the harbour's edge before part of shallow Table Bay was reclaimed to create space for the city's commercial and administrative district. Buitenkant Street (Outer Edge) marks the easternmost boundary of the old city; its intersection with Strand Street guarded by the old military sentinel that is the Castle of Good Hope. Buitengracht Street (Outer Canal) marks the western boundary of the old city, beyond which once lay the 'menace of wild animals [and] the depredations of marauding Hottentots', the alien natives who inhabited the Cape (Murray 1964, 3).

The early colonists ventured past these very first frontiers long ago; yet the erstwhile boundaries between self and other continue to haunt the city in unexpected ways. Follow Strand Street and, at the point where it intersects the old west boundary, it becomes the main drag of a chic precinct named Green Point, presently considered to be 'some of the most sought-after real estate in the country' (Moodie 2004). Just below the main road, nestled between an old school that remains from Green Point's days as a coloured working class neighbourhood and the now fashionable restaurants and clubs of the area, stands a cordoned-off construction site.

In mid-2003, demolition and excavation on this site, subsequently to become known as Prestwich Place, came to a sudden halt as the dull white bone of human remains was revealed. Here, like the unexpected surfacing of memory, emerged the remains of thousands of slaves and poor residents of colonial Cape Town. During the 18th and 19th centuries their burials took place beyond the city boundaries, as if this were a geographical marker of the non-citizenship that followed them even to the grave. Prestwich Place is just one section of a network of unmarked graveyards that now lie buried beneath much of the west precinct's desirable real estate.

Archaeologists stood at this site and wrote: 'Cities are built on their pasts, constructed by the living on top of the dead. It is both a physical and a political process' (Malan et al. 2003). The dead, they might have added, surface at odd moments. The discovery of the bones and the subsequent debates about their identity and fate might be seen as a metaphorical unearthing of the city's unfinished business (Jonker 2005). For those who claimed to have descended from the dead, exhumation and development was seen as a perpetuation of their ancestors' abjection, a sign that some people still had no place in the city (Henri and Grunebaum 2004, Grunebaum 2004).

On the opposite side of the city from Prestwich Place lies one of the nation's most remembered sites of forced removals. Once stretching out from Buitenkant Street, District Six's empty expanse is a visible haunting. Protracted forced removals of black residents took place in the early 20th century, and began again in 1966, ending only in the early 1980s when all had been removed to the far periphery of the city. The land was cleared of houses, shops and streets by bulldozers. An activist campaign endeavoured to prevent development on this vacated land, calling it 'salted earth'. The activists were successful to an extent, and District Six remains largely empty, memorialized as an 'open wound' (Layne and Till 2005).[4]

District Six and Prestwich Place anchor a memorial cartography of Cape Town, acknowledging that the present day city can be mapped by spectral traces of absence and loss. District Six reminds us that Cape Town was once a place of creolization and creative ferment, a busy port city that knew no cultural purity. Apartheid and its legislation of group identity halted history's carnival. Through racial identification and geographical segregation the authorities banished the cultural promiscuity of the

---

4   The land has been returned to a trust representing dispossessed residents, and money is currently being sought to build houses and return ex-residents and their descendants.

city's living, creative communities, sending black residents out to the periphery. The empty plots of District Six mourn this loss.

Sites such as District Six and Prestwich Place represent a broader cultural landscape that has become visible after 'transitional justice' has run its course. This landscape is what remains: history etched into the very land on which we live.

These sites mark, like hauntings, the 'unfinished business' of transitional justice, markers on a cartography of incomplete political transformation. They remind us that the true work of transition is re-inhabiting a broken landscape. How do we become citizens again of a traumatized city? How do we adopt it as our own? How do we learn to live with its ghosts?

Living with Ghosts

Nominally, Cape Town has two universities: a historically black one in the bush and a historically white one on the mountain. Judy, a drama teacher at the university in the bush, explains her theory about the university on the mountain. She tells me she sees trauma in the bodies of the students who attend its steep campus. Their bodies are haunted as by some unseen handicap. No wonder there is comparatively little creative flourishing at the university on the mountain, a lack of confidence, she seems to say.

Why should this be so? It's all about location, she explains. The university's location places a heavy burden on people. It nestles at the foot of the mountains, overlooking the sprawl of Southern Suburbs and Cape Flats. When it's dark and rugby is being played on the fields, the spotlights can be seen for kilometres, so that it looks as if a dazzling spaceship has landed at the foot of the mountain. The university shares this vantage point with a stone memorial dedicated in the name of Cecil John Rhodes, the infamous colonizer who wished even to 'annex other planets' (Millin 1933, 138).

Considering Rhode's spectral gaze over the city brings to mind the figure of the colonial settlement as panopticon, that architectural device of observation that Jeremy Bentham invented to control 19th century England's criminal population. The panopticon was based on the idea that the threat of constant surveillance might produce effortless control of a population. Meanwhile Foucault, who saw how the principle of the panopticon might be assimilated into everyday architectures of power, haunts the highways of Cape Town. We eventually embody structures of power, adopting them into the disciplines of everyday living. These roads, canalized rivers and railway tracks describe lines of force that divide, conquer and thereby construct social identities that are as intimate and inalienable as the mental roadmap one follows in order to get home. We silently obey these ghostly forces.

We sit around a conference table at the university on the mountain. It is a comfortable room with glass windows on two sides looking out onto breathtaking views of Cape Town and the slopes of Table Mountain. Just out of sight of the window, the city's poor black areas sprawl. From this side of the glass, the blue of sky and mountain's green are tranquil, smugly silent in their wisdom of ages. We sit with our backs to this dramatic scene, our small scholarly group intently discussing reconciliation, ten years after the establishment of the TRC. The questions are numerous: should big business be liable to pay reparations in the absence of the TRC being able to pay substantial reparations to victims? What is the status of amnesty and the possibility of convicting those who were not awarded amnesty? Are we more reconciled as a nation since the TRC hearings have run their course? Does everyone want reconciliation? What is reconciliation anyway?

The group, comprised mostly of lawyers, speaks of reconciliation in terms of institutions, rules, responsibilities. But when psychologist Pumla Gobodo-Madikizela joins us, the tone of the conversation changes. It is no longer about what rules will reproduce what results, which institutions are better suited to this or that, or whether forgiveness should be regarded cynically or strategically. She talks instead of personalities, of the alchemies that occur in a room with closed doors. How, we wonder again, are we to regard the forgiveness shown at the commission? Gobodo-Madikizela, who sat as one of the commissioners, talks of Archbishop Desmond Tutu, and his tears. I think of a poem written by Ingrid de Kok:

> It doesn't matter what you thought
> of the Archbishop before or after,
> of the settlement, the commission,
> or what the anthropologists flying in
> from less studied crimes and sorrows
> said about the discourse,
> or how many doctorates,
> books and installations followed,
> or even if you think this poem
> simplifies, lionizes
> romanticizes, mystifies.
>
> There was a long table, starched purple vestment
> and after a few hours of testimony,
> the Archbishop, chair of the commission,
> laid down his head, and wept (de Kok 2002).

It is enough to realize that whatever reconciliation South Africa has achieved has been the gift of singular personalities, passions and difficult choices. I am reminded of Paul Ricoeur, who says that, 'forgiveness can find refuge only in gestures incapable of being transformed into institutions' (Ricoeur 2004, 458). Unlike Derrida, Ricoeur does not believe that forgiveness is impossible, only that it is difficult. It is not the same as amnesty; it cannot be formulated but is found only in inimitable gestures. Forgiveness cannot be granted by an institution but only, truly, by the secret alchemy of a gesture that cannot be transformed into an institution. This is why reconciliation surely must not hinge on forgiveness – for what possibility is there then of reconciliation with the dead, who make no more gestures and are capable of shedding no tears?

Antjie Krog is another considered chronicler of South Africa's pursuit of transitional justice. Published in 1998, her *Country of My Skull* presented a personal travelogue of the emotional topography of South Africa during the TRC hearings.

A Change of Tongue (2003) picks up the story in order to negotiate the more complicated terrain of post-TRC transition and reconciliation. It's 1999, and Krog has set out on the election campaign trail to interview Nelson Mandela. Mandela insists that the interview take place in Qunu, the place of his birth, and the village in which he set about building his house after gaining his freedom.

Krog writes of this house in Qunu, 'When Mandela was still a poor attorney he bought himself a plot in the Transkei, because he believes that a man must have a place to live close to where he was born'. Much later, after many years in prison, Mandela approached the chief of the area to re-acquire a plot in the area. Here he at last built his house, 'on the same design as the prison warder's house in which he had lived for the last years of his imprisonment at Victor Verster' (Krog 2003, 241).

If Cape Town's monuments are not made solely by man, then what strange iconoclasm is needed to transform the intimate history of water and mountain? In 2002, with relatively little fuss, Mandela established the Mandela Rhodes Foundation, which would take on Cecil John Rhodes' bequests, such as that institution of British colonial education, the Rhodes Scholarship (now a Mandela Rhodes Scholarship).

If Mandela can rehabilitate Rhodes, re-inhabit his name, establish (a) trust with him even – then must we not learn to re-inhabit the roads and railway lines and faux garden cities surrounded by their broken houses and emptinesses? Rewrite the city's text-ure with new words? If we are no longer colonist or native but hybrid, in the manner of Mandela-Rhodes, then how do we name our city? Do we re-inhabit the name of the city, like Mandela re-inhabited his old prison house? How do we re-inhabit this texture that is the memory of water and of rock?

Goedegift

At first I can't find it. My tattered map doesn't show that the old road beneath the quarry has become a pedestrian-only service access way. When I do finally find it, Goedegift silences me. The road itself is still there but her house is long gone. The resolute homes of the wealthy leave no space for memory here, actual or imagined.

I have to reconstruct my mother's childhood milieu from a bench stationed at the bottom of the road, a concession to the idea of the public domain, squeezed in between tasteful modernist residences and the impending horror of a three level housing complex. 'Invest now!' says the billboard. But the view from the bench makes horror, even hatred, dissipate. From here the world is an idyll. The harbour is a sheet, boats anchored, sails gently unfurling like unspoken clichés. Dusk is falling and the mountains stretching to Muizenberg recede into a light haze.

She used to tell stories, every now and then, about baboons coming down from the mountain to play-steal her tea set; of picking fruit; of her father almost drowning them all in the midnight sea the night he drunkenly took them into the harbour on a leaking boat – bizarre fragments of childhood offset with the warm wonder of nostalgia. They never applied to the land claims commission because, she claims, they rented and didn't have full ownership. The commission accepted rights less than ownership, I insisted one day, but she seemed not to hear. I figure she is engaged in the more complex politics of family relations, pride and stoicism. So now there is just this bench, halfway between the mountain and the water below.

References

de Kok, I. (2002), 'The Archbishop Chairs the First Session', in *Terrestrial Things* (Cape Town: Kwela/Snail Press).

Dialogues Across Cultures Conference, hosted by the Centre for Australian Indigenous Studies, Monash University (Melbourne, 11–14 November 2004).

Dispatch (1998), 'TRC Harms Race Relations: Survey', *Dispatch,* 28 February, <http://www.dispatch.co.za/1998/07/28/southafrica/trc.htm>

Gibson, J.L. (2004), *Overcoming Apartheid: Can Truth Reconcile a Divided Nation?* (New York: Russell Sage Foundation).

Grunebaum, H. (2004), 'Invisible Synchronicities, the "New" and the Politics of Time', (unpublished paper).

Henri, Y. and Grunebaum, H. (2004), 'Re-historicising Trauma: Reflections on Violence and Memory in Current-Day Cape Town' (unpublished paper).

Hope, C. (2005), 'Now Everyone Lives in the Townships', *Guardian Unlimited* (Website), 28 February, <http://www.guardian.co.uk/southafrica/story/0,1426812,00.html>

Jonker, J. (2005), 'Excavating the Legal Subject', *Griffith Law Review*, 14, 187.

Krog, A. (1998), *Country of My Skull* (Cape Town: Random House).

Krog, A. (2003), *Change of Tongue* (Cape Town: Random House).

Layne, V. and Till, K. (2005), 'Keynote Lecture on Memorialisation, World Heritage, and Human Rights', presented at the *Hands On District Six: Landscapes of Postcolonial Memorialisation Conference* (Cape Town, 25–28 May).

Malan, A. et al. (2003), (unpublished conference paper) (available from Cultural Sites and Resources Forum, University of Cape Town).

Mbembe, A. (2004), 'Aesthetics of Superfluity', *Public Culture*, 16:3, 404.

Mbembe, A. and Nuttall, S. (2004), 'Writing the World from an African Metropolis', *Public Culture*, 16:3, 354.

Millin, S.G. (1933), *Rhodes* (London: Chatto and Windus).

Moodie, G. (2004), 'Old bones of Contention: Historians Want Development of Slave Graveyard Halted', *Sunday Times*, 25 January.

Murray, M. (1964), *Under Lion's Head* (Cape Town: A.A. Balkema).

Rassool, C. et al. (2000), 'Burying and Memorialising the Body of Truth: the TRC and National Heritage' in James, W. and van de Vijver, L. (eds), *After the TRC: Reflections on Truth and Reconciliation in South Africa* (Cape Town: David Philip).

Ricoeur, P. (2004), *Memory, History, Forgetting*, Blamey, K. and Pellauer, D. (trans.) (Chicago: University of Chicago Press).

van Onselen, C. (2001), *New Babylon, New Nineveh: Everyday Life on the Witwatersrand, 1886-1914* (Johannesburg: Jonathon Ball).

PART II
Sites of Reconciliation

Chapter 9

Lead Essay
Reconciliation: From the Usually Unspoken to the Almost Unimaginable

Paul James

Around the world today, numerous communities face an immediate future of intense violence and social upheaval. The Congo, East Timor, Israel-Palestine, Kashmir, the Solomon Islands, Sri Lanka, the Sudan and Tibet are examples amongst many others. In zones of chronic tension, politics characteristically lurches back and forth from hope to despair to hope ... to despair. Peace talks, road maps and new elections descend into a quotidian hell of missiles, armoured vehicles and suicide-martyrs – and then new maps are drawn again. In Sri Lanka and Israel-Palestine, violence erupts in remembrance of past violence. In Tibet, dissent is met with tanks. In East Timor, after the high expectations of independence and the rigorous work of the Reception, Truth and Reconciliation Commission (CAVR), an unexpected political divide emerges as the brothers and sisters of *Lorosa'e* and *Loromonu* become enemies, willing to kill and die over status and resources (Grenfell 2008).

At the same time, in other places, there are signs of slow reconciliation. After years of tension, ranging from hot and cold sporadic violence to tepid non-recognition of the depth of difference, there are moments and processes that suggest that reconciliation is possible – Australia, Bosnia and Herzegovina, Kosovo, Northern Ireland and Rwanda. Does this mean that political recognition, reconstruction and recovery are proceeding productively in such places? Does it mean that now at least in theory we understand the optimal pathways to reconciliation and positive peace? Contemporary history suggests not. Despite developments such as the national truth and reconciliation commissions and the International Criminal Court, the connection between grass-roots security and national and global governance has in practice gone backwards over the last half-century. Despite the gains in regions that years ago left their wars behind, reconciliation and recovery are hindered by numerous problems: global and local inequalities; attempts by governments to paint over problems; lack of systematic connection between different government bureaucracies, non-government agencies, and international interventions; too many attempts at quick fixes; and disjointed, self-serving and limited support from most countries in the world.

And for all of that, there is an even darker side of the planet that has not yet been mentioned. Firstly, even taking seriously the most optimist prognoses for older post-war countries such as Bosnia and Herzegovina, the hopes for reconstructing the new war-zones devastated by the global War on Terror – particularly Iraq and Afghanistan – require a projection of at least a generation or two into the future (Shadid 2005). Secondly, genocide and ethnic cleansing are not practices of the past based on a return to primordial madness, but a phenomena of the rational, modern (and democratic) present (Mann 2005).

While a lot can be said about what does not work, we need affirmative answers to what might be alternative pathways to peace. Inter-state wars may be declining as a global phenomenon, but localized transnational violence and divisive identity politics are more intense, with more impact on non-combatants than ever before (Hironaka 2003). In such a context, and despite the need to say something positive, it is crucial to begin by addressing the quandaries of reconciliation that in the main continue to be either unspoken or haphazardly insinuated by cynics. It is only by taking these issues seriously that we can get beyond high-sounding rhetoric.

The Usually Unspoken

I believe that there are possible pathways to political reconciliation but, at the risk of being misunderstood, let me begin with a series of interconnected propositions about the problems associated with any reconciliation process. None of these propositions are remarkable in themselves, but it is unusual for them to be spoken about together by an advocate of reconciliation processes.

Dialogue is not the answer – at least not in itself (Burton 1969). Neither is reconciliation furthered by simply concentrating on testimony, listening or memorializing the past. Reconciliation is not simply about individuals feeling better. Confronting oppressors with their victims, or bringing victims into ritual structures of testimony, are as likely to cause deep pain to the traumatized as bring about reconciliation (Humphrey 2002).

Moving from the individual level to that of the community-polity, reconciliation is not about the transcendence of the universal over the personal. Reason and interest, the universalizing affirmations of the liberal Enlightenment, the freedoms of capitalism or the hopes of free market democracy, are as likely to lead to bloody conflict as to peace (Friedman 2003; Chua 2003). Existing liberal multiculturalism, tolerance and democratic pluralism are more likely to lead to self-satisfied, empty, thin or pleasantly repressive societies than they are to underpin complex negotiation over the dialectic of identity and difference (Wolff et al. 1969). Truth and reconciliation commissions tend to be successful only in very limited circumstances and only then when linked to both fundamental political change (for example, the end of apartheid) and systematic juridical action (the trying of serious human rights violators as criminals). Most national courts are conducted at the legal direction of the winners of a particular conflict. All of the international tribunals from Nuremberg to the Former Yugoslavia have been conducted by or from the perspective of the winners. Most tribunal hearings are more concerned with individualized justice appearing to be done than with the oft-cited 'collective conscience of humanity'.

The list goes on. It could be a never-ending litany of propositions that confront commonsense understandings of peace-making. The key point here is that, either we are usually so concerned, as cosmopolitan humanists, to find the virtuous pathway from violence to reconciliation, or as realist pragmatists, to fault the whole endeavour of reconciliation as foolish idealism, that we rarely address such points of grey complexity with direct passion.

There is no single pathway and, as other writers in this volume argue, there is no way of overcoming the ambiguities and ambivalences of reconciliation (see Rothfield this volume). Positive reconciliation is ongoing and always in process. It is not an ultimate state. Such an approach thus hints at a parallel approach to the classical discussion of the distinction between positive and negative liberty. Positive reconciliation is defined here not as the final resolution of difference nor as a process of forgiving and forgetting – this can be called negative reconciliation – but rather as a never-concluding, often uncomfortable process of remaking or bringing together (from the Latin – *reconcilare*) of persons, practices and meanings in ongoing 'places of meeting' (from the Latin – *concilium*). The definition, relevant to both personal and political reconciliation, is thus careful not to presume that differences will be resolved, dissolved or settled once and for all time, nor to presume an ultimate truth or transparency about the source of conflict. Contingent judgements and carefully framed statements of best available understandings need to be made and witnessed (this relates to the argument below for a Global Truth, Reconciliation and Justice Forum), but they remain open to revision. 'Places of meeting', in this sense, require the active possibility of return over time and the possibility of the layering of truths and the contestation of meaning. In this essay then, I want to take this issue about the irresolution of the reconciliation process as a starting point and suggest a social framework in which the constant tensions of violence and peace, trauma and recovery can be understood and worked through across a number of levels.

The present approach focuses on political reconciliation. In particular, it focuses on political as opposed to personal reconciliation after recognized structural or embodied violence. It draws heavily on the work of Geoff Sharp and others who talk of the constitutive levels of the social.[1] Here, I want to focus upon two different but related ways of conceiving of the social. At the risk of summarizing a complicated method in a few condensed sentences, the social can at one level be expressed in terms of modes of integration and differentiation, or 'ways of relating', from face-to-face relations through institutionally-extended relations to disembodied-extended relations. It can also be understood via a second and more abstract conception of the social in terms of 'ways of being' – in particular ways of living in relation to the nature of time, space, embodiment and knowing. Examining the manifold formations of ways of being allows us to talk about overlaying and cross-cutting 'formations of being' – namely, the tribal, the traditional, the modern and the postmodern (James 2006, 65–96).

---

1   See Sharp 1993. For other examples, drawing upon the 'constitutive abstraction' or 'levels' method associated with Arena Journal see Cooper 2002, Ziguras 2004, Cregan 2006, and James 2006. Here 'the social' is taken to be the encompassing ground of human being including domains analytically separated out as the political, the economic, the cultural and the ecological.

Understanding sociality in these terms of layers of relating and being, I suggest, has consequences for thinking about reconciliation as an ongoing process and for understanding the ways that this process can be positively institutionalized so as not to empty out the face-to-face. Two underlying arguments connect all of this discussion. The first is that a sustainable process of political reconciliation requires a regime of practice that is systematically interconnected across different levels of social integration or 'ways of relating'. For example, reconciliation conducted as a series of institutional encounters without care about the way in which it resonates with the embodied complexity of face-to-face relations or the symbolic politics of more extended relations is likely to be deeply counter productive. The second argument is that a sustainable process of political reconciliation needs to be conducted with an active sensitivity to different 'ways of being', including the tensions and contradictions between them. For example, to address an issue such as the Israel-Palestine question – that requires consideration of both modern sovereignty issues around territory and neo-traditional claims to place – in a setting framed by the modern juridical sense that problems can be resolved by talking about political roadmaps and abstract lines of demarcation, misses out on the tensions among different ways of being for both sides.

Ways of Relating and Being

If we begin with basic questions of sociality and with the proposition that social relations can best be understood in terms of the layering of ways of relating and being, then the other side of that proposition is, firstly, that reconciliation is all too often understood as a one dimensional practice set within the dominance of a single ontological formation – the modern. Secondly, the strengths of reconciliation are often lost in confusion about the intersection of different modes of integration. The dominant tendency is to treat the face-to-face as primary in the theory and practice of reconciliation, while at the same time reducing those face-to-face relations to thin (even if momentarily passionate) encounters situated within a technique driven enactment of what might be called 'reconciliation as one-dimensional peace'. That is, most enactments of reconciliation have really only been interested in the face-to-face as a symbolic gesture for a brief bounded period and within an overwhelmingly disembodied framework of ambiguous forgiveness/'othering' aimed at achieving abstracted peace/justice. Peace – that is, negative peace – occurs when 'the victims' have testified and been given fifteen minutes of fame and the world can safely move on.

In this process, there is a tendency for deponents to be constructed as victims who have forgiven and who themselves can now be forgotten. In other words, for all the importance of face-to-face testimony, or facing the other and 'saying sorry', as a base level of the process of reconciliation, face-to-face engagement tends to be left with little support or with limited time to carry the substantial weight of on-the-ground practice. In East Timor, for example, after an initial Herculean stage of collecting testimony for the *Chega* Report (2005), the process of community-based hearings was ended and the international community stopped sending the money.

At the same time, practices at the level of the institutional integration tend to be reduced to modern juridical proceduralism, notwithstanding its symbolic effect, around questions involving individual guilt or innocence. For example, the International Criminal Tribunal for Rwanda, dealing with the genocide of approximately 800,000 persons has, over its first ten years from 1997, made only 22 judgements involving 28 accused.[2] Equally, practices at the level of disembodied integration are largely left to a sensationalizing global media which, fuelled by the propaganda of self-invested states, tends to turn 'the face of the enemy' into an icon of evil – an abstract other – while 'the face of the victim' becomes a living martyr. For example, Saddam Hussein was constructed as evil personified with little sense of the complexity of what underpinned the emerging and violent dominance of the Ba'ath Party in Iraq from 1968 to 2003.

Each of these points needs more illustration and elaboration. The core problem is not how reconciliation tends to be limited to the abstract symbolic – symbolic politics can be important and achieving personal reconciliation and extending particularistic justice to everyone is simply not possible given the complexity of contemporary zones of violence. The problem is rather that there tends to be little energy given to relating and coordinating the different levels of engagement. The following discussion moves in turn across the three levels of integration introduced earlier: face-to-face relations, institutionally-extended relations and disembodied relations.

The Level of Face-to-Face Integration

The trope and the actuality of the face, as well as the concepts of face-to-face 'interaction' and 'integration', are important to rethinking the nature of the kind of engagement that needs to occur in processes of reconciliation. Emmanuel Levinas writes: 'the relation to the face is straightaway ethical. The face is what one cannot kill, or at least it is that whose *meaning* consists in saying: "thou shalt not kill"'. The point here is not that looking into another's eyes stops one from killing. The possibility of murder, as Levinas adds, 'is a banal fact: one can kill the Other; the ethical exigency is not an ontological necessity' (Levinas 1985, 87). However, it does provide a ground for human engagement. It is this fundamental and messy sense of ethical exigency – facing the pain and having that pain acknowledged – that occurs at the base of a positive reconciliation process.

By contrast, the dubious hope of final and complete resolution (negative reconciliation) can only be achieved either though a fog of remembering-then-forgetting or through a rationalization of remembering that denies the issue that

---

2   This is not to criticize legal rationality and the slow process of procedural justice in itself. It is rather to question the way in which truth and reconciliation at this level of institutional extension tends to become confined to modern proceduralism. The South African and East Timorese national reconciliation processes were, for the time of their enactment, partial positive exceptions to this concern. The Jakarta Ad Hoc Human Rights Court, which concluded in 2004, was an exception on the profoundly negative side. Of the 16 Indonesian military and police defendants, all were acquitted under dubious circumstances.

subjective pain continues to be embedded in the bodies of the aggrieved long after the act of truth-telling. By the same process, the notion that 'time heals' is dependent on a modern conception of abstract empty time. Within a traditional or even neo-traditional ontology of time, healing occurs within ongoing practices of both intense remembering, including carrying past pain into the present as real now (such as through the trans-substantiated body of Christ) and ritually distancing that pain. By comparison, the use of a title such as *Burying the Past* for a book on reconciliation and justice is indicative of the modernist framing of the very different pathways to reconciliation (Biggar 2003). The past cannot be buried in the modern sense of covering over. Equally inappropriate is modern memorializing. The fixed marble monument in Denpasar to the victims of the Bali bombing was erected with no sensitivity to the traditional cosmology known as the *rwa bhineda,* which 'delicately suspends the forces of good and evil in an infinite and irresolvable dialectical combat' (Lewis and Lewis 2008, 194).

There can be no categorical imperative to find reconciliation. Nevertheless, in the messy humanness of pain and suffering, guilt and remembering, a pressing need arises to find an ethically framed and positive way forward. The problem is that if political reconciliation (as distinct from personal reconciliation) occurs only at this level of the face-to-face it is bound to fail. Part of the fundamental irresolution of the political reconciliation process is that the ending of trauma effectively requires the 'renewal' of a sense of face-to-face integration that has been cut to pieces by 'the enemy'. This kind of renewal simply cannot be achieved through face-to-face interaction, including testimony or forgiving the other. Neither can the other saying 'sorry' remake that remembered past; often, in fact, it serves to accentuate the loss or to create a spectral presence of the past. More fundamentally, the other is rarely someone that can be drawn into such a relationship of integration.

In summary, reconciliation needs to be built from the ground up while being supported from the top down. Reconciliation conducted as face-to-face testimony and acknowledgement is fundamental, but unless it is at once re-embedded in the continuing moments and projects of the everyday and lifted to a level of more abstract engagement (usually as a series of institutionalized practices) with a larger community or civil sphere then it is likely to fail. In other words, reclaiming the face-to-face as one level of engagement is crucial, but it needs to be held in a clear and negotiated relation to more abstract levels of integration, including the institutionally-extended and disembodied or mediated level of mass communications.

The Level of Institutionally-Extended Integration

Lifting face-to-face testimony to the level of civil society (local, regional, national and global) has been the putative task of tribunals as spaces of truth-telling. However, in practice, they rarely become what I have been calling 'places of meeting'. In these formal venues, victims tend to be selectively chosen for their unambiguous innocence or the illustrative nature of their suffering (Humphrey 2002, Ch. 8). While they sometimes face the alleged perpetrators of violence, as persons, they also tend to be subordinated to the process of legally churning through the material. There are important exceptions where symbolic politics and institutional framing has been handled well. For example, the first of the national hearings of CAVR in 2002 was given the title of 'Hear our Voices' (*Rona Ami-nia Lian*) and the subsequent hearings had thematic foci such as political imprisonment or forced displacement. This meant that while only a few were able to testify, the symbolic purpose of speaking to the nation was recognized for what it was – a partial process that had to be linked to other places of meeting. Such places were participatory workshops in villages or the Healing Workshops held in Dili at CAVR's national office, the ex-prison Comarca Dalide previously used by the Indonesians to hold and interrogate political detainees. For all the strength of that process however, only six such healing workshops were held and they were wound down in 2004 with the task of reconciliation barely begun.

The concept of 'places of meeting' or *concilium*, introduced earlier, is used here across the layers of meaning of spatiality from its expression as designated 'places' to meet face-to-face and negotiate over differences, to abstracted institutionalized or technologically-extended 'spaces' where communities and polities negotiate over differences. Tribunals and commissions in theory should provide such places. However, whether they are criminal courts such as the International Criminal Court on the Former Yugoslavia or reconciliation venues such as the *Nunca Mas* (Never Again) tribunals in Argentina, such institutions tend not to have the capacity to provide either the institutional stewardship required or the capacity to reach beyond juridical process and individual testimony. *Nunca Mas*, for example, was skewed towards a legalistic understanding of testimony in order to collate the truth as part of the larger project of bringing alleged perpetrators to trial. The Court on the Former Yugoslavia brought persons from the villages of Bosnia Herzegovina and Kosovo to testify in The Hague. They then had to face as their legal interrogator the man that stood in the dock, symbolic of all the horror, Slobodan Milošević. And, for all that, the Court had only two support staff to look after the psychological wellbeing of such displaced deponents. These were people who in many cases had never before been out of their local region. They came to The Hague wanting to talk about what they experienced but were cross-examined on such issues as the trajectory from which a bullet entered the body of the person they saw murdered before their eyes.

What is needed in reconciliation meeting places is personal testimony and political practice that breaks down the binaries of victim and perpetrator. This needs to be done without detracting from the possibility of individual criminality on the one hand and collective culpability on the other. Firstly, from the perspective of individuals, this requires a negotiated and articulated division and relationship between forums of testimony/admission and courts of evidence and judgement. This is different, for example, from the South African 'trading' of peace for justice where full testimony was enough for a perpetrator of torture or illegal killing to be given amnesty. Secondly, from the perspective of the collective, whether community or polity, this requires a movement beyond either individual testimony or judgement of guilt or innocence to the possibility that an abstracted entity such as a nation or state or institution or corporation or even global community can be taken to task for deeds of commission and omission. In the current regimes of truth, reconciliation and justice, only individuals are called to account (Broomhall 2003). Positive reconciliation requires a challenge to the dominant notion that only perpetrated action can be adjudicated upon and that only individuals can be brought to task. This issue will be addressed a little later through a proposition that we need a global truth and reconciliation forum that addresses collective rather than individual responsibility. However, I still need to elaborate my concerns about how reconciliation figures at the most abstract level of integration – the disembodied – a level at which social relations are carried on the wings of mediated interchange such as through the media of electronic communications.

The Level of Disembodied Integration

While at this level of integration the bodies and faces of personally known others become technically irrelevant, the great irony is that modern universalizing polities, processes and connections always seem to require particular faces to mark their existence – from the faces on our currencies to the 'photo-op' representations of our leaders' faces on the front page of newspapers. These faces are variously abstracted beyond the particularities of the individuals from whom the images are taken. The face of the body politic, for example, tends to draw on the possibilities of the female face where the person is available because her gender can be abstracted from particularistic history into an iconic form of history. Joan of Arc, Bodicea and Marie as historical figures, though to 'Liberty' and 'Justice' and 'Peace through Justice' as iconic figures, are taken out of history and come to express a collective entity. Similarly, the faces of innocence and victimhood are abstracted from the particularities of their experience and dependent upon being 'unknown' persons, so to speak – for example, a child screaming as she runs from a village being attacked became the icon of pain during the Vietnam War. Again, even if the faces of evil remain individualized in a way that the faces of the body politic do not, they are similarly turned into empty icons to be filled with public prejudices – this time of one-dimensional blame. There are counter-examples to this process, but when the violence cannot be carried in the face of a single person, significatory chains of connection tend to be treated as an homogenized entity: Al-Qa'ida becomes the name of evil and a group linked with them becomes evil simply by association.

The point is not that the abstraction process is bad in itself, but that in treating more abstract levels of integration and representation as if they are ontologically continuous with the face-to-face, collectivities get away with murder. In the context of the globalizing mass media, responses to crimes against humanity are as likely to turn into star-chamber theatrics as to work through the complex meaning of causation, guilt, criminality and forgiveness. Adolf Hitler, Joseph Stalin, Pol Pot, Slobodan Milošević, Saddam Hussein and Osama bin Laden remain figures of particularistic intrigue, but by being lifted into the realm of abstracted communication they are paradoxically turned into pseudo-traditional scapegoats to be sent into the wilderness carrying our collective guilt. Their abstracted presence (to use an oxymoron to describe the ambiguity) allows us to escape the necessity of dealing with the complexities of reconciling past periods of pain, including those not named by association with such figures. Who is responsible for the destruction of approximately one million Ottoman Armenians? What rationale can there be for the death of 600,000 civilian Germans at the end of World War II by British firebombing when such tactics were irrelevant to winning the war (Sebald 2003)? Why is it that the only country to use atomic weapons against civilians has still not sought a process of atonement? These questions, and dozens of others closer to home, take us to the final part of this essay, the question of reconciliation at a collective level.

Towards the Almost Unimaginable: A Global Truth, Reconciliation, and Justice Forum

There are many issues that continue to remain misunderstood, both as general phenomena and as events. We can add to the earlier list of general propositions that usually remain unspoken. For example, putting in place an occupying external force to stop immediate violence may be necessary to save lives, but it tends to confirm the axiom of peace through repression, while necessitating a long-term military presence that is often counterproductive (Paris 2004). Or to give another example, more wars have been fought 'in the name' of peace, order and long-term justice than in the name of greed, interest or acquisition. These are general issues that need to enter public dialogue and debate. To get to a deeper level of understanding I suggest that we need a process of global learning that moves beyond the current shallowness of the mass-mediated civil sphere. When media commentators, for example, blame nationalism, civilizational difference, religious adherence, traditionalism or tribalism as the cause of violence, they tend to be contributing more to the self-confirming process of violence-begetting-violence than to the task of understanding peace-making and the possibilities of reconciliation.

One way of providing an institutional *concilium* that brings together relations from embodied to the mediated and disembodied would be to develop a Global Truth, Reconciliation and Justice Forum. This would build upon and go beyond the approach of the Permanent Court of Arbitration in The Hague, formed in 1899 to adjudicate on international problems between nations, corporations and organizations. Institutional funding might take a similar form to the Permanent Court with its activities supported by an annual payment from institutional members. However, in other respects the Forum's way of operating would cut across the dominance of modern juridical concerns to become an institution of social dialogue in the global public sphere.

It could be set up with the following aims:

1. To provide a meeting place, witnessed by the world, where civil society groups could bring the issues that underlie contemporary grievances and pain forward for public documentation, debate, dialogue and deliberation. At the end of that four-dimensional process there would not be a definitive deliberation on guilt or otherwise, but a voicing of 'majority' and 'minority' judgements by learned arbiters based on both supported testimony and expert research.

2. To provide the conditions for a global learning process about the effects and consequences of conduct during past international crises. The aim would be to learn from the past by investigating the causes of crises, conduct during those episodes and the consequences of the global community's response. In

this process the aim would not be criminal prosecution or to bring particular regimes, institutions or corporations to legal task, but rather to provide an institutional base for thinking through how international practice might have been conducted otherwise.

3. To provide for an institutionalization of ethical authority about the need for deep consideration of the relationship across different levels of extension – global, regional, national and local – and to provide ways of approaching the articulation of practices of truth, reconciliation and justice.

4. To provide a clearinghouse for collecting material on current international crises.

5. To provide information, considered social and legal frameworks, critical reflections on past tribunals and moral support for local and national truth and reconciliation tribunals currently in process, or being established or discussed. This dimension would have to include critical reflection on the Forum's own long-term effects.

Such a Forum need not be located in a single centralized venue, but could be coordinated as a series of interconnected places. It could be asked to conduct enquiries into past breaches of the principles of good international citizenship, particularly in relation to massacres, genocide, the death of civilians in military conflict, the state-sanctioned or institutionally-perpetrated use of terror, including torture, violent regime-change including coups and invasions of national sovereignty. This could include acts of intentional harm, acts that unintentionally contributed to harm and inaction that allowed harm to escalate in dangerous ways. Working on the basis that most nation-states do not release sensitive state documents for a period of 30 years, the Commission could investigate those events with ongoing, unresolved and intense international symbolic importance. For example: the fire-bombing of Germany, the timing of the D-Day invasion, the bombing of Hiroshima, the Cuban Missile Crisis, the 1965 massacre in Indonesia; the 1973 coup in Chile; the systematic killings in Kampuchea and so on. In relation to current events, it could also develop an ongoing auditing of the recent history of international responses to global crisis. This would entail an ongoing research department with the task of documenting and setting up the conditions for seeking the 'truth' on what actually happens during contemporary or recent crises that involve extended violence or systematic harm to a significant population.

There is, of course, very little chance in the immediate future that powerful governments and regimes would support the formation of such a forum. Fear of adverse deliberation will keep them wedded to councils and assemblies where vetoes can be enacted, votes can be influenced and power can be exercised more comfortably. A Global Truth, Reconciliation and Justice Forum, or some variation, remains however one of the forms of institutionalization that should be considered in taking this complex area of reconciliation more seriously.

References

Biggar, N. (ed.) (2003), *Burying the Past: Making Peace and Doing Justice after Civil Conflict* (Washington: Georgetown University Press).

Broomhall, B. (2003), *International Justice and the International Criminal Court: Between Sovereignty and the Rule of Law* (Oxford: Oxford University Press).

Burton, J.W. (1969), *Conflict and Communication: The Use of Controlled Communication in International Relations* (London: Macmillan).

Chua, A. (2003), *World on Fire: How Exporting Free Market Democracy Breeds Ethnic Hatred and Global Instability* (New York: Doubleday).

Commission for Reception, Truth and Reconciliation, Timor Leste (2005), *Chega! Executive Summary* (Dili: CAVR).

Cooper, S. (2002), *Technoculture and Critical Theory: In the Service of the Machine* (London: Routledge).

Cregan, K. (2006), *The Sociology of the Body: Mapping the Abstraction of Embodiment* (London: Sage Publications).

Friedman, J. (ed.) (2003), *Globalization, The State and Violence* (Lanham, MD: AltaMira Press).

Grenfell, D. (2008), 'Reconciliation: Violence and Nation-Formation in Timor-Leste', in D. Grenfell and P. James (eds), *Rethinking Insecurity, War and Violence: Beyond Savage Globalization?* (London: Routledge).

Hironaka, A. (2005), *Neverending Wars: The International Community, Weak States and the Perpetuation of Civil War* (Cambridge: Harvard University Press).

Humphrey, M. (2002), *The Politics of Atrocity and Reconciliation: From Terror to Trauma* (London: Routledge).

James, P. (2006), *Globalism, Nationalism, Tribalism: Bringing Theory Back In* (London: Sage Publications).

Lewis, J. and Lewis, B. (2008), 'Recovery: Taming the Rwa Bhineda after the Bali Bombings', in Grenfell, D. and James, P. (eds).

Mann, M. (2005), *The Dark Side of Democracy: Explaining Ethnic Cleansing* (Cambridge: Cambridge University Press).

May, L. (2005), *Crimes Against Humanity: A Normative Account* (Cambridge: Cambridge University Press).

Paris, R. (2004), *At War's End: Building Peace after Civil Conflict* (Cambridge: Cambridge University Press).

Shadid, A. (2005), *Night Draws Nigh: Iraq's People in the Shadow of America's War* (New York: Henry Holt).

Sebald, W.G. (2003), *On the Natural History of Destruction* (London: Hamish Hamilton).

Sharp, G. (1993), 'Extended Forms of the Social: Technological Mediation and Self-Formation', *Arena Journal*, 1, new series, 221–37.

Wolff, R.P. et al. (1969), *A Critique of Pure Tolerance* (London: Jonathan Cape).

Ziguras, C. (2004), *Self-Care: Embodiment, Personal Autonomy and the Shaping of Health Consciousness* (London: Routledge).

Chapter 10

Accountability, Remorse and Reconciliation: Lessons from South Africa, Mozambique and Rwanda

Helena Cobban

Between October 1992 and July 1994, three countries in sub-Saharan Africa had the opportunity to terminate internal conflicts characterized by the widespread commission of atrocities. In October 1992, the leaders of Mozambique's Frelimo government and the Renamo insurgency concluded a General Peace Agreement (GPA) ending a violent 15-year rebellion. In April 1994, South Africa held its first one-person-one-vote election, marking the close of four centuries of subjugation of the country's non-white majority;[1] and in July 1994, the Rwandan Patriotic Front (RPF) seized power from the genocidal clique that ruled Rwanda and brought hope of an end to the pervasive Hutu-Tutsi divide.

Each of these transitions from conflict to peace had the potential to transform a rights-abusing political order. In Rwanda, the genocide did not erupt again in the 12 years that followed, but in all other respects, hopes for an improvement in the rights situation remain unfulfilled. By contrast, in South Africa and Mozambique, the political promise of the transition era was largely met. Between 1994 and 2006, South Africa registered an impressive 6-interval improvement on the 12-interval index that Freedom House uses to assess a countries' standing in the field of political rights and civil liberties, while Mozambique showed a 4-interval improvement.[2]

These experiences are thought provoking since each country used a different approach to dealing with the challenge of post-atrocity or 'transitional' justice. In Rwanda, individuals accused of participation in the genocide at the highest levels were sent for trial at the United Nation's International Criminal Tribunal for Rwanda (ICTR). Parallel to that process, national prosecutors and police began jailing suspects in anticipation of trials to come. When the number incarcerated reached 2 percent of the population, with little hope of cases being heard within less than several decades, the government established an alternate mechanism. However, the new courts took a long time to set up and by mid-2006 their work had barely started.

---

1 I use the racial categories imposed on South Africa's citizens by the apartheid since it is impossible to discuss the apartheid and post-apartheid periods in South Africa without doing so. This in no way implies that I subscribe to the racial theories that underlay them.

2 Rwanda's status on both counts remained static over the same period.

In South Africa, after a government dominated by the African National Congress (ANC) came to power in April 1994, the main mechanism used to deal with the legacies of apartheid was the Truth and Reconciliation Commission (TRC). The TRC offered amnesties to perpetrators of politically motivated acts of violence from both sides of the conflict, conditional on the submission of full accounts of 'the truth' about their own acts of atrocity and those of others. The architects of the TRC sought to reveal facts that had long been suppressed about past atrocities, while publicly acknowledging the suffering endured by victims and survivors.

Mozambique used neither of these mechanisms. Instead, a blanket amnesty was granted to all who had committed acts of violence during the civil war. Meanwhile, in local communities, where brother may have taken up arms against brother or a son may have raped a neighbour's daughter, the country's religious and community leaders successfully worked together to bring about a psychosocial form of healing.

The contrasting pictures presented by these three attempts at transcending conflict and achieving transitional justice intrigued me. Over a number of years I conducted documentary research and between 2001 and 2003 I undertook research trips to each country and to ICTR's headquarters in Arusha, Tanzania. Some of my most valuable findings concern the challenges these experiences raise to the notion of 'individual accountability' upheld by rights activists in Western countries, and the alternative approaches they suggest for how inter-group and inter-personal reconciliation may be achieved.

Notions of Accountability

With roots in the Enlightenment philosophy of those such as Thomas Hobbes and John Locke, the dominant Western worldview holds that individuals are able to make considered, autonomous choices about their actions under most circumstances and should therefore be held individually accountable for the consequences. These assumptions underpin both the prescription of criminal prosecution as the best policy response to the commission of atrocities and the processes of most truth and reconciliation commissions. An immediate concern with this paradigm is that it has come to be understood as representing a universal truth, seamlessly applicable on an international scale. At the same time, it has generated demand for forms of accountability that can be judged as insubstantial. For example, in a criminal justice proceeding such as that undertaken by the ICTR, the defendant is not required to undertake any of the following 'personal accountability' tasks:

- acknowledge the factual truth of the court's findings;
- acknowledge personal responsibility for the crimes committed;
- express repugnance or repudiation toward such acts in general;
- recognize that such acts harm other members of society;
- express remorse or regret for undertaking such acts and for inflicting harm;
- ask for forgiveness from victims or society in general;
- offer to undertake reparatory action;
- promise not to commit these or similar actions again.

Thus, even a convicted *génocidaire* (perpetrator of genocide) can emerge from a criminal proceeding denying the factual basis of the court's findings, whilst expressing an attitude of disdain toward his victims, the court and the political-social order it represents.[3] In the United States, the manoeuvre of 'plea-bargaining' requires an admission of guilt and acknowledgement of the illegality of some of the crimes committed but participation is optional, as is the expression of remorse during sentencing. Fundamentally, the defendant's attitude toward the crime or to the people harmed is peripheral to the technical 'success' of the trial. Indeed, it could be argued that moral engagement with the perpetrators of violent acts is as peripheral to the concerns of a criminal proceeding as is the rehabilitation of victims.

Why then is there continued belief within the rights movement in the West that such proceedings are the best way of pursuing accountability? Perhaps a more abstract form of it is sought: accountability to the broad sweep of the historical record, such as that achieved (imperfectly) at the Nuremberg Trials following the Second World War, rather than accountability to the existing institutions and members of the society in which the atrocities were committed? Or perhaps this support is based on the view that 'accountability' is simply the same as punishment? But even in this latter regard the kind of accountability attained can seem thin and formulaic if punishments commensurate with the crimes in question are what is sought: international criminal courts have become notably more focused on due process and more squeamish about punishment since the days of Nuremberg.[4]

Truth commissions like that held in South Africa do not generally dispense punishment but they nonetheless operate according to the same notion of accountability required by criminal prosecution. In one sense, the form of accountability that the South African TRC required was more concrete than that demanded by the ICTR. Applicants to the TRC's Amnesty Committee did have to satisfy its members that they had 'told the whole truth' about their role and that of others in committing human rights violations. This roughly corresponded to carrying out the first two of the eight 'personal accountability' tasks listed above. However, the TRC never required perpetrators to undertake the third to the eighth task, despite public pleas made by commissioners in several high profile cases. Thus, a non-repentant perpetrator could completely satisfy the demands of the committee simply by 'telling the truth'. By contrast, at East Timor's Commission for Reception, Truth, and Reconciliation (CAVR), in addition to telling all they knew about the commission of atrocities, amnesty applicants needed to undertake a 'Community Reconciliation Act', usually described as, 'Apologize, bound not to repeat' (CAVR 2004). Also, South Africa's TRC was not wholly limited to considering the cases of individuals. It convened

---

3 At the International Criminal Tribunal for former Yugoslavia (ICTY), Slobodan Milosevic exhibited all of these traits until his death in early-2006, as did Saddam Hussein in his trial before the Iraqi Special Tribunal and prior to his execution.

4 After a single joint trial at Nuremberg that involved 22 defendants and lasted just over ten months, 12 were sentenced to death, and hanged a few weeks later. One defendant, Hermann Goering, 'cheated' the hangman by swallowing a suicide pill the night before the scheduled group execution. For reference to the inhumane manner of these executions see: West 1955, 72.

'institutional' hearings with the aim of demonstrating the part played by broad social sectors in underpinning the apartheid system.[5] However, the work of the Amnesty Committee was still organized around the cases of individual applicants and operated on a strict assumption of individual accountability.[6]

Accountability, Individualism, and Manicheanism

The notion of individual accountability for actions undertaken during a time of mass violence made little sense to most people I spoke to in Mozambique in 2003. In the provincial town of Belavista, the idea of punishing people for violent acts during war was dismissed by civil leaders, who generally felt that 'in civil wars, terrible things happen'.

In the same year, I spoke with Afiado Zunguza, the Executive Director of a Mozambican church-based organization called Justapaz, about the challenges facing a society recovering from war. I based this conversation on a list of eight such 'meta-tasks' compiled by Martha Minow (Minow 2000, 253). The second item on Minow's list is, 'Obtain the facts in an account as full as possible in order to meet victims' need to know, build a record for history, and to ensure minimal accountability and visibility of perpetrators'. Zunguza's response to this was critical. He said that most elders in Mozambican society would say, 'Pointing fingers won't help. Perpetrators are a part of us. We believe they didn't want to go to war. They are our sons, and we want them back. To accuse them would mean that they would continue to be bandits.'

The Rwandan Attorney-General, Gerald Gahima, viewed the matter similarly during conversations I had with him in 2002 and 2005. Gahima described the difficulty of making judgments during times of mass violence that are based on the application of the 'normal' rules of individual accountability. One of the examples he offered involved the case of a Hutu woman who had denounced her Tutsi husband and children to the *génocidaires* in her neighborhood – who were her own brothers. Having faced many dilemmas of this nature, Gahima concluded that the greatest priority was to try to prevent the kind of mass violence that produces complex situations such as these.

The understanding that in the midst of grave violence moral truths that appear easy to discern in everyday life can become indecipherable is not new. Primo Levi's *The Drowned and the Saved* is a reflection on his experience of Auschwitz (Levi 1986). The book contains a chapter on the 'Grey Zone' inhabited not only by the Jewish and Ukrainian sub-officials in the Nazi Lager (camp) system, but by other prisoners as well. Levi argues that acts of atrocity committed at such times are often

---

5   This was in conscious imitation of the Nuremberg approach, where the 22 defendants were chosen specifically to 'represent' certain leading sectors of Nazi society rather than according to the prosecutors' prior ranking of their supposed degrees of culpability as individuals.

6   The view of victims as having been harmed mainly as individuals rather than as members of a more broadly oppressed group also prevailed, although this was widely criticized in South Africa, including by members of the new ANC-led political elite.

the result of coercion or extreme mental stress and fear – and also, that many of the immediate victims are themselves not perfectly 'innocent'.[7]

> Before discussing separately the motives that impelled some prisoners to collaborate to some extent with the Lager authorities … it is necessary to declare the imprudence of issuing hasty moral judgments on such human cases. Certainly, the greatest responsibility lies with the system, the very structure of the totalitarian state; the concurrent guilt on the part of individual big and small collaborators (never likable, never transparent!) is always difficult to evaluate. It is a judgment that we would like to entrust only to those who found themselves in similar circumstances and had the opportunity to test for themselves what it means to act in a state of coercion … The condition of the offended [against] does not exclude culpability, which is often objectively serious, but I know of no human tribunal to which one could delegate the judgment (Levi 1986, 43–4).

In *Beyond Retribution: Seeking Justice in the Shadows of War*, Rama Mani goes a step further, urging policymakers to consider all people involved in mass violence as 'survivors', rather than dividing them into 'perpetrators' and 'victims':

> [A]n exclusive focus on individual accountability, and on the individual identification of perpetrators and victims, is not helpful … as it denies both the guilt and the victimization of the vast majority of society [in situations of grave violence]. Moreover, it ignores what all citizens in society share in common: that they are all survivors, whatever their past role, and that they now have a common stake in building a future together.

> [Martha] Minow observed the need to define the entire society as one of victims. While this is an advance as it acknowledges the real impact of conflict on an entire society rather than a targeted few, to do so would only entrench the notion of victim-hood, and concomitant helplessness. Rather, it is more useful to recognize that in such circumstances, to emerge alive, regardless of one's role and affiliation during conflict, is to be a survivor. More useful than Minow's notion of collective victim-hood is a redefinition of the entire society as *survivors* …

> Adopting a common identification which embraces all members of society may render more feasible the task of (re-)building a new political community that overcomes divisiveness between perceived perpetrators and victims (Mani 2002, 123).

This was the approach used in Mozambique after 1992, where the national discourse about the civil war contained little reference to either 'perpetrators' or 'victims'. Instead, Mozambicans talk about *affetados* or *affetadas* – those 'affected by' the war's violence. While this term might be useful to adopt more broadly, it carries the passive connotation that Mani rightly rejects regarding Minow's suggested use of the term 'victim'. Indeed, Mani stresses how the term 'survivor' carries the sense of having lived through something, and surmounted obstacles in doing so.

The diagnosis of Post Traumatic Stress Disorder (PSTD) is one realm within Western discourse in which a more nuanced understanding is applied to the

---

7   In Hannah Arendt's 1946 correspondence with Karl Jaspers, she expressed similar concerns regarding the moral climate in Germany during the Nazi era. For example, see her 17 August 1946 letter (Arendt and Jaspers 1992, 54).

commitment of violent acts under conditions of mass violence or war. Previously known as 'neurasthenia' or 'shell shock', PSTD reflects the recognition among the medical community that returning soldiers are frequently in need of psychosocial care in dealing with the trauma of war. Also, most former combatants view the moral and existential climate of war as markedly different from that of settled civilian life. Unfortunately, this recognition is not frequently extended to soldiers and other perpetrators of violence in countries beyond the West.

Remorse, Accountability and Ritual: Paradigms of Reconciliation

Another criticism of procedures that seek to establish strictly individual accountability is that where they try, they fail to elicit a strong expression of remorse from 'perpetrators'. Yet during my research I found that credible expressions of remorse make a significant contribution to the process of reconciliation. For example, South Africans used the TRC to initiate a national conversation in which the predominantly Afrikaner implementers of apartheid were confronted with the facts attributable to the system, reproached on that account, and invited to respond with meaningful expressions of remorse.[8]

TRC Staff Psychologist Pumla Gobodo-Madikizela has considered with great wisdom the contribution that remorse and its credible public expression can make to social healing:

> When perpetrators <u>feel</u> remorse, they are recognizing something they failed to see when they violated the victim, which is that the victims feel and bleed just like others with whom they, the perpetrators, identify. Remorse therefore transforms the image of victim as object to victim as human... (Gobodo-Madikizela 2003, 130).

> When perpetrators <u>express</u> remorse, when they finally acknowledge that they can see what they previously could not see, or did not want to, they are re-validating the victim's pain – in a sense, giving his or her humanity back. Empowered and re-validated, many victims at this point find it natural to extend and deepen the healing process by going a step further: turning round and conferring forgiveness on their torturer (Gobodo-Madikizela 2003, 128).

Gobodo-Madikizela writes about the personal journey undertaken by the infamous Afrikaner organizer and perpetrator of atrocities, Eugene de Kock, following his appearances at the TRC's Human Rights Violation Committee. After testifying about his role in the murder of three black policemen, de Kock met the widows of two of the officers. Gobodo-Madikizela recounts their description of this encounter:

> Both women felt that de Kock had communicated to them something he felt deeply and had acknowledged their pain. [Mrs. Faku said] "I couldn't control my tears. I could hear him, but I was overwhelmed by emotion, and I was just nodding, as a way of saying yes, I

---

8 The TRC gave a weightier voice to victims than is provided in most criminal proceedings. Many used the opportunity to add their reproach of perpetrators to that made by the commissioners.

forgive you. I hope that when he sees our tears, he knows that they are not only tears for our husbands, but tears for him as well... I would like to hold him by the hand, and show him that there is a future, and that he can still change" (Gobodo-Madikizela 2003, 14–15).

The emphasis placed on remorse and reproach by the TRC was part of the wider effort in South Africa after 1994 to 're-socialize' the country's whites by encouraging them to reconsider their view of their non-white compatriots. This effort reflects the South African approach to reconciliation, which I identify by the broad paradigm of Reproach-Rethinking-Remorse-Reparation (RRRR). In Rwanda, the paradigm might be identified as Accusation-Confession-Punishment (ACP), with the aspect of confession recognized as optional.

Both the RRRR and ACP paradigms rely on verbalized forms of interaction. Conversely, Mozambicans pursued a different paradigm through the use of healing rituals, which are based on performance. Sociologist Alcinda Honwana explains that the objective of these traditional rituals 'is not to ignore past trauma, but to acknowledge it symbolically before firmly locking it away and facing the future' (Honwana 1998). According to Honwana, the appeal of performance over word in Mozambican culture emerges from the belief that, 'Recounting and remembering the traumatic experience would be like opening a door for the harmful spirits to penetrate the communities' (Honwana 2001, 139).

João Paulo Borges Coelho compares the approach used after the 1992 peace agreement with that used by Frelimo in the early days of Mozambique's independence from Portugal (Coelho 1998). In the aftermath of the first transition thousands of people were required as a condition of re-integration into post-independence society to reveal their record of service as workers for the colonial authority. Coelho writes that:

...the effect of coming clean was often humiliation. 'Collaborators' were persecuted for their past and saw their careers and attempts to rebuild their lives blocked. As a result, many fled the country, with some subsequently offering their services when Renamo was formed by the Rhodesians in 1977 (Coelho 1998).

In contrast to this, he notes that the 1992 peace accord 'avoided a "winner-takes-all" scenario' and that, 'a fortunate combination of local circumstances also ensured that the principle of "purification" adopted by Frelimo following the colonial war would be replaced by a more conciliatory stance towards Renamo' (Coelho 1998). This is a possible sign that Frelimo had learned from its previous error of judgment.[9]

This 'fortunate combination of circumstances' occurred at both the national and international levels. At the national level, Frelimo had been forced to end its conflict with Renamo through negotiations rather than outright victory and the Mozambican people had a cultural preference for performative rituals to mark the resolution of conflict and generate reconciliation. At the international level in 1992, there was still

9   In 1945 the Allies also made a firm decision not to repeat the mistake they had made in 1918 of imposing a strong punitive policy on the defeated Germans, which had helped to incubate the rise of Nazism.

no general expectation – far less a requirement – that perpetrators should be held 'accountable' in a criminal court after the conclusion of a peace settlement. Taken together, these circumstances led to the country's broad use and public acceptance of performative, re-integrative approaches in dealing with the legacies of the civil war.

In 1996, Priscilla Hayner visited Mozambique to research attitudes toward the idea of a 'truth-establishment' mechanism. She summarizes the responses given to her interlocutors as follows:

> No, we do not want to re-enter into this morass of conflict, hatred, and pain. We want to focus on the future. For now, the past is too much part of the present for us to examine its details. For now, we prefer silence over confrontation, over renewed pain. While we cannot forget, we would like to pretend that we can (Hayner 2001, 185).

In 2001 and 2003 it appeared that this view continued to dominate. Further, it seemed that many Mozambicans had managed to remove many details of the civil war from their memories. In several conversations I had, Mozambicans could not even recall facts such as which side of the war a friend had fought on. It was not that they had forgotten the war; rather they had chosen and carefully framed what it was they wanted to remember and discuss. As Zunguza told me, they remembered the ways in which it had been a disaster for the entire nation, not individual experiences. By contrast, in Rwanda in 2004 and 2005, survivors of the genocide were still being pressed by the ICTR and the national justice system to remember and describe traumatic events that had occurred ten years earlier.

Lessons from Mozambique

Why has Mozambique's transition from a violent civil war to sustained peace been so successful? The focus on healing in the national culture and belief system are certainly significant. In addition to these context specific factors, I have identified seven lessons that indicate alternatives to the common mechanisms of post-atrocity justice that may prove constructive if adapted elsewhere.

The first lesson is found in the strong commitment, made prior to negotiation of the GPA and during the transition period of 1992–1994, to prioritizing the demands of the future over the desire to re-examine the past.

Second, the rituals undertaken at all levels signaled the existence of a clear temporal and existential transition from war to peace. Several people have described a highly publicized handshake between President Chissano and Renamo Leader Afonso Dhlakama in October 1992, as the key transformational act at the national level. At the local level, cleansing and re-integration ceremonies brought the experience of this transition to the fore.

Third, an agreement on the establishment of an egalitarian and fundamentally democratic political system was central to the GPA.

Fourth, the treatment of people who had come into direct contact with the violence of war as *affetados* meant that no attempt was made to distinguish among them: all were viewed alike and all participated in cleansing and re-integration ceremonies.

Fifth, there was concern that examining atrocities committed during the war might cause renewed trauma and violence. This created resistance to attempts to re-visit the past and sustained a strong ontological distinction between the times of war and peace.

Sixth, because people were never singled out as 'perpetrators' or 'victims', the same expectation was made of all to participate in building a new order.

Finally, all the resources of Mozambican society were made available for re-integration. These included: relationships with ancestors, the spirit of their sacred home places, extended family and the broader community, and economic resources – all of which was based on an understanding of the contribution that a stable family life within a supportive community and a decent livelihood makes to the rehabilitation of people who have survived war.

Building Peace and Preventing Atrocity in the 21st Century

The 1990s were a period in which the United States and its allies enjoyed unrivaled power. Political elites in those countries sought to use this position to implement their ideas on how to end the commission of atrocities, reverse the impunity of perpetrators in positions of power, and extend respect for the basic principles of the rule of law. However, their views had been influenced by a slightly mythologized, deeply de-politicized and often aridly legal-technical understanding of what had been accomplished during the Nuremberg Trials. For many, Nuremberg was a beacon in the campaign to end the sovereign immunity of national leaders and sent a warning to the highest officials of various governments that they could be held responsible for atrocities carried out by subordinates under their command. The establishment of ICTY in 1993 and ICTR in 1994 was seen as building directly on the precedents of Nuremberg and the momentum gained in this campaign also led to the founding of the permanent International Criminal Court (ICC) in 2002.

My research suggests the value of a more political and more deeply historical view of the nature of atrocities when identifying ways to end mass violence and instil the rule of law (and therefore, end impunity) in places where it has hitherto been disregarded. The differing trajectories that South Africa, Mozambique and Rwanda have taken show that the provision of amnesties secured a sustainable peace and strengthened the rule of law in South Africa and Mozambique, while a reliance on prosecutions in Rwanda has failed to bring about respect for the rule of law.

A focus on the politics of terminating conflict requires attention to the politics of making and building peace. Parties to a conflict who are able to achieve peace through negotiation, as in Mozambique or South Africa, have the opportunity to prepare long-term foundations for peace. Meanwhile, the record of the victorious (Western) Allies at the end of the Second World War shows that even a party which achieves a formal 'peace' through outright military victory can also succeed in building peace, provided it pays due attention to the vital tasks of social and political reconstruction.[10]

In Rwanda, South Africa and Mozambique, people frequently highlighted the importance of meeting basic economic needs and of establishing a stable socioeconomic order in the aftermath of conflict. Mani's analysis of post-war justice gives equal weight to the needs of distributive justice (economic), legal justice (restoration the rule of law) and rectificatory justice (the remedying of wrongs) (Mani 2002, 38–46 and Ch. 5). Roland Paris identifies the adoption of conflict-reducing economic policies as one of the six key tasks to be addressed in any successful effort to build peace (Paris 2004, 188). Indeed, in societies reeling from conflict, when asked to define the kind of justice they would like to see, many people speak about economic justice before they consider matters of prosecutions, trials or punishments. To this extent, perhaps the Western concept of individually applicable prosecutorial 'justice', as upheld in societies that have already enjoyed economic stability for many decades, is inappropriate. Those living in deprived communities are more liable to refuse any reductive understanding of justice in terms of orderly criminal proceedings. For them, justice must also include social and economic sustainability.

References

Arendt, H. and Jaspers, K. (1992), *Correspondence: Hannah Arendt, Karl Jaspers, 1926–1969* (New York: Harcourt Brace Jovanovich).

CAVR (2004), 'Community Reconciliation', *CAVR Update*, December 2003/January 2004 (published online) <http://www.easttimor-reconciliation.org/cavrUpdate-Dec03Jan04-en.html>.

Coelho, J.P.B. (1998), '"Purification" versus "Reconciliation" amongst Ex-Combatants', Epilogue to Honwana, A., 'Sealing the Past, Facing the Future'.

Freedom House Country Ratings <http://www.freedomhouse.org/ratings/index.htm>.

Gobodo-Madikizela, P. (2003), *A Human Being Died That Night: A South African Story of Forgiveness* (New York: Houghton Mifflin).

Hayner, P.B. (2001), *Unspeakable Truths: Confronting State Terror and Atrocity* (New York and London: Routledge).

Honwana, A. (1998), 'Sealing the Past, Facing the Future', in Armon, J. et al. (eds), *The Mozambique Peace Process in Perspective* (London: Conciliation Resources).

Honwana, A. (2001), 'Children of War: Understanding War and War Cleansing in Mozambique and Angola', in Chesterman, S. (ed.), *Civilians in War* (Boulder: Lynne Rienner).

Levi, P. (1986), *The Drowned and the Saved* (New York: Summit Books).

---

10 These comments are also relevant to the position of the U.S. occupation authorities in Iraq after 2003.

Minow, M. (2000), 'The Hope for Healing', in Rotberg, R.I. and Thompson, D. (eds), *Truth v. Justice: The Morality of Truth Commissions* (Princeton and Oxford: Princeton University Press).

Mani, R. (2002), *Beyond Retribution: Seeking Justice in the Shadows of War* (Malden MA: Polity Press, Cambridge and Blackwell Publishers).

Paris, R. (2004), *At War's End: Building Peace After Civil Conflict* (Cambridge and New York: Cambridge University Press).

West, R. (1955), *A Train of Powder: Six Reports on the Problem of Guilt and Punishment in our Time* (Chicago: Ivan R. Dee).

Chapter 11

Community Reconciliation in East Timor: A Personal Perspective

Patrick Burgess

Historical Background

The eastern half of the island of Timor was historically a Portuguese colony, while many of the surrounding islands, including West Timor, came under Dutch control. Following the war of independence in 1945, the Dutch islands became the state of Indonesia and in 1960 East Timor was recognized by the United Nations as a non-self-governing state administered by Portugal. In 1974 the Carnation Revolution in Portugal established a new policy to release colonial holdings. The absence of a plan for the colony's transition to independence, and resulting opportunity to seize power, led to the rapid formation of political parties in East Timor. The two major parties, UDT and Fretilin, rapidly became involved in a short civil war, which claimed the lives of several thousand. Both sides to the conflict committed human rights violations, including the massacre of unarmed detainees, although the number and severity of the Fretilin violations was significantly higher (CAVR 2006, Pt 3; Pt 8).

Fretilin unilaterally declared the independence of the Democratic Republic of Timor L'Este in November 1975. Ten days later Indonesia mounted an invasion of the territory, joined by some of the thousands of East Timorese that had fled the civil war. During this period, in which the United States was involved in both the Cold War and the Vietnam War, Fretilin's leftist philosophy had little appeal in comparison with President Suharto's anti-communist, pro-free market agenda. As a result, the major western powers politically supported East Timor's integration into Indonesia, despite their international obligation to uphold the new republic's right to self-determination and the knowledge that the Indonesian military forces had been implicated in the killing of up to one million alleged Indonesian Communist Party sympathizers in 1965 (CAVR 2006, Pt 7).

The divisions among East Timorese created by the civil war deepened during the 24 years of Indonesian military occupation. Indonesian security forces used local paramilitaries, known as *Hansip*, to gain intelligence and contribute to operations. Some East Timorese also joined the army and police force and were involved in human rights violations committed against supporters of Falintil, the relatively small pro-independence guerrilla force, and others that resisted integration. Torture, forced disappearance and rape were systematically used with almost total impunity. Between 100,000 and 180,000 East Timorese are estimated to have died as a result of the conflict (CAVR 2006, Pt 6).

In 1999 the Suharto regime fell. The temporarily appointed President, B.J. Habibie, unexpectedly invited the United Nations to organize a referendum on East Timor's secession from Indonesia. This appears to have been contrary to the wishes of senior members of the Indonesian security forces, as the military mounted a major operation to force the East Timorese to vote against independence (CAVR 2006, Pt 8). In carrying out the operation, they armed, directed and funded over 20 different East Timorese militia groups.

In defiance of the campaign of terror undertaken by the military before the ballot, 78.5 percent of voters chose independence, sparking an angry rampage of revenge. In three weeks more than 1,500 civilians were killed, hundreds of women were raped, more than 60,000 houses were burned, most government and private infrastructure was destroyed, almost all vehicles and items of value were looted and 250,000 East Timorese were deported to West Timor, many of them forcibly. Following a direct request by President Clinton of the United States, Indonesia finally agreed to intervention by international peace-keepers. The security forces and militia then moved to West Timor with whatever items of value were left.

UNTAET, Justice and Reconciliation

In October 1999 the United Nations Transitional Administration in East Timor (UNTAET) was established with an unprecedented mandate to administer the territory and prepare it for independence. The mission was faced with the enormous challenge of reconstruction. Among the multitude of pressing tasks, were the need to draft a constitution and write laws, establish institutions – courts, prisons, government departments, defence services, port and taxation authorities – build schools and hospitals, and prepare for an election and the administration of the first parliament.

One of the mission's fundamental goals was to mitigate the desire for revenge for past violations. The events of 1999 were particularly problematic, as much of the violence had involved East Timorese militia groups acting under the direction and protection of the Indonesian military. In the absence of this protection there was little to prevent victims, their families and communities from seeking their own form of justice.

Within UNTAET the United Nations (UN) established the Serious Crimes Investigations Unit (SCU) and the Special Panels of the Dili District Court. These bodies were charged with the investigation and prosecution of 'serious criminal offences', to be undertaken by UN staff under the authority of a Deputy General Prosecutor for Serious Crimes. The Special Panels consisted of one East Timorese and two international judges. 'Serious crimes' included crimes against humanity, genocide, war crimes, murder, sexual offences and torture. The Regulation that provided the mandate of the Special Panels limited it to acts committed between 1 January and 25 October 1999.[1]

---

1 Investigation of pre-1999 crimes such as crimes against humanity, genocide and war crimes could have been undertaken as they are covered by universal jurisdiction. However, the Serious Crimes Investigation Unit restricted itself to crimes committed during the period set out by the mandate because of the size of the caseload.

The Dili District Court held jurisdiction over all other crimes, past or present, known as 'ordinary crimes'. The tens of thousands of ordinary crimes that had been committed presented an intractable challenge. The entire system of justice including the court buildings themselves needed to be re-established. This not only meant deciding upon and clarifying the law but training and appointing court administrators, police investigators, judges, prosecutors and defence counsel, as there were less than a hundred East Timorese with law degrees and fewer than a handful with courtroom experience. As the prisons grew overcrowded it became obvious that the system would be unable to deal with even the new crimes being committed, much less those of the past.

The UN Commission of Inquiry into violations committed in East Timor had recommended that the major perpetrators, many of whom were suspected to be senior Indonesian military and civilian officials, be brought to justice through the establishment of an international tribunal (UN 2000). However, Indonesia was first given the opportunity to try its own citizens and an ad hoc tribunal was established in Jakarta. Over time it came to be regarded as a sham: eventually all the individuals indicted and tried for crimes against humanity were acquitted.

Origins of the East Timor Truth and Reconciliation Commission

In August 2000 the First National Congress of the East Timorese (CNRT), an umbrella body including representatives of all parties that had supported independence, passed a unanimous resolution to establish a commission for truth and reconciliation. Shortly before this, I was appointed Director of the UNTAET Human Rights Unit (HRU) and subsequently, the late Sergio Viera de Mello, who led the UNTAET mission from October 1999 until independence on May 2002, asked me to take the lead role in the establishment of the commission from the UN side.

The workload of the HRU at that time was overwhelming. Our human rights officers were busy helping refugees return safely to their villages, monitoring the police, military, prisons and the development of the justice system, participating in the drafting of a range of laws with human rights implications, investigating complaints of rights violations, assisting in drafting a constitution and, with 'serious crimes' investigations, establishing a data base of people killed during the violence in 1999, training civil society groups, police, military and government workers on human rights issues and myriad other tasks.

In building the foundations of a reconciliation mechanism it was essential to ensure that the Timorese owned the process. A Steering Committee was formed of representatives of 11 East Timorese groups – non-government organisations (NGOs), political parties, Falintil and the Church – and of the United Nations Commission for Human Rights (UNHCR) and UNTAET. Paul van Zyl and Priscilla Hayner, two experts in transitional justice, assisted. As Sergio Viera de Mello's representative, I chaired the committee and the secretariat was based at the HRU.

This was the first time that a UN peace-keeping mission had been directly involved in the establishment of a truth and reconciliation commission. This led to differences of opinion, even within the HRU, as to whether this was appropriate work for the mission to undertake. What was clear was that reconciliation is a fundamental aspect of peace-keeping and is directly related to past, present and potentially future human rights violations. Further, UNTAET was a *de facto* government as well as a UN peace-keeping mission. The HRU was the section best equipped to help initiate a body that would become self-sufficient, though it required substantial efforts and resources in order to do so.

The Steering Committee began by developing a general framework, which was canvassed through public consultations in each of the 13 districts. Among the range of suggestions received, there were a number in common across the territory, including:

- Victims and witnesses needed to tell their stories and have them recorded to ensure that lessons of the past were learned and atrocities would not be repeated. There was concern that uncovering past events would lead to renewed violence. While acknowledging this risk, the vast majority of people consulted said that the painful process of establishing the historical truth was essential for them to move forward;
- The need to bring to justice those responsible for the commitment of major crimes;
- Those involved in less serious crimes could be dealt with at the community level. They must tell the complete truth, apologize to their victims and the community and be ready to make repayments or to undertake work to prove the sincerity of their apology. This process should involve elders entrusted with traditional justice and spiritual matters and community leaders (CAVR 2006, Pt 1, 11).

The HRU's work with returning refugees strongly supported the need for a process of peaceful resolution of past differences. Only a relatively small number of returnees were suspected of committing major crimes and UN peace-keepers and police were ordered to detain them as they crossed the border. However, thousands were suspected of beatings, burning homes, looting and other lesser crimes committed not only in 1999 but also during the Indonesian occupation. These individuals were susceptible to revenge attacks, which if begun, could quickly re-ignite the previous cycle of violence and destroy any hopes of a lasting peace.[2]

The Challenge of Recruitment

While a framework was being designed, there were logistical matters to consider. The former head of the UNAMET mission, Ian Martin, identified one of our most pressing concerns when he asked how we were going to find the people to staff the commission. The usual recruiting frenzy had taken place in Dili with the arrival of the UN and international NGOs and the small number of educated East Timorese had been absorbed into relatively well-paid jobs. Additionally, the police, military and government departments had completed their personnel intake and few experienced

---

2 Initially, District Human Rights Officers tried to attain advance notice of the arrival of 'problem cases' and negotiate an agreement of safe return with local leaders pending formal legal examination of the case. If negotiations were successful, the suspect was accompanied on their homecoming and visited regularly to ensure their safety. This strategy was formulated on the basis that a functioning legal system was being developed to deal with these cases.

individuals were left in need of work. Consequently, I was enormously relieved when it became clear during a public consultation where the human resources to run a successful reconciliation program were going to be found.

The consultation was being held in the Suai district, about 8 hours by car from Dili. Approximately two hundred people were gathered beneath the thatched roof of a traditional building. The suggestions being made were similar to those we had encountered elsewhere and as I listened, the voice of experience in my head warned that we may have bitten off more than we could chew with our ideals of healing past wounds.

As discussion led to the need for perpetrators to 'confess their sins' and for the community to be involved in the process, I decided to test the suggestions with a role-play. Walking into the audience I asked for volunteers and delegated roles that represented those common to a hearing: perpetrators, victims, members of the victim's community and panel members representing the community and the Church. The other members of the Steering Committee and I stood back, watched and were stunned. The participants took to their roles naturally and were at ease in their exploration of such a difficult situation. Both laughter and sombre moments were shared as they re-created experiences shared by those present. No reticence to appear in public or awkwardness was shown. The participants engaged with the issues, participated vigorously and thoughtfully and concluded with a workable solution. What we witnessed was the result of the participatory, community-based way that the East Timorese, in the absence of any trustworthy formal legal mechanisms, had been resolving problems for centuries.

Local communities were where we would find the people to do the work of the commission, as long as it was based on a realistic assessment of capacity and was designed to utilize the strengths of those involved. Arguments about a lack of capacity would be right in relation to a western model requiring a high level of formal education, but with this approach we had seen how a low-level of literacy could be compensated by a high-level of verbal ability.

Armed with the information and understanding gathered during the public consultations, the Steering Committee drafted the legislation for the establishment of the East Timor Commission for Reception, Truth and Reconciliation (CAVR).[3] Part IV of the legislation dealt with a central aspect of the commission, the Community Reconciliation Procedures (CRPs).[4] According to the UNTAET Regulation, the CAVR would not have the power to impinge on the exclusive jurisdiction of the Office of the General Prosecutor (OGP) over 'serious crimes'. However, it would have the authority to deal with 'criminal or non-criminal acts' in a community-based setting, on receipt of permission from the Prosecutor General. A strict definition of

---

3   The *Comissão de Acolhimento, Verdade e Reconciliacão de Timor Leste* (CAVR) was established in July 2001 by UNTAET Regulation: UNTAET/REG/2001/10, 13 July 2001. The International Centre for Transitional Justice provided technical assistance in the drafting exercise, which meant the process benefited from the experience gained in establishing other commissions.

4   Paul van Zyl and Priscilla Hayner developed the concept on which this mechanism was based during a workshop held in Dili in early 2000.

what the CRPs should deal with was not included, but in practice the SCU dealt with murder, rape, torture and the organization of mass violence and less serious matters were referred to a CRP.

Community Reconciliation Procedures in Practice

In line with the Regulation, CAVR staff members visited villages to provide information and assist perpetrators in writing a short statement on their involvement in the acts under consideration. After being considered by an in-house committee, statements were forwarded to the OGP, which had two weeks (with the possibility of extension to one month on notification) to consider the case and advise the CAVR of its intention to exercise exclusive jurisdiction over the matter or proceed by way of CRP. This short time frame for the Prosecutor's response was essential given the Commission's ambition of making the mechanism available to all of the 65 sub-districts in East Timor, an aim it eventually achieved.

Once a case was approved, a presiding panel was formed in the village where the violation had occurred. A CAVR Regional Commissioner and local leaders from the church, women's groups, youth committees or other representative groups chaired the panels. A hearing date was then arranged, usually to allow for the inclusion of a number of perpetrators. On the day of the hearing perpetrators were required to make a formal public acknowledgement and apology for their actions, and victims were given the opportunity to ask questions of the perpetrator and to make comments. Community members could also participate with questions and comments. After hearing from all parties, the panel negotiated an agreement on 'acts of reconciliation' for the perpetrator to undertake, which might include payment of reparations, a direct apology or community service. The signed agreement was forwarded to the appropriate district court and, on completion of the acts of reconciliation, the perpetrator received immunity from further civil or criminal liability.

I participated in designing the procedures and training staff and, fuelled by the repeated accounts of the merits of the mechanism that I gave to potential donors, I became increasingly excited by its potential. However, there were times when I harboured doubts. This was an entirely new process that had never been attempted before. I was putting my professional reputation on the line by stating my belief that it would work, but would it?

At the conclusion of the first round of field activities I met with a group of field staff and regional commissioners and enthusiastically asked whether we were going to be able to make this a successful program. I was expecting a resounding 'yes' in reply, accompanied by lots of wonderful Timorese smiles. Instead there was silence and shaking heads, definitely a bad sign. The problem was that perpetrators did not want to participate. Why should they volunteer to take part in a painful and embarrassing process that obliged them to apologize for their actions in public and make payments or work to repay their social debt?

In drafting the Regulation we had been aware that without including requirements that were logistically impossible, such as access to legal advice, people could not be compelled to take part in a CRP. We had reasoned that in the absence of a legal obligation, perpetrators would volunteer to participate to avoid the alternative of arrest and formal trial. At the time, this accorded with reality. However, the establishment of the CAVR took longer than expected. By the time the CRPs were ready to begin, it was clear to everyone that the justice system was struggling to cope with the new crimes being committed and that it would certainly not have the capacity to handle 'less serious' past violations.

On seeing the disappointment among the staff at the initial response to the program, I was uncertain about what could be done next but I knew we needed to continue. On a whiteboard I drew a rough bridge with a victim represented at one end and a perpetrator at the other. I explained that, like the bridge, our role was simply to bring people together by organizing the hearings and providing a safe place for people to meet. From there, it was up to them to reconcile with each other. The staff remained unmoved. The perpetrators were both afraid of the hearings and they did not feel compelled to come. I thought this over and asked the group what tools they would need to build the bridge and bring the perpetrators to it. It was from here that the answers began to flow. For the mechanism to work, the field staff and regional coordinators wanted much greater insistence on participation from the government, the Church, local groups and community elders. Further, seating and a meal at the end of the hearing would ensure that things ended in a positive spirit with everyone eating together.

'OK then, if the national office helps you with these things, can you run the program successfully?' I asked. 'Yes!', came the reply, and the reward of flashing, white Timorese smiles.

Meetings between Aniceto Guterres Lopes, the Chair of the Commission, and senior Timorese leaders resulted in repeated public support for CAVR programs from President Xanana Gusmao and Bishop Nascimento. Priests across the predominantly Catholic country told their parishioners to 'go to the CAVR and confess your sins'. The Prime Minister and Foreign Minister also showed support. Logistical assistance for hearings was increased and the CAVR district teams secured the help of local civic leaders, who placed indirect pressure on perpetrators in their communities to participate.

In the first sub-districts the program began slowly, with only a few perpetrators brave enough to come forward. However, the hearings became more than a process for dealing with individual wrongdoing as they progressed. They represented a symbolic closure to the conflict for communities and a chance to explore various aspects of what had taken place through questions directed to the participants and wider public discussion. Perpetrators took advantage of the opportunity not only to explain their actions but also to dispel rumours and misinformation. In this way, actual rather than supposed offenders were sometimes identified. Further, victims were able to vent their anger and seek consolation in an explanation of what had taken place.

Adat and spiritual practices took on a major role in the hearings, particularly the practice of *biti bot*. According to this tradition a large mat was unfurled in front of the panel's table. Spiritual leaders and elders, often dressed in costumes of colourful traditional weavings, silver horns, chest plates and calf boots of long horse hair, chanted to rhythmic drums and ritually chewed betel nut while seated on the mat. The mat could not be rolled up until the dispute had been settled.

As the number of villages completing successful CRPs increased, opinions about their importance to the perpetrators, victims and their communities passed by word of mouth and demand grew rapidly. By the end of the 18-month operational period approximately 1,400 individual cases had been finalized.[5] The smallest hearing involved one perpetrator; the largest dealt with 55, was attended by over a thousand villagers and lasted several days. By the closure of the program the CRPs became a victim of their own success. Due to the temporal mandate and limited available funding, it was estimated that several thousand additional cases were excluded.[6]

The United Nations Development Program (UNDP) conducted a study of the CRPs in 2004 based on more than 70 interviews. In his report on the assessment, Piers Pigou concluded:

> In terms of impact, there is a widespread feeling that the CRPs have definitely contributed to building social cohesion and relieving tensions in many places ... There is broad acknowledgement from victims and deponents that the commission played its neutral role with considerable dexterity. When compared with the formal justice system, the CRP is seen to be relatively quick and a visibly just resolution of the problem. In addition, it expedites the possibility of returning to normal life, which is important in a context where violence is regarded by some as a legitimate problem-solving mechanism (Pigou 2004, 76–7).

Following the process of community reconciliation, perpetrators were generally accepted back into their communities. In several cases victims volunteered to join them in completing their community service as a demonstration of forgiveness and solidarity. However, if victims felt that the perpetrators had not genuinely apologized or did not tell the whole truth, their request to be re-admitted to the community was rejected.

A number of people who had been convicted and served prison sentences for offences applied to have the same set of actions dealt with through a CRP. Court proceedings and prisons in Dili were perceived as too removed from the local context and unable to offer the same opportunity for explanation and peer-judgement. Nor did they provide the security of a CRP. The entire community was bound by a decision that community and *adat* leaders participated in making. Beating a perpetrator as revenge for their actions would be a serious contravention of such an agreement.

Some victims who participated in CRP hearings complained that they felt pressured to accept the apology of the perpetrator because the community wanted settlement of the dispute. The 'acts of reconciliation' were in general less severe than had been expected and in many cases did not amount to more than a public apology. It is unclear if individual victims' needs were superseded by community desires in this regard, especially in the context of communal villages where the two

---

5   For detailed statistics on the CRP program see: CAVR 2006, Pt 9, 31.

6   Author interview with Jamito da Costa, Director of the CRP Program, Dili, April 2005.

are often merged. CRPs were also much more effective in rural villages, which tend to maintain strong community structures.

It is important to remember that the CRPs were but one aspect of an integrated approach to reconciliation, informed by a strategic plan that maintained the importance of addressing the issue at both local and national levels.[7] The Final Report of the CAVR was based on approximately 8,000 victim and witness statements. Public hearings, involving evidence given by national leaders including the President, Prime Minister, Head of the Armed Forces and other senior political leaders, were covered live on national television. Local public hearings were held in each sub-district. Also, a radio program on reconciliation issues was broadcast weekly and healing workshops were conducted for victims, as part of a comprehensive victim support program that was integral to the Commission's work.

Conclusion

The problems experienced by the formal justice sector following East Timorese independence are common to post-conflict situations. The CRPs temporarily filled this vacuum, providing the only contact with any process of justice for most people because they were faster, cheaper, more accessible and easier to understand. They relied on voluntary participation and did not entail lengthy investigations or the costly roles of professionals and administrators. Cases were usually finalized within a day and they produced a higher level of community participation than would have been possible in the courts.

On the other hand, the CRPs could not offer the uniformity, appropriate matching of sentences to crimes and support for the concept of the rule of law provided by a formal justice system. However, in the early years following independence, East Timor bore little resemblance to the perfect world in which a formal justice system is a necessary foundation for a new society. In the muddy bog of post-conflict reconciliation, where every wobbly step forward is painful, hard-won and brings with it a risk of falling face-down, small practical gains are like gold and academic hyperbole seems as abundant and useless as desert sand. In this context the CRPs made a remarkable and practical contribution.

Nations emerging from long periods of conflict have no choice but to make progress on the issue of reconciliation if they are to succeed in breaking the cycle of violence. Even slow progress will not take place without a serious effort, resources and specifically targeted programming. There are few examples of how to assist in the generation of reconciliation in post-conflict situations. The principles of the CRPs hold some valuable lessons: look deeply into local conditions, resources and needs; do something more than just talk; and do not to be discouraged by the massive, inevitable difficulties or the critical voices from comfortable armchairs far away. There will be many failures and some successes, even in the most optimistic scenario. The effort required will often seem too much but, when considered in relation to the consequences of inaction, little choice remains.

---

7   For a full account of CAVR's reconciliation program, see: CAVR 2006, Pt 1.

Postscript

Violence re-erupted in Timor Leste in May 2006, resulting in the deaths of 30 people and the dislocation of more than 150,000.

Did the work of the CAVR and the CRPs in particular have any relationship to the renewed violence? Is this an indication of failure or does it show that they delayed or minimized an inevitable resurgence of conflict and anger? It is impossible to answer these questions conclusively, however, no voices critical of the work of the CAVR have yet been raised. In accepting the position of Prime Minister, following Mari Alkatiri's resignation as a result of the crisis, Jose Ramos Horta asked his people to study and learn the lessons set out in the Report of the CAVR. The commission was also mentioned favourably by then President Xanana Gusmao. In the middle of the crisis an East Timorese woman said to me, 'See what happened because the CAVR closed down'. The story is of course not as simple as that.

In my opinion these events underline the difference between the governance structures suitable for post-conflict settings and those relevant to nations with a history of peace. A semi-permanent institution responsible for reconciliation should be included in the government of all societies recovering from long-term conflict. Such institutions could follow on from the work of truth and reconciliation commissions but should not be limited to dealing with the past: their work should aim to resolve the transitional issues of reconciliation that inevitably arise.

References

East Timor Commission for Reception, Truth and Reconciliation (CAVR) (2006), *Chega! Final Report of the Commission for Reception, Truth and Reconciliation in East Timor* <http://www.ictj.org/en/news/features/846.html>.

Pigou, P. (2004), *CAVR's Community Reconciliation Process: Report for UNDP*, April.

United Nations (UN) (2000), *Report of the International Commission of Inquiry on East Timor to the Secretary-General*, UN Document A/54/726 – S/2000/59, 31 January.

UNTAET Regulation 2001/10, Sections 22.2 1; 22.2 2; 24.6; 24.7; 31.

Chapter 12

The Role of Economic Development in Reconciliation: An Experience from Bosnia and Herzegovina

Vince Gamberale

Since the outbreak of war in 1992, the fledgling nation of Bosnia and Herzegovina (BiH) has endured the trauma of armed conflict, displacement of approximately 1.8 million people and continuing polarization of its existing population along the ethnic divides of Serb, Croat and *Bosniak* (Muslim Slav) created by the collapse of the former Yugoslavia. The war was brought to an end in November 1995 with the 'General Framework Agreement for Peace in Bosnia and Herzegovina' reached in Dayton, Ohio. As the country struggles to come to terms with the consequences of a war that resulted in the deaths of at least 100,000 people, it also faces the challenge of much needed political and economic reform.[1]

Compounding the difficulties of reform in a divided and post-socialist nation is the complex political and administrative structure inherited from the Dayton Accords and the Washington Accords that preceded them.[2] The State of BiH consists of two entities roughly equal in territorial size – the predominately Bosniak / Bosnian Croat 'Federation of Bosnia and Herzegovina' (FBiH) and the predominately Bosnian Serb 'Republika Srpska' (RS) – and a joint multi-ethnic central government (BiH State) charged with conducting foreign, diplomatic, defence and indirect tax policy.[3] The cumbersome nature of this structure has obstructed economic reform and stifled economic development. While the post-war period has seen the stabilization of the currency, establishment of the private banking sector and tax reforms, high levels of unemployment and poverty persist, even with considerable levels of post-war international development assistance.

---

1   For further information, see: The Research and Documentation Center Sarajevo, The Status of Database by the Centers <http://www.idc.org.ba/aboutus/Overview_of_jobs_according_to_%20centers.htm>.

2   The Washington Accords, signed on 18 March 1994, led to a ceasefire between the Bosniaks and Bosnian Croats that eventuated in the creation of the 'Federation of Bosnia and Herzegovina' Entity.

3   In addition to the entities of FBiH and RS, the District of Brcko was established in 1999. It falls under the exclusive sovereignty of the BiH State and is governed by a single, multi-ethnic, democratic government. BiH State has had responsibility for defence policy since 2005 and for Indirect Tax Policy since 2006.

This chapter offers a review of the 'Municipal and Economic Development Initiative' (MEDI), implemented from 2001 by CHF International in Bosnia and Herzegovina with funding from the United States Agency for International Development (USAID) and the Swedish International Development and Cooperation Agency (SIDA). MEDI was designed to create democratic, non-profit associations serving a variety of community needs, including small business development, government advocacy, quality of life improvement and financial services. It is possible now to consider the outcomes of this program and the role of economic development in relation to reconciliation in a post-conflict environment. Drawing on lessons taken from MEDI, I examine correlations between economic development in BiH and increased tolerance and cooperation between its people, who have been polarized around ethnicity and brutalized by war.

Overview: Issues for Economic Development

The war devastated a country that had enjoyed stability and relative prosperity through industrialization following the Second World War. The unfavourable environment for economic development that now exists can be attributed to the destruction of much of the national infrastructure, displacement of the population and the introduction of criminal activity and corruption into the market, as well as halting attempts at privatization and the difficulties of making the political transition from socialism to democracy. While these issues present significant obstacles for economic development, mitigating forces can also be found to be at work.

Although the Dayton Accords were welcomed in 1995 for bringing peace, in the years since they have come to be perceived as laying the foundations for a failed state. In 1995, the structure of governance they established includes: the Office of the High Representative (OHR), an ad hoc international institution responsible for overseeing implementation of civilian aspects of the accord, with power to enforce laws and remove government representatives; BiH State, the central government, which has responsibility for foreign policy but extremely limited capacity to raise taxes and create laws; the RS and FBiH entity governments, which have greater capacity to raise taxes and make laws, 10 cantonal governments within FBiH, also with tax and law-making capacity; and 148 municipal governments with extremely limited tax-raising and by-law capacity.[4] The central, state, entity and cantonal levels of government support an executive branch, headed respectively by a prime minister, assembly/legislature and judiciary. Therefore in 2006, the some 3.9 million citizens of BiH were burdened by one weak central government, 13 powerful entity or cantonal governments – dominated by political parties based on ethnicity or motivated by

---

4   In June 2006 the Steering Board of the Peace Implementation Council, the international body guiding the peace process, called on national authorities to take full responsibility for peace implementation and announced that the OHR would close on 30 June 2007. Due to political instability in 2007 this deadline was prolonged without a clear date. The High Representative, who is also the European Union Special Representative in BiH with a mandate to promote overall EU political coordination, will remain in the country after the closure of the OHR.

nationalism – and 148 limited municipal governments. [5] With the OHR adding yet another layer to this already cumbersome structure, widespread confusion regarding the responsibilities and jurisdiction of the various levels of governments has resulted in public cynicism and a view that: 'Everyone is in charge and no one is in charge!' Contributing to this general sense of disenchantment are the disproportionate amounts spent on government administration – estimated in 2006 to consume some 70 percent of budget expenditures – as opposed to the provision of services to citizens. Compounding this concern is the stigma of petty and systemic corruption. The governance structure hinders the prevention of corruption, as does domination by the agendas of political parties, lack of transparency in the privatization process and the low level of the average wage.[6]

In a rare display of consensus, a movement to reform the constitution was initiated in 2005 by the eight main political parties. Despite compromises on the nature of reforms, the vote in parliament in 2006 for constitutional reform narrowly failed to receive the necessary two-thirds majority. Attempts to reform the Dayton based BiH governance structures have since been linked to the long term EU Accession process. In the three and a half years of conflict that engulfed BiH, many buildings, roads, bridges, railway lines, medical facilities and the means of energy generation and distribution were damaged or destroyed. From 1995, multilateral and bilateral donor agencies provided over US$5 billion for reconstruction. When this began to rapidly contract from 2001, entity and cantonal governments and the private sector increased their contributions. Lines of micro-credit and remittances from the Bosnian diaspora have helped to re-establish housing, an estimated 60 percent of which was also damaged or destroyed. The diaspora is comprised of some 700,000 refugees who continue to live in the Balkan region or further abroad. Up to 30 percent of BiH's Gross Domestic Product (GDP) in the immediate post-conflict period is estimated to have come from remittances. While these funds were initially used to support consumption some are gradually being shifted towards private investment. The LRC Credit Bureau (provision of credit and financial debt information), Prizm Research (social and market research), and Pharmamed (pharmaceutical product manufacturer) are examples of successful entrepreneurship and investments in human capital initiated by the diaspora and returnee community.

While investment in the economy is welcomed, another source of private investment raises ethical and political concerns. Criminal activity within the economy is encouraged by the general nature of war, and in BiH war lords or organized crime controlled lucrative smuggling routes in and out of conflict areas. People were forced to pay exorbitant prices for basic necessities such as vegetables, meat, fuel, and in the case of Sarajevo during the siege, even water. Vast amounts of money were amassed in this way and also through the illegal trade in weapons. In the period since, many of those who profited have converted their contraband fortunes into legitimate business

---

5   According to the 1991 census the population of BiH prior to the war was 4.3 million. As no census has been conducted since then and 2006 (the time of writing), all current population figures are estimates. In 2005, World Bank data estimated the population to be 3.9 million.

6   At the end of the war the World Bank reported the average monthly net wage to be US$57, by 2005 it was estimated as US$332.

activities and investments. As a consequence, several have positioned themselves among the country's new economic elite and use their influence to lobby government for changes to laws and regulations.

Unfortunately, this is only one of a number of areas of concern surrounding the post-war process of privatization, which has been mired in delays and allegations of political corruption and nepotism – the successful privatization of the banking sector and the steel plant in Zenica being notable exceptions. However, the restitution of housing property and its privatization, overseen by the OHR, has largely been hailed as a success. The process established a twentieth century precedent of completely returning property to its original owners/occupants in a post-conflict environment: as of 2006 approximately 97 percent of properties have been returned. While this has not meant the re-establishment of pre-war multi-ethnic communities, it has made it possible for people to return to their homes should they wish, or to initiate sale of their property.

Despite the many negative economic issues impacting upon BiH's potential for growth, there are trends that show promise for the future. These include the commencement of negotiations towards the European Union (EU) Structural Accession Agreement (SAA) – the first step towards EU membership; establishment of the Regional Development Agencies (RDAs) and their respective economic zones; conduits for EU economic development funding, and a means of filling the void in economic governance; improvements generated by the BiH Central Bank in inflation and the overall efficiency of the financial services sector; and the establishment of the Indirect Tax Authority (ITA) – as a consequence of which the State government will receive its first taxation revenue base due to the conversion of all entity/cantonal sales taxes into the state-level Value Added Tax (VAT).

MEDI: Methodology and Outcomes

The vision of the MEDI project is encapsulated within the following statement: 'Through Private Public Partnerships (using credit as the hook) create a critical mass of association members that will utilize pressure to ensure a more responsive government that will seek an environment that encourages economic development.'

Methodology

Between 2001 and 2004 the MEDI program was implemented in 14 municipalities within the Lasva and Bosna Valleys of Central BiH. After 2004, it was expanded to include additional municipalities within the Vrbas Valley and the city of Sarajevo. Combined, these geographic areas saw some of the most intensive fighting and suffering during the war. The overarching aim of the program was to improve the economic environment at the municipal level by establishing and encouraging partnerships between municipal governments, the private sector and civil society (owners of farms and homes).

The methodology according to which the program was designed and run was as follows:

1. Identify or create small business and farm/home owners associations in target communities, known as 'Business Associations' or 'Community Development Corporations', and provide capacity building in sustainable activities such as: developing a membership base, providing membership services, improving advocacy techniques, and assessing and pursuing income generating opportunities.
2. Offer direct credit to association members for small business development and shelter/quality-of-life improvements. This simultaneously supports membership growth, familiarizes members with credit mechanisms and creates a peer group within the association.
3. Engage the mayor of the municipality in the program by establishing an agreement that they will regularly meet association leaders to ensure that the parties work together to improve the municipal processes affecting local small business and farm/home owners.
4. Work with the municipality to design, build and operate accessible and highly visible 'Municipal Customer Service Centers', generally located at the entrance to city halls. This includes producing necessary business and citizen information materials, such as application forms, lists of required documents, an outline of key processes and the names and contact details of relevant staff. It also involves re-engineering and automating the processes within local governments to make them more efficient and responsive to the needs of citizens.
5. Create a regional 'Enterprise Network' comprised of representatives of local small business and farm/home owner associations to create a collective membership base among local associations and the critical mass for changes such as reductions in fees and taxes and the refinement of bureaucratic processes.
6. Create a regional 'Mayor's Coalition' comprised of mayors from partner cities to bring mayors together to address issues such as the delivery of services and to advocate for change.
7. Develop a regional 'Private Public Partnership' (PPP) between the Enterprise Network and the Mayor's Coalition to address shared interests (such as greater responsibility for local government), develop regional economic development objectives and target major investment opportunities to improve regional economic conditions.

Outcomes

As of August 2005, the outcomes of the MEDI program were as follows:

1. 16 Business Associations or Community Development Corporations had been established, representing a base of 3,000 businesses (also representing 14,000 employees) or farm/home owners.[7]

---

7   The ethnic demographic of the membership base roughly reflected that of the Central Region of BiH.

2. The Lider Micro-Credit organization had been established and disbursed some 5,500 small business, housing and consumer loans valued at approximately US$10 million with a repayment rate of no less than 98.5 percent.[8]
3. Over 300 advocacy actions had been undertaken to improve the economic environment, resulting in 130 economic reforms at the municipal, cantonal, entity and state levels.
4. 18 Municipal Customer Service Centres had been established, improving service efficiency and leveraging additional municipal government funding for the same effect.
5. As a consequence of the Regional PPP created under MEDI the 'REZ Regional Development Agency' (REZ RDA) was established by the MEDI stakeholders to facilitate the economic development of the Central BiH Economic Region. By August 2005 it had begun to implement or monitor some 30 economic development projects linked to the Central BiH regional economic strategy and had facilitated almost US$2 million in business linkages and credit referrals.[9]

Economic Development and Reconciliation: Possible Correlations

The aim of many CHF International programs is to build constituencies and progressive leadership to enhance stability through positive change in fragile environments. Within these programs we develop strategies for sustainable reconciliation, conflict management and community mobilization by identifying and supporting individuals and groups with a stake in ongoing stability. Under the MEDI program, those stakeholders were business people, owners of farms or homes and members of government at the municipal level. Our goal was to provide a framework in which stakeholders could realize their interest in bringing about a policy and regulatory environment in which individual assets could thrive and common needs would be met.

The implementation of the MEDI program was a significant success. By 2005, we had substantially exceeded targets and our expectations. However, while it was clear that participants understood the benefits of maintaining peace and improving governance, given the brutal nature of the war and the bitter memories of those who had survived it, we remained uncertain about the possibility of sustained, meaningful cooperation. We were encouraged to find that the desire to improve the local potential for economic development was strong enough to motivate people to work together. Several factors underlie this desire, including tolerance and the will of the silent majority, the potency of economic factors in generating cooperation and

---

8 For further information on the Lider Microfinance Organisation, see: <http://www.lider.ba>.

9 The REZ Regional Development Agency is comprised of representatives of regional municipal and cantonal governments and business associations and is sanctioned by the OHR and EU as the designated RDA for Central BiH. For further information, see: <http://www.rez.ba>.

advocacy, the roles of local leadership and economic institutions and efforts made to avoid a 'Cyprus Effect'.

We witnessed a great degree of cooperation in the MEDI program in the formation of associations at the municipal level, regional networks and coalitions and in the processes of joint decision-making and collective action, including: advocacy, economic-planning and the development and implementation of projects ranging from road improvements to the establishment of industrial parks. Behind much of this cooperation was an understanding of tolerance that might be stated as: 'I'll tolerate our differences, but I'll never reconcile them. I might eventually put aside the sense of injustice I feel about the past, but I'll never forgive you.' Though this remains far from the acts of reconciliation to which we might aspire in the future, given the recent and violent nature of the war in BiH, a shift towards such tolerance is nonetheless remarkable. Despite the polarization fomented by nationalist and other political parties, it seems that the majority of citizens want to move forward and build a future for themselves and their children. People want the opportunity to work and to increase income, businesses want access to markets and the opportunity to improve profitability. The process of association and mobilization provided an opportunity to put aside differences in order to pursue needs.[10]

Once associations and partnerships with municipal governments had been developed, stakeholders identified their cantonal and entity governments as the focal point for their economic grievances. Municipal governments were frustrated by the expectations imposed on them regarding service delivery without allocation of necessary resources. Bureaucracy and corruption smothered the ability of business, farm and home owners to function and productively manage their assets. Economic reform proved to be a powerful, neutral force in the promotion of cooperation across ethnic divides. Once this mobilization began, the higher levels of government found it difficult to deny the voice or ignore the desires of the previously silent majority. This was especially the case with the REZ RDA, where representation of this voice was institutionalized within its governance structure. The advocacy process that mobilization set in train was certainly not without flaws, but a shift in municipal, cantonal and entity priorities from issues based on ethnicity to those based on economics had been triggered.

Of significance to these outcomes was the role played by local leadership. In all but one municipality, mayors, council members, business and community representatives set an example of tolerance and cooperation in accepting the challenge of economic reform. In setting aside their ethnic and religious affiliations they encouraged their communities to cooperate and demonstrated the value of tolerance in laying the foundations for the future. A great deal of courage was required by these leaders in refusing to engage in the politics of fear and hatred which allows

---

10   To formally ascertain why businesses and the owners of farms and homes joined the Business Associations and Community Development Corporations, we conducted an annual survey of participants for each of the years in which the program was implemented. In the first year, the majority of people joined in order to access micro-credit. In the second year, it was to advocate for economic reform. By the third year, the main reason for joining was to participate in improving the economic environment within their community.

previous adversaries to be blamed for current circumstances. Local leadership of this kind is invaluable: it cannot be replaced by the international community but should certainly be supported by it. One way that the international community has fulfilled this need in BiH has been by helping to establish or support apolitical economic institutions, such as the Central Bank, and the RDAs.[11] Economic institutions that act as 'honest brokers' can bridge the ethnic divide that is otherwise an obstruction to the processes requiring trust and cooperation. To increase financial transparency, the Central Bank established a credit registry in 2006 for all bank credit clients and the private LRC Credit Bureau compiles data on the credit-worthiness of persons and companies. The Central Bank and the LRC are examples of public and private institutions respectively that have fulfilled the role of 'honest brokers' and apolitical institutions that have alleviated the fear of sharing sensitive information across the ethnic divides.

At the end of the war, BiH was broken into entities and cantons, separated by the Inter-Entity Boundary line (IEBL), which was monitored by the Stabilisation Force (SFOR) led by NATO. However, unlike other divided lands, physical walls and border points were not constructed and the international community encouraged free movement throughout the country and a single economic space. Refugees and internally displaced persons (IDPs) were encouraged to return to their homes. The OHR introduced generic car license plates to replace those displaying the owner's municipality and in doing so encouraged many people to cross the IEBL without immediate fear of attack. Where opportunities arose, businesses began to operate across the IEBL, thus re-establishing markets or beginning new ones. Further, municipal governments have begun to work together on development issues and other matters of common concern.

This contrasts enormously with the ongoing situation in the island of Cyprus. Since 1974, Cyprus has been divided by a physical boundary known as the 'Green Line'. It straddles the country, separating the economically 'under-developed' Turkish Cypriot north and 'developed' Greek Cypriot south. In 2004, the United Nations' 'Annan Plan for Cyprus', generated a great sense of optimism that the island would finally be reconciled.[12] The plan proposed the creation of the 'United Cyprus Republic', a loose confederation of the two component states joined together by a minimal federal government. A referendum on the plan was to be held prior to Cyprus being granted membership of the EU, with the expectation that if the majority voted for unification, the island would enter the EU as a unified state. If the majority voted against it, the Greek Cypriot south would gain membership alone. The common fear in the weeks preceding the referendum among those supporting unification was that Turkish Cypriots would be against it. It therefore came as a

---

11   During the election year of 2006 politicians from the RS resisted the cross IEBL activities of the five RDAs within BiH. Threats of obstruction were made, including cutting RS Entity budget allocations to RS Municipal governments that cooperated and engaged with these RDAs. For further information on the RDA network, see: <http://www.eured-sme-bih. org/eng/red_process/red_network.html>.

12   For further information on the 'Annan Plan for Cyprus', see: <http://www.hri.org/ docs/annan/>.

surprise when the Turkish Cypriot population overwhelmingly voted for unification and the Greek Cypriot population overwhelmingly voted against it.

In retrospect, the basic foundations for the unification of Cyprus can be found to have been lacking: the process of generating tolerance across the physical and national divide had not begun. In a show of goodwill the Green Line was opened by the Turkish Cypriot State in April 2004. This gave Greek Cypriots their first opportunity in 30 years to visit the homes that had been theirs before the war. Although peace has been maintained in Cyprus, the complete separation of the island's ethnically divided people has prevented the emergence of tolerance and the implementation of the kinds of confidence building measures taken in BiH that both promote tolerance, and are promoted by it.

My experience with the MEDI program in BiH has led me to believe that economic and business development activities can encourage tolerance, mutual confidence and cooperation across entrenched ethnic divides. These activities provide an incentive to act on a deeply held desire for stability in post-conflict communities. Although tolerance does not guarantee reconciliation it represents a significant foundation from which the process can take root over the long-term. Perhaps this process will follow the precedent of the European Union, which was originally founded as The European Coal and Steel Community (ECSC) in 1951 by Germany, France, Italy, Belgium, Netherlands and Luxembourg. Established to encourage economic development, the ECSC also initiated a peace-building project that created an environment of tolerance and cooperation between previously warring nations that has been sustained to this day.

References

CHF International (2004), *Stable Society Study: Effects on Conflict Dynamics and Peace-Building* (Maryland: CHF International).

CHF International Bosnia and Herzegovina <http://www.chfbh.ba>.

CHF International Website <http://www.chfinternational.org>.

District of Brcko <http://www.brcko.org>.

Divjak, B. (2006), 'Case Study: Bosnia and Herzegovina', *Local Business, Local Peace: the Peace-Building Potential of the Domestic Private Sector* (London: International Alert).

European Union Special Representative (EUSR) <http://www.ohr.int>.

EURED II Project <http://www.eured-sme-bih.org>.

Government of Republika Srpska <http://www.vladars.net>.

Government of the Federation of Bosnia and Herzegovina <http://www.fbihvlada. gov.ba>.

Lider Micro-finance Organisation <http://www.lider.ba>

Office of the High Representative (OHR) in Bosnia and Herzegovina and European Organization for Security and Co-operation in Europe (OSCE) Mission to Bosnia and Herzegovina <http://www.oscebih.org/oscebih_eng.asp>.

Research and Documentation Center Sarajevo <http://www.idc.org.ba/aboutus>.

REZ Regional Development Agency <http://www.rez.ba>.

United Nations Development Program (UNDP) in Bosnia and Herzegovina <http://www.undp.ba>.

United Nations Website for the Secretary General's Comprehensive Peace Plan for Cyprus: The 'Annan Plan' <http://www.hri.org/docs/annan>.

World Bank (1997), *Bosnia and Herzegovina: From Recovery to Sustainable Growth*, (Washington DC: World Bank).

World Bank Group Bosnia and Herzegovina <www.worldbank.org/ba>.

Chapter 13

Between Denial and Reconciliation: Lessons from South Africa to Israel and Palestine

Daphna Golan-Agnon

Might it not make sense for a group of respected historians and intellectuals, composed equally of Palestinians and Israelis, to hold a series of meetings to try to agree a modicum of truth about this conflict, to see whether the known sources can guide the two sides to agree on a body of facts – who took what from whom, who did what to whom, and so on – which in turn might reveal a way out of the present impasse? It is too early, perhaps, for a Truth and Reconciliation Commission, but something like a Historical Truth and Political Justice Committee would be appropriate (Said, 1991).

In 2003, I attended the Global Reconciliation Network conference, 'Thinking Through a Collapsing World', in London. I went there to ask for help and advice. I was scared every morning when I sent my children to school and when I went to work. tried to guess which route would be the safest – should I drive through areas that had seen repeated suicide attacks or detour around them? Five years have passed since then and I am still scared. I am scared because both Palestinians and Israelis have elected governments that do not recognize the other side's rights, hopes and dreams. I am scared by the experience of yet another war, the Second Lebanon War, and by the destruction, fear and hate that permeates the region.

It gave me hope to meet people at that conference who came from countries that had gone through reconciliation processes. Charles Villa-Vicencio, the former National Research Director of South Africa's Truth and Reconciliation Commission (TRC), spoke about the similarity between personal and political reconciliation. He explained that in South Africa this process had just begun, for immense and growing economic gaps were yet to be resolved. Nevertheless, the resolution of material problems would be achieved through the search for reconciliation. The process does not begin with forgiveness, he said, but rather it gives the two communities a time and a place for anger and grieving, for expressing pain and healing of wounds. Villa-Vicencio related that a Sudanese elder had told him: 'Reconciliation is when you are ready to sit down with your enemy under the same tree.' I thought of the countless olive trees that Israel has uprooted in the occupied territories. With our own hands, we have cut down that potential meeting place, along with the hope it might have represented. In its place, we increasingly erect walls and build roads on confiscated Palestinian lands, where Palestinians are not allowed to go.

In this essay I ask what Israeli peace activists can learn from the South African process of truth and reconciliation.

Comparing the Israeli–Palestinian Conflict with Apartheid

The Injustice of Legal Discrimination

For most Israelis, the comparison of Israel with the apartheid regime is unacceptable. It angers and threatens Israelis in general, and liberal Israelis in particular, because it challenges the basic belief that the Israeli–Palestinian conflict was imposed upon Israel, and is unlike any other conflict in the world.[1]

Indeed, there are many differences between the two, the major one being that in South Africa a small minority controlled the nation's resources and power and denied the majority its rights. In Israel-Palestine, the number of Jews and Arabs is similar. Israelis stress this difference because as long as there is a Jewish majority within the non-existing 1967 borders, they can continue to claim that Israel itself is democratic.

Another difference is religion. Israel is situated at the heart of numerous sacred places for Christianity, Islam and Judaism. The struggle for control of these holy sites is a focal point of the struggle over land and resources. Furthermore, the importance of religion and the religious struggle in the Israeli–Palestinian conflict is related to another difference: the degree of international involvement and commitment on the part of other countries. The international community imposed sanctions on the South African regime to end apartheid, while Israel gets billions of dollars every year from the United States, and economic privileges from the European Union. In part, international support for Israel stems from a Western sense of guilt and responsibility for the persecution of Jews in the Second World War and the history of anti-Semitism that preceded it.

These differences recognized; there is a significant similarity in the use of the legal system to normalize a state of discrimination. During apartheid, not only did millions of people live without minimal rights and in ongoing poverty but the discrimination that gave rise to these conditions was anchored in a complex system of laws. The Occupied Territories are also governed by a complex system of laws, hundreds of them. Some are left over from the British others are the legacy of Turkish, Jordanian and Egyptian legislation. There are Israeli and international human rights laws, as well as military edicts, *shariah* law and the legislation enacted by the Palestinian Authority. As in South Africa, Israel employs many lawyers and

---

1   After many years reporting from Jerusalem and Johannesburg, the award winning Middle East Correspondent for *The Guardian*, Chris McGreal, published an assessment of the comparison between Israel and South Africa. McGreal's articles were not published in Israeli newspapers but *Haaretz*, the liberal Israeli paper, did publish a scathing response by Benjamin Pogrund, claiming the comparison was unjustified (see McGreal 2006; McGreal 2006a; Pogrund 2006).

consultants to explain how, in this convoluted system, things may be unjust but are nevertheless legal. Hundreds of laws do not make discrimination just. It does not matter how we explain it. There are two groups of people living on a small piece of land: one enjoys rights and liberties and the other does not.

Further, anyone who has visited both apartheid South Africa and Israel cannot help but perceive the shared use of imaginary and real borders alongside physical evidence of separatist laws. In the mid-1980s when I travelled in South Africa, the roads connecting parts of Kwazulu to white South Africa were unmarked. All the water sources, the factories, the paved roads were in white South Africa. The poverty, hunger and anger were in Kwazulu, a state composed of 49 units and dozens of disconnected pieces of land. Travelling through the West Bank, when it was still possible, was very similar. Areas A, B and C have been defined by the Oslo Accords so as to grant incremental autonomy to the Palestinians. Area A is completely controlled by the Palestinian Authority, while Palestinians ostensibly administer Area B, though Israelis control it militarily. Area C is controlled by Israel alone. Area C, which comprises more than 60 percent of the West Bank, is home to the Jewish settlers, some 250,000 of whom live scattered among more than two million Palestinians. Some other 250,000 Jews live in confiscated Palestinian land in East Jerusalem. This draft map, agreed upon in the Oslo negotiations, is very much like the map of the South African Bantustans. The Palestinians call it the Swiss cheese map: 'We got the holes', they say.

Just as the opponents of apartheid did not recognize the borders imposed by the government of South Africa, Palestinian and Israeli peace activists do not accept the small, divided cantons that have been allocated to the Palestinians. However, while the international community in its entirety was opposed to segregation and oppression in South Africa, opposition to the oppressive regime in Israel has not brought the Israeli occupation to an end. On the contrary, over the years Israel has been building a giant wall around the Palestinian areas and establishing checkpoints that divide the West Bank into cantons, or perhaps large prisons, which Palestinians are not permitted to leave.

These new walls are part of a larger Israeli government program. They say the 590 kilometre system of cement walls, electric and barbed wire fences, trenches, patrol roads, trace paths, guard towers, lookouts and cameras are built to secure Israel. This security fence, also called the 'apartheid wall', separates Palestinian families, bars farmers from picking their olives and obstructs the way to work, to school, to hospitals. These walls, built on Palestinian lands, are the manifestation of the Israeli policy of segregation, which is supposed to afford Israelis security. If there is a lesson we might learn from the South African example, it is that forcibly imposed segregation does not bring security.

In the summer of 2005, Israel withdrew from the Gaza Strip, and evacuated some 8,000 Jewish settlers who had held approximately 22 percent of the land in what is one of the most populated areas in the world – home to some 1.5 million Palestinians. But the withdrawal from the Gaza did not end Israeli control over the area. Gaza is like a prison and Israel controls all the entrances. Thousands of people wait months for permission to enter Egypt and ailing and wounded people on the other side of the border with Egypt wait to return to their homes. Gaza is poorer and hungrier than ever before. If the unilateral withdrawal from Gaza was seen as a move towards peace, it turned out to be a tragic example of how peace cannot be achieved without negotiations.

One Step Forward, Two Steps Back

In the last 20 years there has been a growing peace and human rights movement in Israel – Women in Black, *Gush Shalom* and Peace Now; human rights organizations such as *B'Tselem*; *HaMoked* (The Center for the Defence of the Individual); The Association of Civil Rights; Physicians for Human Rights – all are working, along with others, to end the violation of Palestinian human rights. There are also an increasing number of reserve soldiers who refuse to go on duty in the Occupied Territory.

Today most Israelis understand that we need to share one piece of land between two groups of people. But how do we translate this understanding into actions that might lead to a just and lasting peace? And how do we negotiate peace when the last negotiations brought so much disappointment and violence?

In the 1990s the new South Africa was formed. These were also the years of hope in Israel-Palestine. In September 1993 the signing of the Oslo Accords marked a breakthrough in the Israeli–Palestinian conflict. For the first time, the Israeli Prime Minister Yitzhak Rabin and the Palestinian leader Yasser Arafat recognized that there are two nations claiming possession of the same land, that compromise was necessary. In spite of objections from the Israeli right and the radical left, the Oslo Accords constituted an important recognition by the Israeli leadership: that the oppression of Palestinians could not continue indefinitely.

While the accords were not as meaningful as the first free elections in South Africa, held at the same time, they did bear a certain similarity to an earlier attempt made in 1984 by the South African apartheid government to reform parliament and allow some 'non-whites' to vote. In both places, there was an attempt to reduce the pressure, to adapt a little without changing the power relations between those with rights and those without. In both cases, despite the inadequacy of the offers made, the psychological impact was significant. For years, whites in South Africa believed they had special privileges by virtue of their race. Suddenly, the people they had taught their children to regard as sub-human were given the right to vote. The destruction of the lie had been initiated, and it paved the way to a larger transformation. The Oslo Accords had a similar effect on Israelis, yet they did not pave the way to peace.

When I was growing up there were no Palestinians in Israel. Prime Minister Golda Meir said so, our teachers and parents told us so and we all believed it. We were told that Palestinians had no special connection to this place, and that they had the option of going to live in one of the nearby Arab countries. Years later, when I joined a minority of Israeli peace activists and called for talks with the Palestinians, I was labelled a traitor and prohibited by law from speaking with most Palestinians on the grounds that they identified with the Palestinian Liberation Organization (PLO). The only legal way to talk with Palestinians who lived ten minutes away was to travel to conferences in Europe or the United States. Then, all of a sudden, Yitzhak Rabin was talking with Yasser Arafat and with these same Palestinians. Despite their patronizing tone, the Oslo Accords were a breakthrough in Israeli consciousness. They allowed Israelis to see how peace might feel. The country experienced economic prosperity. Millions of tourists came to Israel. Investments flourished. For the first time in my life I was able to travel to Arab countries. But while we were celebrating, the Palestinians were still living under occupation and their situation was only getting worse. Israel continued to build settlements (doubling the number of settlers during the period of the peace talks) and added more checkpoints, which prevented Palestinians from travelling in their own territory.

There are different interpretations of why the negotiations that followed failed (Hammami and Tamari 2000). Hussein Agha and Robert Malley, President Clinton's Special Assistant for Arab-Israeli Affairs between 1998 and 2001, wonder if there was ever a generous Israeli offer made at Camp David (Agha and Malley 2001). Even former Israeli Prime Minister Ehud Barak, one of the chief negotiators in the late 1990s, acknowledges that he did not offer the Palestinians anything real (Barak 2003, 84–7). Despite the different readings of why the negotiations failed, reconciliation was never on the table.

Lessons from South Africa

In May 2003 a Palestinian friend, Dr. Rema Hammami, and I, invited twenty Israelis and Palestinians to a conference in Cape Town.[2] We met with past and present South African leaders and they gave us a lesson in the restoration of hope. I returned to Israel with three questions, whose pursuit may help us to understand some of the obstacles to reconciliation in the Middle East.

Finding a Shared Vision of the Future

The first question is one that I was asked time and again in South Africa: Why is there no Israeli–Palestinian peace movement? While we have asked this of ourselves and considered various answers, in post-apartheid South Africa, after hundreds of organizations and movements – women, youth, church groups and professional unions – had joined forces in the struggle against apartheid, the question took on a new significance. Why do social activists and peace movements across and within Israel and Palestine not work together? I can only conjecture that the answer lies somewhere in the fundamental difference between the vision that most anti-apartheid activists had – that of a united democratic South Africa – compared to the vision most Israeli and Palestinian peace activists share – that of two separate sovereign states. The dream of one state unified South Africans, enabling the various anti-apartheid factions to overcome differences and work together. In Israel-Palestine, like in every divorce negotiation, we are still quibbling over details, over the division of assets. Optimism, generosity and love are elements of marriage but not of divorce. What is our common dream? A wall? What is our common vision? We have none.

---

2 'Restoring Hope: Building Peace in Divided Societies', organized by the Human Sciences Research Council (Western Cape, May 4–6 2003).

The more we repeat the need for a democratic Jewish state alongside a Palestinian state, the more like a nightmare it sounds. The issues over which we are divided arise immediately. Where exactly will the fence between these two states be situated and what will be done about the Israeli settlers and the right of return of Palestinian refugees? If we had a clearly defined and shared vision with which to identify our common future we could begin to negotiate the details. For now, the details are all we have.

Many of the South Africans we met in Cape Town did not understand why we want two states and not one bi-national state. George Merring, the last Chief of Staff of the South African military under apartheid and the first during the transition period – a man who can by no means be considered a 'radical left winger' – asked why we don't consider the option of a single state. For him, and many South Africans, the map of the future of Palestine is too reminiscent of the Bantustans, and if that did not work for them, why would it work for us?

I am not sure that a two-state solution is still viable and I do not think we should aspire to this model. The concept of transitional justice and reconciliation might help us progress in thinking creatively about different solutions. When they began the process of change in South Africa, there were many differences of opinion: How to create economic equality after years of discrimination? Was nationalization the answer? Did redistribution of land mean all the land that had been expropriated? These and other questions were not resolved to the satisfaction of all concerned and differences of opinion remain to this day. Nevertheless, since the Freedom Charter, the vision of a South Africa that belongs to all who live in it has made it easier to present a united front. It is a simple, clear, single vision that we in Israel and Palestine lack.

Continued Negotiations, No Matter What

The second question that I returned with was what we can learn from the South African insistence on maintaining negotiations despite attacks, assassinations and killings. How and why did they manage to keep negotiations going regardless of everything that could have obstructed or concluded them? F.W. de Klerk, the former President of South Africa, claimed that it became clear there was no other way. South African students were not being accepted for tertiary education abroad and many young white people were leaving the country, the Olympic Games and other sports tournaments were closed to them and the economic situation had deteriorated. The government was brought to a point where it could not deny that perpetuating the apartheid regime would destroy South Africa financially and that white hegemony was destined to end. What Mr. de Klerk did not say, but his former opponents did, was that when he began the process of negotiation, he thought that he could change the white regime without bringing it down altogether. However, once the process of democratization had begun, there was no stopping it.

Why have talks on peace between Israel and Palestine been failing for years? We could learn something from the way the negotiation process in South Africa was managed and from the role of the international community in making certain it took place. How can we translate the insight of most Israelis and Palestinians

– that we have to reach a compromise – into negotiations involving genuine dialogue between the two sides? How can we make sure these negotiations involve broad public representation from both societies and not just military officials? How do we persuade Israelis and Palestinians that negotiations must continue no matter what happens? These questions became more pressing in 2006 when both peoples elected governments who refuse to recognize each other. It became evident during the Second Lebanon War that the whole region is unstable as long as there is no peace between Israel and Palestine.

Peace negotiations need the regional support of Arab leaders in order to be successful. However, when the United States has declared a 'Civilization War' against Islam, and Israel is playing a role, regional reconciliation seems less attainable than ever.

Planning for Change

My third question is how we begin to prepare for what happens after the talks, after the compromise, after the struggle. It seems change is not possible unless preparation occurs well in advance. The TRC was established on the understanding that there would eventually be a public process of reconciliation. It was made possible with the knowledge that the signing of the agreement was not the end of the conflict, rather the beginning (TRC 1998, 1999; Krog 1998; Tutu 1999). In the Middle East, we need to begin thinking about how we can formulate our future.

These three questions draw together the main obstacles before us: we have no shared vision of the future, most of us do not believe a shared future is possible and the world colludes with our failure to persevere in the search for justice and reconciliation.

The road to reconciliation runs through memory, recognition and pain. I hope that we will eventually take it. For Israeli Jews, it requires that we ask ourselves how we see our future in the midst of an Arab world. How we find a way to apologize to Palestinians for taking their land in 1948, deporting them and from 1967, not allowing them the freedoms that we want for ourselves. The failure of the Oslo Accords and all the agreements that have almost been signed since, lies in the failure to talk about the past and about the hopes and dreams of those who lost their past in the Palestinian villages upon which we built our state. It is a major discussion – one that Israelis and Palestinians, Jews and Arabs, the Germans who brought the Holocaust on the Jews and the millions of people who incite and supply arms to the conflict here – are yet to begin.

Unlike in South Africa, a country that was banned from international sports, Israeli teams play in European leagues. Unlike the cultural boycott of South Africa by artists, thousands are eager to perform in Israel. Israel competes in the Eurovision song contest each year as if it were part of Europe.

Israelis do not search for the road to reconciliation because they do not want to be a part of the Arab world in which they live and the United States and Europe support them as 'the only democracy in the Middle East'.

Israelis live in fear and they cannot find the way to reconciliation because legal language dominates the public discourse. Are the territories occupied or 'held'?

Do human rights conventions or humanitarian laws apply in the territories or, for various complicated legal reasons, do they not? This language facilitates the cloaking of terrible deeds according to an ostensible justice. Israeli Jews do not look for reconciliation because they say they 'do not believe there is a solution to this conflict'. This possibly means that they do not believe there is a solution that will preserve their privileges as Jews.

South Africa's experience teaches us that in order to move towards a better future we have to return to old wounds. Israeli Jews do not want to look at the past and acknowledge the wrongs they have and continue to perpetrate against the Palestinians. They feel that these Palestinians, were they to return, would threaten the Jewish majority and thus also the democratic self-perception of Israel. They do not do more because most Palestinians, as well as many Arabs, do not acknowledge the historical connection of Jews to the piece of land on which Israel has been built and see them only as foreign conquerors.

I am not sure how Israeli's Jews and Arabs will manage to consolidate a shared vision of how we see ourselves in the future, how Jews and Arabs will live together, enjoying justice and reconciliation on the same piece of land, nor how we will atone for the pain of the past, how we will ask for forgiveness. How will we as Jews live in the midst of an Arab region that has never accepted us, a region which we have done very little to be accepted by? I do not know when we will begin to talk about these issues. But I am sure that we need the help of the international community to find the way. The struggle for justice in Israel and Palestine is not only ours to solve. We need help, and time is running out.

References

Abel, R. (1995), *Politics by Other Means: Law In The Struggle Against Apartheid, 1980–1994* (New York: Routledge).

Adam, H. and Moodly, K. (2005), *Seeking Mandela: Peacemaking between Israelis and Palestinians* (Philadelphia: Temple University Press).

Agha, H. and Malley, R. (2001), 'Camp David: The Tragedy of Errors', *The New York Review of Books*, 48:13, August 9.

Barak, E. (2003), 'I Did Not Give Away a Thing', *Journal of Palestine Studies*, 33:1.

Baskin, G. (December 21, 2002), 'Why Oslo Failed', <http://www.mideastweb.org/log/archives/00000017.htm>.

Benn, A. (2001), 'PA Economy to Top Powell's Agenda Here', *Ha'aretz*, February 22.

Bloomfield, D. et al. (eds) (2003), *Reconciliation after Violent Conflict: A Handbook* (Stockholm: IDEA).

Boraine, A. (2000), *A Country Unmasked: Inside South Africa's Truth and Reconciliation Commission* (Cape Town: Oxford University Press).

Boraine, A. et al. (eds) (1994), *Dealing with the Past: Truth and Reconciliation in South Africa* (Cape Town: IDASA).

Coetzee, J.M. (1999), *Disgrace* (London: Secker and Warburg).

Cohen, S. (1991), 'The Human Rights Movement in Israel and South Africa: Some Paradoxical Comparisons', *The Harry S. Truman Institute, Occasional Papers*, 1 (Jerusalem: Hebrew University).

Cohen, S. (2001), *States of Denial: Knowing About Atrocities and Suffering* (London: Polity).

de Klerk, F.W. (1998), *Last Trek – A New Beginning: The Autobiography* (London: Macmillan).

Edelstein, J. (2002), *Truth and Lies: Stories from the Truth and Reconciliation Commission in South Africa* (New York: The New Press).

Eldar, A. (2000), 'So Close to Total War, So Close to a Peace Agreement', *Ha'aretz*, November 28.

Elon, A. (2001), 'The Deadlocked City', *New York Review of Books*, 48:16, 6–12.

Golan-Agnon, D. (2005), *Next Year in Jerusalem: Everyday Life in a Divided Land.* (New York: The New Press).

Golan-Agnon, D. (2006), 'Separate but not Equal: Discrimination against Palestinian Arab Students in Israel', *American Behavioural Scientist*, 49:8, 1075–84.

Gross, A.M. (2004), 'The Constitution, Reconciliation, and Transitional Justice: Lessons from South Africa and Israel', *Stanford Journal of International Law*, 47.

Hadland, A. and Jovial, R. (1999), *The Life and Times of Thabo Mbeki* (Rivonia: Zebra Press).

Hammami, R. and Tamari, S. (2000), 'Anatomy of Another Rebellion', *Middle East Report*, 217, Winter.

Hass, A. (2001), 'Palestinians Condition Talks on Halting Settlement Growth', *Ha'aretz*, April 3.

Hayner, P.B. (2001), *Unspeakable Truths: Confronting State Terror and Atrocity* (New York: Routledge).

Henkin, A.H. (ed.) (2002), *The Legacy of Abuse: Confronting the Past, Facing the Future* (New York: Aspen Institute, NYU School of Law).

Kritz, N. (ed.) (1995), *Transitional Justice: How Emerging Democracies Reckon With Former Regimes*, 1:Iii (Washington DC: United States Institute for Peace Press).

Johnson, S. (1994), *Strange Days Indeed: South Africa from Insurrection to Post-Election* (London: Bantam Books).

Kimmerling, B. (2003), *Politicide: Ariel Sharon's War against the Palestinians* (New York: VERSO).

Krog, A. (1998), *Country of My Skull* (Johannesburg: Random House).

Mamdani, M. (1997), 'Reconciliation without Justice', *South African Review of Books*, 46 (November/December).

McGreal, C. (2006), 'Worlds Apart', *The Guardian*, 6 February.

McGreal, C. (2006a), 'Brothers in Arms: Israel's Secret Pact with Pretoria', *The Guardian*, 7 February.

Morris, B. (2002), 'Camp David and After: An Exchange (An Interview with Ehud Barak)', *The New York Review of Books*, June 13, <http://www.nybooks.com/articles/15501>.

Morris, B. (2000), *Righteous Victims: A History of the Zionist-Arab Conflict, 1881–1999* (New York: Knopf).

Pogrund, B. (2006), 'Why Depict Israel as a Chamber of Horrors like No Other in the World?', *The Guardian*, 8 February (also published in *Ha'aretz*).

Rouhana, N.R. (2001), 'Reconciliation in Protracted National Conflict: Identity and Power in the Israeli–Palestinian Case', in Eagly, A.H. et al. (eds), *The Social Psychology of Group Identity and Social Conflict: Theory and Practice* (Washington D.C: APA Publications).

Ross, M.H. (2004), 'Ritual and the Politics of Reconciliation', in Bar-Siman-Tov, Y. (ed.), *From Conflict Resolution to Reconciliation* (Cape Town: Oxford University Press).

Roy, S. (2002), 'Why Peace Failed: An Oslo Autopsy', *Current History*, 101:651, January.

Rubinstein, D. (2001), 'Adding New Weight to an Old Demand', *Ha'aretz*, April 5.

Rubinstein, D. (2001), 'The Palestinians See an Israel Not Ready for Peace', *Ha'aretz*, December 20.

Said, E. (2004), *From Oslo to Iraq* (New York: Pantheon).

Shavit, A. (2003), 'Reality Bites', *Ha'aretz*, January 10.

Truth and Reconciliation Commission (TRC) of South Africa, *Report*, 1998–1999, 5 Volumes (London: Macmillan).

Tutu, D. (1999), *No Future Without Forgiveness* (London: Rider).

Villa-Vicencio, C. and Verwoerd, W. (eds) (2000), *Looking Back Reaching Forward: Reflections on the Truth and Reconciliation Commission of South Africa* (London: Zed Books).

Waldmeir, P. (1998), *Anatomy of a Miracle: The End of Apartheid and the Birth of a New South Africa* (New Brunswick, NJ: Rutgers University Press).

Chapter 14

The Australian Reconciliation Process: An Analysis

Andrew Gunstone

In 1991 the Australian Commonwealth Parliament unanimously passed the *Council for Aboriginal Reconciliation Act 1991* (CAR Act), instituting a ten-year process of reconciliation between Indigenous and non-Indigenous people. The process, which was to be achieved in time for the centenary of Australian federation in 2001, had three broad goals: to educate the wider Australian community about reconciliation and Indigenous issues; to foster an ongoing national commitment to address Indigenous socioeconomic disadvantage; and to investigate the desirability of developing a document of reconciliation and, if favoured, provide advice concerning its content. These goals were to be promoted and advanced by the Council for Aboriginal Reconciliation (CAR) (Tickner 1991, 2–3; CAR Act 1991, 3–4; CAR 1994, 182–4).

Despite some positive outcomes, I argue that none of these goals were achieved and explain how several interrelated factors obstructed the reconciliation process. I maintain that these factors need to be addressed for substantive reconciliation to be achieved in Australia.

The Goals of the Reconciliation Process

Education

CAR did achieve several successful outcomes related to the goal of education, including the production of a range of accessible resources to educate the wider Australian community about reconciliation and Indigenous issues. One of the major resources was the 'Study Circles' project, which distributed over two thousand kits throughout Australia to church groups, trade unions, community-based organizations and groups of interested people, enabling participants to undertake a self-managed course that discussed Indigenous cultures, histories, contemporary issues and reconciliation (AAACE 1993, 4–9). Another major resource was CAR's quarterly publication *Walking Together*. With a circulation of 75,000, it was published throughout the reconciliation process and was the main means of communicating with interested parties (CAR 2000a, 23). Other CAR resources included brochures, leaflets, reports, videos, television and radio promotions and information supplements for magazines and newspapers.

CAR also developed the 'Australians for Reconciliation' program to consult with the Australian community and encourage involvement in reconciliation (CAR 1995, 2). The involvement of communities is imperative in national reconciliation movements (Gastrow 1999, 108–9; Phillips 2001, 171). By the conclusion of the process, hundreds of small reconciliation groups were operating throughout Australia (Nettheim 2000, 63). The signing of 'Sorry Books', displays of the 'Sea of Hands' and the 250,000 people who marched for reconciliation across Sydney Harbour Bridge during 'Corroboree 2000' are prominent examples of this broad community involvement.

Despite these positive outcomes, a number of factors restricted the overall success of the education goal. One factor was the significant confusion over the meaning of 'reconciliation' within the wider Australian community (Saulwick and Muller 2000, 5–6). One reason for this was that the reconciliation process did not articulate a clear concept of reconciliation beyond broad, non-specific definitions, such as 'building bridges', 'developing partnerships' and 'working together' (Tatz 1998, 1–2). There were also a multitude of differing definitions advocated by individuals and organizations that emphasized issues as diverse as Indigenous rights, religion, assimilation, acknowledging history and the need for Australians as a whole to accept the current political situation (Dodson 2000a, 269; Johns and Brunton 1999, 4). Moreover, an acrimonious debate over the comparative importance of practical and symbolic reconciliation occurred following the election of the Howard Liberal/National Government in 1996 (Howard 2000, 88–90; Pearson 2000, 166). In addition to exacerbating the confusion, this debate also assisted in obscuring or ignoring any discussion on substantive reconciliation.

The influence of nationalism also impacted upon the education goal. Significantly, the aim of the process was to achieve reconciliation by the centenary of Australia's federation in 2001 (Tickner 1990, 6). The reconciliation process was framed in terms of Indigenous and non-Indigenous people 'sharing' a single national identity, culture and history (Moran 1998, 108–9). Other issues, such as sovereignty, land rights, power relationships and a treaty, that are not easily accommodated within a nationalist framework were marginalized, thereby narrowing the scope of the education campaign (Pratt et al. 2001, 146).

The reconciliation process also focussed on changing attitudes towards Indigenous issues and reconciliation rather than increasing knowledge (Mansell 1992, 20). Slogans exhorting Australians to 'walk together' and be 'united', as well as images of holding hands, took precedence over information about the historical, political and moral consequences of the invasion and subsequent policies of massacre and genocide. This enabled non-Indigenous people to support reconciliation without 'serious self-examination' (Foley 2000, 26). Further, even the efforts made to change attitudes were largely unsuccessful. Several opinion polls on Indigenous issues conducted throughout the reconciliation decade showed no 'marked change' in attitudes toward Indigenous people (Markus 2001, 208–14).

Finally, the Commonwealth Government had a significant influence over the reconciliation process, including selecting CAR members, approving CAR Strategic Plans and situating CAR's Secretariat in the Department of the Prime Minister and Cabinet (CAR Act 1991, 5–7; Gunstone 2007, 50–51). This influence restricted the breadth of the education campaign. Publications, such as *Walking Together*, were predominantly written by non-Indigenous people who adhered to a nationalist discourse that did not mention issues, such as sovereignty or a treaty, that might offend or criticize the government (CAR 1997, 6–9). Further, toward the end of the process, the Labor Opposition accused the Howard Government of influencing opinion polls that had been commissioned by CAR (Taylor 2000, 2).

Socioeconomics

CAR also failed to achieve its socioeconomic goal. The founding documents of the reconciliation process and CAR both identified health, deaths and overrepresentation in custody, education, housing and employment as relevant to this goal (Tickner 1991, 6; CAR 1993, 8–10). Overall there was no significant positive change in these indicators throughout the reconciliation process.

In relation to health, life expectancy for Indigenous people did not improve during the 1990s, remaining at 56 years for men and 63 years for women in 2001, compared to 77 years for non-Indigenous men and 82.4 years for non-Indigenous women in 2001 (AMA 2002, 2; Taylor 2000, 4; ABS 2001c). Further, the Indigenous infant mortality rate has remained about two and a half times that of the total Australian population's rate since the early 1980s (AMA 2002, 2).

As for deaths in custody, from 1990 to 2000, approximately 18 percent of all deaths in custody were of Indigenous people, a 50 percent increase from the 12.1 percent of the previous decade (Collins and Mouzos 2001, 2; Neill 2002, 212). Further, the overrepresentation of Indigenous prisoners increased between 1991 and 2001 from 14 percent to 20 percent of the total prison population (ABS 2001b, 9).

In relation to education, the number of Indigenous people aged 15 years and over who did not have post-secondary qualifications dropped from 90.7 percent in 1991 to 85.2 percent in 2001, compared to a greater improvement for the wider community from 73.6 percent in 1991 to 65.3 percent in 2001 (Gray and Auld 2000, vi, 26; ABS 2001a, 4; ABS 2002b, Tables I01, I14). Further, Indigenous retention rates improved from 25 percent in 1993 to 34 percent in 1999 compared to a greater improvement for non-Indigenous students from 50 percent in 1997 to 73 percent in 1998 (AMA 2002, 6; Ring and Brown 2002, 629).

In relation to housing, the rate of Indigenous home ownership only increased from 31 percent in 1996 to 32 percent in 2001, compared to 71 percent for non-Indigenous people in 1996 and 2001 (ABS 2002a, 233; ABS 2003, 249). Further, a 2001 survey revealed that 33 percent of Indigenous communities failed water quality tests; 7 percent had no electricity supply; 91 percent, with populations under 50, had no sewerage system; and 48 percent, with 50 or more people, reported sewerage overflows (ABS 2002c, 16–22, 59).

As for employment, the proportion of working age Indigenous people neither employed nor on employment creation programs declined from 71.4 percent in 1991 to 66.8 percent in 2001 (Gray and Auld 2000, 6, 24; ABS 2002b, Table I16). Further, in 1991, the Indigenous adult median weekly income level was only 70 percent of the non-Indigenous income level; in 1996 this figure had fallen to 65 percent and in 2001 it had fallen further to 59 percent (Altman and Hunter 2003, 6, 8).

The reaction from both government and the wider community to these appalling statistics illustrates the failure to achieve a national commitment to address Indigenous disadvantage. Neither the Keating Government (1991–1996) nor the Howard Government (1996–2000) adequately addressed Indigenous socioeconomic disadvantage during the reconciliation decade (Pearson 2002a, 11). Further, neither government recognized that self-determination remains a vital component of improving Indigenous socioeconomic conditions (Clark 2001, 12).

The attitudes of many non-Indigenous people towards this issue also hindered the attainment of the goal. Many refused to recognize the connection between history and current socioeconomic conditions and showed a general apathy toward Indigenous disadvantage (Manne 2001, 104; Cowlishaw 2000, 21–22). A 2000 *Newspoll* survey on non-Indigenous attitudes to Indigenous issues found that only 41 percent of respondents thought Indigenous people were a disadvantaged group and that 60 percent felt Indigenous people received too much government assistance (Newspoll 2000, 34). Some within the media demonstrated similar views by reinforcing negative stereotypes, reporting in a sensationalist way and showing a lack of concern for reporting on Indigenous social issues (Neill 2002, 87–8; Gordon 2001, 19–21).

A Document of Reconciliation

From 1991 to 1997, CAR consulted widely in investigating the desirability of a document of reconciliation and discerned a favourable response (CAR 2000a, 72). CAR also commissioned research involving non-Indigenous people that found almost 75 percent of respondents supported a formal agreement, although one that created unity and did not contain separatist language was emphasized (Johnson 1996, 2–7).

On 3 June 1999, CAR released its *Draft Document for Reconciliation* and spent the following months seeking feedback from within the Australian community (CAR 1999, 1).

Following the release of the Draft Document, several Indigenous leaders, including Geoff Clark and Patrick Dodson, argued that any document of reconciliation should be a formal agreement between Indigenous people and governments that specifically discussed issues such as rights, a treaty, self-determination, customary law, land, power relationships, sovereignty and constitutional recognition (Clark 2000, 233; Dodson 2000a, 269–73). Also, several Indigenous leaders, including Parry Agius, Mick Dodson, Olga Havnen and Lowitja O'Donoghue, criticized the proposed Preamble at the 1999 Constitutional Referendum for similarly failing to acknowledge any specific Indigenous rights (Agius et al. 1999, 15).

Further, Patrick Dodson argued further, that CAR should recommend to the government that a treaty be developed and that it should be based on certain core principles, including: 'political representation, reparations and compensation, regional agreements, Indigenous regional self-government, cultural and intellectual property rights, recognition of customary law and an economic base' (Dodson 2000b, 19–21). On 25 May 2000, Geoff Clark, Aden Ridgeway, David Ross and Patrick Dodson met with Prime Minister John Howard in an unsuccessful attempt to place these issues on a reconciliation agenda (Saunders and Shanahan 2000, 5).

CAR released its final *Documents for Reconciliation* at Corroboree 2000. This consisted of the 'Declaration Towards Reconciliation', an 'aspirational statement', and the 'Roadmap for Reconciliation', an outline of national strategies for reconciliation designed to 'implement the principles of the Declaration' (CAR 2000a, 71, 74).

The 'Declaration Towards Reconciliation' made no substantive commitments to issues that Indigenous people had long been campaigning for; contained several nationalist phrases, such as 'we share our future and live in harmony', 'move on together' and 'united Australia'; and linked the term 'self-determination' with the phrase 'within the life of the nation' (CAR 2000g, 3). As Monk argued, the term 'self-determination, whilst upheld in the "Declaration Towards Reconciliation", was not part of the process of arriving at a document, and had largely been included as a political catch-phrase' (Monk 2001, 22). Finally, the Declaration stated that as 'one part' of the nation apologizes, 'another part accepts the apologies and forgives' (CAR 2000g, 3). This fell significantly short of a genuine apology offered with no conditional expectations that the offender should automatically be forgiven (Gaita 2000, 286).

The 'Roadmap for Reconciliation', with its four national strategies, similarly failed to substantially incorporate many issues advocated by Indigenous people. Notable for their absence was any concern with addressing fundamental inequalities in power relationships between Indigenous and non-Indigenous people. For example, the 'National Strategy to Sustain the Reconciliation Process' focussed on education and symbolism with only one action discussing power relationships – the need to address low parliamentary representation, and even this was inadequate, as it did not discuss how it might be done (CAR 2000b, 2). Similarly, the 'National Strategy to Promote Recognition of Aboriginal and Torres Strait Islander Rights' did not articulate any specific Indigenous rights beyond intellectual property, the possible recognition of customary laws and a limited notion of self-determination. Sovereignty, genuine self-determination, land rights and a treaty were all ignored (CAR 2000b, 3).

In December 2000, CAR released four booklets that further detailed these strategies, and they also failed to address many longstanding Indigenous concerns. For example, 'Recognizing Aboriginal and Torres Strait Islander Rights' excluded concepts of sovereignty from discussions of self-determination and argued some rights could only be advanced 'over the longer term' (CAR 2000e, 3, 14). Similarly, 'Sustaining the Reconciliation Process' recognized power relationships to a limited extent, including combating racism and inequality, yet focussed on education and symbolism, rather than on issues such as a treaty (CAR 2000f, 5–8, 23–25).

Despite their development, these documents of reconciliation failed to reflect the broad range of views and concerns of Indigenous people, thereby limiting the likelihood that the documents would deliver any significant outcomes and restricting the success of the overall goal.

Factors that Adversely Impacted the Reconciliation Process

Five interrelated factors compromised the effectiveness of the overall reconciliation process. The first concerns how the process was established. After reneging on their commitments to implement two Indigenous demands – national land rights and a treaty – the Hawke Labor Government (1983–1991) proposed the reconciliation process partly as a diversion (Gunstone 2007, 300). While a broad range of non-Indigenous people and organizations were supportive, Indigenous people were less forthcoming, seeing other issues, including land rights and self-determination, as more relevant (ABC 1991). However, the Government largely ignored these concerns and implemented the reconciliation process (Roberts 1993, 16–18). Further, in passing the CAR Act, which empowered the Government to issue directions to CAR and select its members, and in situating CAR's Secretariat in the Department of the Prime Minister and Cabinet, the Government ensured that it could significantly influence the process (CAR Act 1991, 5–7). This influence meant many issues, including sovereignty and self-determination, were marginalized or ignored (Foley 2000, 31).

The second factor was the emphasis on symbolic and practical reconciliation, particularly following the 1996 election of the Howard Government. The Liberal/National Coalition and conservatives emphasized 'practical' reconciliation, a neo-assimilationist view that argued the need to concentrate on improving socioeconomic outcomes (Howard 2000, 88–90; McGuinness 2000, 239). Alternatively, the Labor Party and progressives emphasized 'symbolic' reconciliation that focussed on issues such as apologizing to the stolen generations and marching for reconciliation (Pearson 2002b). In contrast to both, many Indigenous people advocated substantive reconciliation, which would address rights and existing power relations (Dodson 2000; Dodson 2000a, 269). While recognizing the importance of an apology and addressing socioeconomic conditions, neither symbolic nor practical reconciliation was seen as sufficient for reconciliation. Unfortunately, the debates that occurred concerning the most appropriate approach to reconciliation focussed on the symbolic and practical, and governments and the wider community largely ignored substantive reconciliation (Brennan et al. 2003, 122).

The third factor was the emphasis on nationalism. As stated earlier, the strong link between reconciliation and nationalism encouraged Indigenous and non-Indigenous people to become 'united' and to 'walk together' by sharing histories, cultures and identities (Moran 1998, 108; Langton 2003, 86–7). This failed to recognize that invasion, colonization, genocide and theft of land and children had continuing repercussions. It also meant that those Indigenous demands that could not be situated within the nationalist discourse were marginalized or ignored (Foley 2000, 31; Ridgeway 2001).

The fourth factor was the limited notion of justice utilized throughout the process. The term 'justice' was largely restricted to addressing Indigenous socioeconomic disadvantage (Tickner 1991, 6–8; CAR Act 1991, 3). Consequently any notions of justice that fell outside this narrow definition – including a treaty, sovereignty, self-determination, land rights and challenging existing power relations – were largely ignored and the process generally failed to recognize the need to involve reparative justice, which recognizes the importance of making reparations for previous injustices (Young 1990, 33; Thompson 2002, xi).

Finally, the reconciliation process emphasized the achievement of better relationships between Indigenous and non-Indigenous people instead of the need to address historical and contemporary injustices by recognizing Indigenous rights and transforming existing power relationships (Wink 1997, 25). This approach contributed to the adoption of a limited notion of justice, and a general failure to acknowledge that legitimate differences exist between and within Indigenous people and non-Indigenous people in terms of rights, sovereignty, self-determination and justice. Instead of advocating the desirability for a 'transcending of disagreement', the reconciliation process could have adopted an approach that accommodated and respected a range of views and differences (Mulgan 1998, 193; Watson 1997, 213).

Conclusion

Despite some limited successes, mainly in terms of education, overall the goals of the Australian reconciliation process – educating the wider community about reconciliation and Indigenous issues, fostering an ongoing national commitment to address Indigenous socioeconomic disadvantage and investigating the desirability and content of a document of reconciliation – were not achieved by the conclusion of the process. Other attempts to explain why the reconciliation process did not achieve its goals have tended to focus on the impact of the Howard Government (Brennan et al. 2003, 122; Pratt et al. 2001, 145). This has obscured the role that several factors, such as the way the process was established, the emphasis on symbolic and practical reconciliation, the nationalist discourse of reconciliation, the restricted notion of justice and the emphasis on improving relationships, played in limiting the effectiveness of the reconciliation process. These factors need to be identified, critiqued and addressed before any substantive reconciliation process can genuinely be advanced in Australia.

References

Agius, P. et al. (1999), 'Media Release 12 August 1999: Drop the Preamble', *Journal of Australian Indigenous Issues*, 2:3.

Altman, J. and Hunter, B. (2003), *Monitoring 'Practical' Reconciliation: Evidence from the Reconciliation Decade, 1991–2001* (Canberra: Centre for Aboriginal Economic Policy Research).

Australian Association of Adult and Community Education (AAACE) (1993), *Australians for Reconciliation: Study Circle Kit* (Canberra: AGPS).

Australian Broadcasting Corporation (ABC) (1991), *Reconciliation* (Sydney: ABC TV).

Australian Bureau of Statistics (ABS) (2001a), *A Snapshot of Australia*, <http://www.abs.gov.au/ausstats/abs%40census.nsf/4079a1bbd2a04b80ca256b9d00208f92/7dd97c937216e32fca256bbe008371f0!OpenDocument>.

Australian Bureau of Statistics (2001b), *Prisoners in Australia*, Cat No. 4517.0 (Canberra: ABS).

Australian Bureau of Statistics (2001c), *Deaths: Australia*, Cat No. 3302.0 (Canberra: ABS).

Australian Bureau of Statistics (2002a), *Year Book Australia 2002*, Cat No. 1301.0 (Canberra: ABS).

Australian Bureau of Statistics (2002b), *2001 Census Indigenous Profile*, Cat. No. 2002.0 (Canberra: ABS).

Australian Bureau of Statistics (2002c), *Housing and Infrastructure in Aboriginal and Torres Strait Islander Communities 2001*, Cat No. 4710.0 (Canberra: ABS).

Australian Bureau of Statistics (2003), *Year Book Australia 2003*, Cat No. 1301.0 (Canberra: ABS).

Australian Medical Association (AMA) (2002), *Public Report Card 2002, Aboriginal and Torres Strait Islander Health: No More Excuses* (Canberra: AMA).

Brennan, S. et al. (2003), 'Rights-Based Reconciliation Needs Renewed Action from Canberra', *Alternative Law Journal*, 28:3.

Clark, G. (2000), 'Not Much Progress', in Grattan, M. (ed.).

Clark, G. (2001), 'Let the White Heat of Anger Glow Again', *The Sydney Morning Herald*, 18 April.

Collins, L. and Mouzos, J. (2001), *Australian Deaths in Custody and Custody-Related Police Operations 2000* (Canberra: Australian Institute of Criminology).

Commonwealth Government of Australia, *Council for Aboriginal Reconciliation Act 1991*.

Council for Aboriginal Reconciliation (1993), *Addressing Disadvantage* (Canberra: AGPS).

Council for Aboriginal Reconciliation (1994), *Walking Together: the First Steps* (Canberra: AGPS).

Council for Aboriginal Reconciliation (1995), *Together We Can't Lose* (Canberra: AGPS).

Council for Aboriginal Reconciliation (1997), *Walking Together*, 20 (Canberra: AGPS).

Council for Aboriginal Reconciliation (1999), *How Can We Advance Reconciliation?* (Canberra: AGPS).

Council for Aboriginal Reconciliation (2000a), *Reconciliation, Australia's Challenge: Final Report of the Council for Aboriginal Reconciliation to the Prime Minister and the Commonwealth Parliament* (Canberra: Commonwealth Government of Australia).

Council for Aboriginal Reconciliation (2000b), *Roadmap for Reconciliation* (Canberra: AGPS).

Council for Aboriginal Reconciliation (2000c), *Overcoming Disadvantage* (Canberra: AGPS).

Council for Aboriginal Reconciliation (2000d), *Achieving Economic Independence* (Canberra: AGPS).

Council for Aboriginal Reconciliation (2000e), *Recognising Aboriginal and Torres Strait Islander Rights* (Canberra: AGPS).

Council for Aboriginal Reconciliation (2000f), *Sustaining the Reconciliation Process* (Canberra: AGPS).

Council for Aboriginal Reconciliation (2000g), *Corroboree 2000: Towards Reconciliation* (Canberra: AGPS).

Cowlishaw, G. (2000), 'The Politics of Scholarship and the Fervour of Friends', *Journal of Australian Indigenous Issues*, 3:4.

Dodson, M. (2000), *Address to Corroboree 2000*, <http://www.austlii.edu.au/au / orgs/car/media/Dr%20Mick%20Dodson.htm>.

Dodson, P. (2000a), 'Lingiari: Until the Chains are Broken', in Grattan, M. (ed.).

Dodson, P. (2000b), *Beyond the Mourning Gate*, <http://www.aiatsis.gov.au/lbry/ digprgm/wentworth/a317361_a.pdf>.

Foley, G. (2000), 'Reconciliation: Fact or Fiction?', *Journal of Australian Indigenous Issues*, 3:2.

Gaita, R. (2000), 'Guilt, Shame and Collective Responsibility', in Grattan, M. (ed).

Gastrow, P. (1999), 'A Joint Effort: The South African Peace Process', *People Building Peace* (Utrecht: European Centre for Conflict Prevention).

Gordon, M. (2001), *Reconciliation: A Journey* (Sydney: UNSW Press).

Grattan, M. (ed.) (2000), *Essays on Australian Reconciliation* (Melbourne: Bookman Press).

Gray, M. and Auld, T. (2000), *Towards An Index Of Relative Indigenous Socio-Economic Disadvantage* (Canberra: Centre For Aboriginal Economic Policy Research).

Gunstone, A. (2007), *Unfinished Business: The Australian Formal Reconciliation Process* (Melbourne: Australian Scholarly Publishing).

Howard, J. (2000), 'Practical Reconciliation', in Grattan, M. (ed.).

Johns, G. and Brunton, R. (1999), 'Reconciliation: What Does It Mean?', *IPA Backgrounder*, 11:4.

Johnson, J. (1996), *Unfinished Business: Australians and Reconciliation* (Canberra: AGPS).

Langton, M. (2003), 'Introduction: Culture Wars', in Grossman, M (ed.), *Blacklines: Contemporary Critical Writing by Indigenous Australians*, (Carlton, Victoria: Melbourne University Press).

Manne, R. (2001), *In Denial: The Stolen Generations and The Right* (Melbourne: Schwartz Publishing).

Mansell, M. (1992), 'Reconciliation by 2001: The White Man's Dream Continues the Aboriginal Nightmare', *The Aboriginal Provisional Government Papers Volume 1* (Hobart: Deep South Sovereign Publications).

Markus, A. (2001), *Race: John Howard and the Remaking of Australia* (Crows Nest, NSW: Allen and Unwin).

McGuinness, P. (2000), 'Reconciliation is a Two-Way Street', in Grattan, M (ed.).

Monk, L. (2001), 'Self-determination, Justice and Australia in the New Millennium', *Journal of Australian Indigenous Issues*, 4:3.

Moran, A. (1998), 'Aboriginal Reconciliation: Transformations in Settler Nationalism', *Melbourne Journal of Politics*, 25:1.

Mulgan, R. (1998), 'Citizenship and Legitimacy in Post-colonial Australia', in Peterson, N and Sanders, W. (eds), *Citizenship and Indigenous Australians: Changing Conceptions and Possibilities*, (Cambridge: Cambridge University Press).

Neill, R. (2002), *White Out* (Crows Nest, NSW: Allen and Unwin).

Nettheim, G. (2000), 'Reconciliation: Challenges for Australian Law', *Australian Journal of Human Rights*, l.7: 1.

Newspoll (2000), *Quantitative Research into Issues Relating to a Document of Reconciliation* (Canberra: AGPS).

Pearson, N. (2000), 'Aboriginal Disadvantage', in Grattan, M. (ed).

Pearson, N. (2002a), 'Addiction Corroding Indigenous Culture', in Healey, J. (ed.), *Aboriginal Disadvantage* (Rozelle, NSW: The Spinney Press).

Pearson, N. (2002b), *Address to the Launch of Don Watson's 'Recollections of a Bleeding Heart*, <http://www.capeyorkpartnerships.com/noelpearson/pdf/paul-keat-1-5-02.pdf>.

Phillips, A. (2001), 'The Politics of Reconciliation Revisited: Germany and East-Central Europe', *World Affairs*, 163: 4.

Pratt, A. et al. (2000), 'Reconciliation: Origins, Policy, Practice, Representations, Meanings, Futures', *Diversity Conference: Imagining Ourselves* (University of Technology Sydney, 1–2 December).

Pratt, A. et al. (2001), 'Papering over the Differences': Australian Nationhood and the Normative Discourse of Reconciliation', Kalantzis, M. and Cope, B. (eds), *Reconciliation, Multiculturalism, Identities: Difficult Dialogues, Sensible Solutions* (Altona, Victoria: Common Ground Publishing).

Ridgeway, A. (2001), *Address to the UN Human Rights Commission*, <http://www.arts.monash.edu.au/cais/events/UN%20SPEECH%202001.pdf.>

Ring, I. and Brown, N. (2002), 'Indigenous Health: Chronically Inadequate Responses to Damning Statistics', *Medical Journal of Australia*, 177:11.

Roberts, D. (1993), 'Reconciliation and the Mabo Factor', *Kaurna Higher Education Journal*, 4.

Saulwick, I. and Muller, D. (2000), *Research into Issues Related to a Document of Reconciliation* (Canberra: AGPS).

Saunders, M. and Shanahan, D. (2000), 'Blacks to Pressure Howard for Treaty', *The Australian*, 25 May.

Tatz, C. (1998), 'The Reconciliation Bargain', *Melbourne Journal of Politics*, 25:1.

Taylor, J. (2000), *Transformations of the Indigenous Population: Recent and Future Trends*, Discussion Paper No. 194 (Canberra: CAEPR).

Taylor, K. (2000), 'PM Swayed Aboriginal Poll: Labor', *The Age*, 11 April.

Thompson, J. (2002), *Taking Responsibility for the Past: Reparation and Historical Justice* (Cambridge: Polity Press).

Tickner, R. (1990), *Backgrounder*, 1:32, Department of Foreign Affairs and Trade.

Tickner, R. (1991), 'Council for Aboriginal Reconciliation Bill 1991 Second Reading Speech', *Hansard*, 30 May.

Watson, I. (1997), 'Reconciliation', in Hinton, M. et al. (eds.), *Indigenous Australians and the Law* (Sydney: Cavendish Publishing).

Wink, W. (1997), *When the Powers Fail: Reconciliation in the Healing of Nations* (Minneapolis: Fortress Press).

Young, I. (1990), *Justice and the Politics Of Difference*, (Princeton, NJ: Princeton University Press).

Chapter 15

Stepping Forward: Reconciliation and the Good Relations Agenda in Organizational Practice in Northern Ireland

Derick Wilson

> The other is the limit beyond which our ambitions must not run and the boundary beyond
> which our life must not expand
>
> (Niebuhr 1952 in Shriver 2005).

Reconciliation activity in Northern Ireland emerged in the early 1960s through students involved in post war European reconciliation, ecumenical church activists, trade unionists, returning development volunteers and teachers and youth workers promoting Catholic-Protestant school programs (Wilson 1994). Later more people committed themselves, motivated by concern for the increasing inter-communal violence and clashes with security forces that accompanied the emergence of the Civil Rights campaign (NICRA, formed on February 1967) and internment on 9 August 1971 (Barton 1998; CAIN Web Service). These 'intentional' reconciliation activities included residential programs outside Belfast, holiday play schemes, 'education for mutual understanding' programs between schools and youth facilities, and support groups for the families of both victims and imprisoned perpetrators of violence. They helped to transform reconciliation from something that occurred on the periphery, narrowly defined in terms of conflict between two opposed traditions, to a task that today makes a significant claim on the policy and expenditure profiles of the governments of the United Kingdom and the Republic of Ireland.

Reconciliation recently became a central policy measure for all departments within the Northern Ireland administration, a legal requirement and the basis for a triennial policy review process (Rt. Hon John Spellar MP 2005).[1] The central role of reconciliation has been strengthened by the Equality and Good Relations legal requirement under the Northern Ireland Act 1998 (Section 75 1 and 2) and the duty placed on public bodies to promote 'good relations' between people of different religious beliefs, political opinions and racial groupings.

---

1 The 'Good Relations' practice evolved from British Race Relations legislation and the Equality and Good Relations legislation (NI).

This chapter outlines the way in which reconciliation in Northern Ireland has been promoted through some civil society groups and actors. It draws on my experience since 1965 with the practice, research and policies associated with trust building and reconciliation. The new policy and strategic framework under the banner of Good Relations has the potential to connect the work of local government and community organizations, regional bodies and Government through the promotion of improved community relations across traditional divides. This means that citizens committed to reconciliation – whether out of civic duty, a moral imperative, a faith perspective or a desire for a more interdependent world – should now be supported by the activities of public institutions, civil servants and community agencies.

However, while the Good Relations agenda draws on a range of compliance measures that did not exist 40 years ago, and is rooted in equality law, human rights standards and other important legal instruments, there is a pressing need to establish commonly supported institutions with the ability to deal with societal issues on a non-partisan basis. Although sensitive issues can now be addressed at a deeper level as meetings between the families of victims and Republican and Loyalist groups and state actors responsible for partisan violence occur, reconciliation is an ongoing, multi-dimensional process which encompasses personal, political, structural, economic, cultural and religious elements. In drawing on the new framework, actors need to be conscious of how reconciliation can be diluted and made complicit with partisan identities, particularly where sponsoring organizations weaken their commitment to secure a baseline of good citizenship.

In addressing these concerns, this chapter focuses primarily on how volunteers, people engaged in community activity and the staff of public institutions and civil society can be helped to maintain a mental model of citizenship that prioritizes equality and difference, and to remain vigilant about the dynamics feeding partisan loyalties. The discussion offers illustrations of practical engagements with reconciliation work in school, youth and community programs, in which people of Catholic and Protestant backgrounds were brought together, and political workshops were held with regional and local politicians from Nationalist, Unionist, Loyalist and Republican traditions. These activities were primarily associated with the Corrymeela Community, an ecumenical reconciliation community with a residential centre in Ballycastle, a fieldwork base in Belfast, and the 'Future Ways' program at the University of Ulster.

Work at these sites was guided by a desire to challenge the persistent operational preference in both government and non-government practice for addressing community relations and reconciliation at its most visible points of failure. An exclusive focus on urban ghettos, victims, paramilitaries, children and young people, condemns community relations activities to a centre–periphery paradigm that presumes a healthy core of society subject to manifestations of sectarian violence on the margins.

In fact, outside the obvious points of greatest stress, it is within organizational and institutional cultures that tension and mistrust in Northern Irish society have been contained, due to silence and legislative exclusion from the public domain. The introduction of the Good Relations agenda provides an opportunity to recognize this operational blindness and to address it via targeted efforts to promote cultures and behaviours that deepen mutual recognition and trust.

This chapter is divided into three sections. The first explores the idea of 'ethnic frontiers' and its application to reconciliation practices in Northern Ireland. The second offers illustrations of how individuals, community groups and civil society organizations can build bridges across painful divides in ethnic frontiers. Drawing on these illustrations, the final section offers some principles for practising reconciliation.

Reconciliation and Good Relations Work in an Ethnic Frontier

The Future Ways program was established in 1985 with support from the Joseph Rowntree Charitable Trust, the Lawlor Foundation and the Understanding Conflict Trust. The purpose of the program was to engage practitioners and academics working in the field of reconciliation to develop:

- A rationale for underpinning community relations practice (1985–1991);
- Community relations practice within the experience of people on the periphery (1991–1996);
- Quality community relations practice to challenge central institutions (1997–2002);
- The operational core to trust building (2002–2007).

Frank Wright, a member of the program, conceived of this reconciliation work as taking place within an 'ethnic frontier' (Wright 1996, 510). Ethnic frontiers are places of divided loyalties and opposed national identities that are geographically close to different and often historically competing national identity centres. They are characterized by the inability of one group to dominate. For this reason peace, such as it exists, can only be an uneasy compromise. The main dynamic in this context is the deterrence of one tradition by the other, alongside attempts to secure the might of historically aligned national neighbours. Conflict emerges mainly in the systems of law and order and opportunities for employment, education and freedom of cultural expression (Wright 1987).

Other members of the Future Ways program, Derick Wilson and Duncan Morrow, in collaboration with Karin Eyben, proposed interweaving the principles of equity, diversity and interdependence into reconciliation practices (Eyben et al. 1997).[2] Wilson and Morrow also developed research that promoted an educational practice of dealing with contested and sensitive issues, and political understandings that underpin learning in an ethnic frontier (Morrow and Wilson1994; Wilson 1994; Morrow 1994). The following draws heavily on these practices, Wright's concept of an ethnic frontier and the practice of visualizing conflictual dynamics, which enables people to explore their place in mixed tradition groups.

---

2   In 2005, this proposal was incorporated as the foundation principles of the 'Shared Future' public policy statement, see: OFMDFM 2005, 1.

Seeing One Another as Equal and Different in an Ethnic Frontier

Recognizing one another as equal and different citizens is hard in a conflict situation. People more readily see members of opposing traditions as 'others' and often learn about them in their absence. This makes it possible to ridicule and demean without being accountable for your views. In an ethnic frontier such as Northern Ireland, the nature of communal conflict is such that institutions and organizations can be experienced as partial to one or other competing group. For example, staff of public and voluntary agencies can unwittingly collude with a narrowed communal identity if they are not encouraged to challenge partisan forms of practice. Partisanship is detrimental to community work and public service practice, since it goes against the principle of inclusive working and the values of the 'public good', which directly oppose bigotry and demeaning others.

A minimum need in a society moving out of conflict is that people are brought into environments in which the other is included. This places an onus on staff to represent or advocate for the other, especially in their absence. In doing so, the conditions are created for the other to take up a place within the structure. This may involve meetings between people from politically opposed traditions where each person is able to experience how their place is secured through the actions and attention of those they view as different (Girard 1977, 1978). Reconciliation between equal citizens is then an outcome of new relationships and structures where each has their place.

The following example of an exchange at a trade union group gives a glimpse into how such new relationships can be formed in practice:

> George (a Protestant) spoke over coffee with the facilitator. He was embarrassed that he did not know that Francis, who was also in the group, had recently had someone in his family killed by loyalist terrorists, "When I met him before, I said nothing about the incident." George spoke of now wondering whether Francis would think that he didn't care, couldn't be bothered or even supported loyalist paramilitaries. The facilitator asked him, if he felt able, to speak to Francis, making his regret and sorrow known and clarify that things were clear between them. It turned out not to be an issue for Francis who said, "How were you to know George?" George spoke about this to the group, provoking group members to look at how sectarian differences get caught up with human life in such ways. They can make relationships tense unless people move beyond the stage of being unsure or embarrassed with each other (Trade Union Group, Wilson 1994).

When people in a contested society are brought together with those they have had no real relationship with, or have experienced only in terms of societal conflict, they readily see them as a danger, as someone to fear. A secure relational environment can be empowering for both parties if it is established with the intention of assisting people to understand the dynamics at work, and enables them to become subjects shaping their own lives, not mere objects of others' manipulations and narrower cultural constraints (Wilson 1994, 142–97).

The following exchange at a Community Relations Group provides some insight:

A young woman spoke: "My brother is in the security forces and one day on patrol they were spat at and called names. That evening a colleague of theirs was shot dead. The next day, when they arrested a Catholic, they took their anger out on that man and gave him a 'good hiding'". Siobhan spoke of her hatred for the security forces: "Even though I don't like it, I have a sense of 'yo' every time a soldier is killed. My earliest memory of a soldier was him dragging my father out of our car and splaying him across the bonnet and beating him up."

Sam said: "Hearing you speak of joy at security force deaths makes me angry and fearful because my family has people in the security forces. They would never do that to anyone."

Seamus said: "I almost resent my father for being a policeman and putting our whole family at risk."

Sinead said: "I don't believe this is happening, we're just getting at it like on that diagram."

Sandy said: "I disagree, for me we are talking together and listening too. I would have been more fearful before this meeting if all this had been said, now I don't feel so much fear" (Community Relations Group, 1990, Wilson 1994).

If people are brought together in an environment that is structurally committed to diversity and guided by a program that promotes an interdependent society they can foster relationships that erode partisan identities. This work can be fragile but successful practice is possible and has been documented (Fitzduff 1989; Wilson 1994; Wilson and Tyrell 1995). The following is such an account:

When a close relative was killed by a paramilitary group, I could feel myself moving away from the mixed friendships I had and move more towards my immediate family circle. The unanimous way they all condemned the action, those in church and all I had known for many years, was a comfort to me. They were such a strong support for me. I even began to agree with sectarian comments they made, which I would never have associated myself with before. Through this all, my Catholic friends kept in touch, they visited me and my relatives. They were not put off by the hardening in my attitudes or the strong feelings against Catholics that developed in the area after the shooting. They saved me from becoming bitter and, in the end, I moved back to them again and away from remaining extreme. Some of my Protestant friends moved this way too and they're grateful the Catholic friends stuck by us (Cross-Community Group, Wilson 1994).

Hope for the future is difficult to sustain when you are engrossed in local conflict, with the fear and uncertainty it generates. Yet the provision of such hope, without trivializing the conflict or overstating the extent to which trust develops, is vital. Everyone has a 'culturally good reason' for the position they take. Often it is based on the personal, political or social beliefs and experiences that surround people. As the example below illustrates, these beliefs are often held firmly and pervade social life:

In our town centre, if you're young and male, you know not to walk on the side of the street that does not belong to your tradition. There are shops we identify as being 'one side' or 'the other' and you stick to them. A boy got his head split when he walked on the wrong side, a gang of boys smashed a hardware shop window, took out a large shaft from it, and proceeded to lay into him with it. Any outsiders on the wrong side get beaten up (Wilson 1994).

Further, the influence of beliefs and traditions about whom to fear or distrust can erode more fragile experiences of meeting people across the divide:

> Few choose to meet each other, unless there is some initiative taken by schools, churches or other organisations to which they belong. At the same time, being together, people began to understand the importance of community relations work taking people beyond separation, avoidance and politeness. At the end of one such discussion between people who had studiously avoided contact back home but became very friendly on a residential course, the advice from one, before the entire group, was: "I give you permission to hit me if I walk past you again back home" (Group Discussion, Wilson 1994).

However, it is possible for people to change their attitudes from ones of violence to peace (Fitzduff 1989). Such transitions occur more often when civic organizations and public institutions prioritize mutual understanding.[3] Relationships develop faster and are more sustainable if the people involved belong to a wider organizational structure that is committed to the same purpose (Wilson and Morrow 1994, Ouseley 2001). As the following example illustrates:

> I am the trade union shop steward in a firm that has always employed people from all traditions. Our boss was killed; he was shot down in his office by terrorists. The car used by the killers was found some time later. Because it was near to where some employees from a different religious tradition to the boss live, some of the work force turned on them. I took it upon myself to drive them home every day after that for some time. I know they had nothing to do with it (Shop Steward, Wilson 1994).

Promoting Equity Diversity and Interdependence

Reconciliation practice that supports good relations needs to be developed within a framework that works as if change is possible. A 'mental model' that promotes equal and different citizenship is one way to establish, or re-establish, a value base that acknowledges others as gifts rather than threats (Senge 1994, 6). After more than 35 years of conflict, the language of reconciliation is still part of the political and institutional discourse of Northern Ireland. However, there is an urgent need to change the way people from competing traditions relate, given the growth in racist attitudes and behaviour over recent years (Institute of Conflict Research 2005).

To enable staff within civic organizations and public institutions to challenge the mental model of partisanship, there must be an organizational insistence that every

---

3 The Probation Board for Northern Ireland (and other public bodies) have developed Good Relations as a strategic and operational objective and proposed a Good Relations policy for staff and client relationships. Ballymena, Belfast and Newry Councils have done likewise. For further information, see: <http://www.pbni.org.uk/>.

person is an equal and different citizen sharing the one place. In a contested society, this is not a simple practice to uphold. Enhanced separation and distinction between cultures, and exclusion among them, can make partisanship appear the easier option, as the following remark shows:

> My house was on the peace line and I have tried for years to keep contact going between the two sides. As a Protestant member of a cross-community project, I came under attack from my co-religionists when the area was tense. My colleague, the chairperson of the project, was Catholic. We stood by each other. We both had our houses petrol bombed, me by hard line Loyalists, she by Republicans (Peace Group Member, Wilson 1994).

In Northern Ireland, it is common to maintain a distance from those viewed as different. Some people prefer outright separation, but avoidance and politeness are practised by almost all. Subsequently, opportunities to meet across lines of perceived difference are held hostage to more broadly held fears, as the following makes clear:

> In our town Catholics and Protestants are not afraid of each other, but there is a certain 'standing off' from each other. Protestants are very much the majority. There are Catholics in the town who are civil servants and a lot of police officers too. All the locals agree that if there is any trouble it is caused by outsiders coming into the town. Any feelings of ambiguity on this, or any people who support political violence, keep quiet (Wilson 1994).

Those facilitating discussions, meetings or other forms of engagement need to help people understand the complexity of individual experiences and the group dynamic at work, in order to promote a recognition that even in a society characterized by an ethnic frontier, people are deeply interdependent. To illustrate:

> In our work we were one community of women who knew each other through and through. There was no mention of politics and religion, and some went to one another's celebrations, weddings and all. When the trouble started, somehow there was a discussion that we did not want any harm to come to anyone on the work floor. When we heard of anything happening in our areas we would tell each other, so no one ran the danger of being ambushed on the way in or out of work (Trade Union Seminar Discussion 1991, Wilson 1994).

Individual staff working to improve community relations, and the organizations and institutions to which they belong, are also at risk of being undermined or influenced by partisan settings and attitudes. Their work is extremely challenging and informal or tacit organizational cultures can weaken the policy and structures designed to promote citizenship and ease with difference (Eyben et al. 2002).

Applying the principles of equity, diversity and interdependence in organizations means: ensuring that boundaries are fair and equitable; affirming the equality and difference of each person; and developing relationships based on mutual understanding. Staff should be encouraged to acknowledge experiences of partisanship, racism or discrimination in their own lives and to recognize the responses that these different dynamics evoke. They also need to be supported in their efforts to generate a more open and shared society.

Supporting and Sustaining Reflective Practice

In current government policy and more broadly, there is increasing engagement with the theme of building a shared society but this needs to be extended and deepened. A mental model of citizenship is essential for linking work with communities to a wider policy program of economic sustainability and future vitality. Public servants and civic leaders in business, trade unions, faith traditions and communities therefore need to question whether they are actively promoting a model of equal and different citizenship or implicitly supporting partisanship.

Northern Ireland remains a country of 'innocent people, in which those who would damage community relations are always others and never us, yet somehow we end up where we are… On the old and well-tried principles of safety first, people profess their commitment to a common future, but first construct their defence' (Morrow et al. 2002). To overcome this, reconciliation and good relations work must be underpinned by the experience of change, of its possibility. Supporting an abstract concept like 'change' is one thing; creating mechanisms that allow people 'to change' is another. The first step is to move away from a pre-occupation with policies that promote change and instead to develop ways in which people can actually experience it.

Generating reconciliation and good relations between people from different traditions is primarily a task for the state, public institutions, civic boards and adult society.

In the experience of the Future Ways program with elected councillors, local councils, voluntary and community agencies and the police service, participants have needed the assurance of support for the reconciliation and good relations agenda from all the policy and institutional levels in which they work.[4]

Reconciliation and good relations practice must be linked to policies and structures that deal with the wider dynamics of violence and the need for community safety.

The system of law and order needs to hold individuals to account, diminish fear within the wider population and erode tendencies towards retaliation and revenge. When this happens citizen based societies are strengthened, when this fails, partisanship grows (Wright 1987).

Day-to-day practice in public and civic institutions and organizations must promote openness, fair treatment and the need for good community relations.

Relationships among staff and with clients need to be open and trusting, and should be underpinned by a structure that is at ease with difference. It also needs to be made clear that solidarity with one tradition or group over another, implicitly or explicitly, diminishes the values of reconciliation and good relations practice.

---

4 For example, PBNI 2006 and Belfast City Council Good Relations Working Group 2006.

Reconciliation and good relations practice works toward real change in people's lives.

Real change means existential change in people's lives, in their being and their actions. This places an onus on the state to examine whether the current systems of law and order, including those governing access to employment, education and cultural expression promote equality or generate conflict.

The need to work 'as if change is possible' demands a new openness within organizations and examination of the changes required to promote a culture of inclusion.

Conclusion

Reconciliation practice is both about healing past relationships and establishing relationships with those on the other side of the force-threat continuum (Wright 1987). It is about creating a new platform on which all previously opposed parties and traditions meet to secure a citizen based society.

From 8 May 2007, Northern Ireland looked into a shared future when the leaders of the historically opposed Democratic Unionist Party and Sinn Fein agreed to lead a devolved Executive and Elected Assembly. Community based reconciliation practices helped to ensure that political reconciliation remained a goal in Northern Ireland. The thread of trust building that has existed within civil society since the early-1960s has informed and, in some cases, facilitated meetings among current political leaders on sensitive and difficult issues.

Against the background of political and civil society, and alongside a willingness to engage across lines of distrust and hatred, there is now an opportunity for the broader good relations agenda to be embraced as 'common sense' between diverse citizens. These citizens are applying their energies to create respectful relationships in which the talents, promise and latent abilities of all are released to embrace the economic, educational, social and intercultural challenges of cementing a new peace and building a sustainable future where past fears are dissolved.

References

Barton, B. (1996), *A Pocket History of Ulster* (Dublin: The O'Brien Press).

CAIN Web Service, *The Civil Rights Campaign: A Chronology of Main Events*, <http://cain.ulst.ac.uk/events/crights/chron.htm>.

Corrymeela Community <http://www.corrymeela.org>.

Eyben, K. et al. (2002), 'Learning Beyond Fear: New Events Seeking New Habits', *Reflections*, 3:4, 42–51 (Massachusetts: MIT Press).

Eyben, K. et al. (2002), *The Equity, Diversity and Interdependence Framework: A Framework for Organisational Learning and Change* (Coleraine: University of Ulster).

Eyben, K. et al. (1997), *A Worthwhile Venture? Practically Investing in Equity, Diversity and Interdependence in Northern Ireland* (Coleraine: University of Ulster).

Fitzduff, M. (1989), *From Ritual to Consciousness*, D. Phil. Thesis (University of Ulster).

Future Ways Programme, University of Ulster, <http://www.socsi.ulster.ac.uk/research/education/furtureways/index.html>.

Girard, R. (1977), *Violence and the Sacred* (Baltimore: Johns Hopkins).

Girard, R. (1978), *To Double Business Bound: Essays on Literature, Mimesis and Anthropology* (Baltimore: Johns Hopkins).

Harding, V. (1983), *There is a River: The Black Struggle for Freedom in America* (New York: Random House).

Jarman, N. et al. (2005), *Community Cohesion: Applying Learning from Groundwork in Northern Ireland* (London: Groundwork UK).

Kaptein, R. (1988), *A Short Survey of the Work of Rene Girard* (Understanding Conflict Project).

Kaptein, R. (1992), 'Ethnocentrism and Northern Ireland', paper presented at the *Conference on Violence and Religion*, 7–9 May 1992, University of Stanford, Stanford.

Kaptein, R. and Morrow, D. (1993), *On the Way of Freedom* (Dublin: Columba Press).

Institute of Conflict Research (2005), *Hate Crime Project* (Belfast: Institute for Conflict Research).

Lorenz, W. (1994), *Social Work in a Changing Europe* (London: Routledge).

Morrow, D. (1991), 'Teaching and Learning With Adults in Northern Ireland', in Poggeler, F. and Yaron, K. (eds), *Adult Education in Crisis Situations* (Jerusalem: Magnes Press).

Morrow, D. (1991), 'The Wrath of God: Churches and the Experience of Violence in Northern Ireland', in Alexander, Y. and O'Day, A. (eds), *The Irish Terrorism Experience* (Dartmouth: Aldershot and Vermont).

Morrow, D. (1994), 'Escaping the Bind in Northern Ireland: Teaching and Learning in the Ethnic Frontier', in Yaron, K. and Poggeler, S. (eds), *Meeting of Cultures and the Clash of Cultures: Adult Education in Multi Cultural Societies* (Jerusalem: Magnes Press).

Morrow, D. (1994), 'Games between Frontiers', in Weisbaden, E.J. (ed.), *Northern Ireland: Past and Present* (Stuttgart: Franz Steiner Verlag).

Morrow, D. and Wilson, D.A. (1993), *Three into Two Won't Go: From Mediation to New Relationships in Northern Ireland* (Washington: National Institute for Dispute Resolution).

Morrow, D. et al. (1994), *Ways Out of Conflict* (Belfast: Corrymeela Press).

Morrow, D. et al. (2002), *Future Ways Submission on Community Relations Policy* (submitted to OFMDFMNI).

Northern Ireland Act 1998, Section 75 (2).

Northern Ireland Community Relations Council Website <http://www.communityrelations.org.uk>.

Northern Ireland Housing Executive (2005), *Corporate Plan 2005–2008* (Belfast: NIHE).

Office of the First Minister, Deputy First Minister (2005), *A Shared Future* (Belfast: OFMDFM).

Ouseley, H. (2001), *Community Pride: Making Diversity Work in Bradford* (Bradford: Bradford Vision).

Probation Board for Northern Ireland (2006), *Strategy on Good Relations Consultation Document* (Belfast).

Senge, P. (1994), *The Fifth Discipline Fieldbook* (London: Nicholas Brealey Publishing).

Shriver, D.W. (1994), *An Ethic for Enemies: Forgiveness in Politics* (Oxford: Oxford University Press).

Shriver, D.W. (2005), *Honest Patriots* (Oxford: Oxford University Press).

Spellar, J. (Rt. Hon MP) (2005), *A Shared Future: Policy and Strategic Framework for Good Relations in Northern Ireland*, published on Monday 21 March 2005 by way of Written Ministerial Statement (WMS) in the House of Commons. See: <http://www.asharedfutureni.gov.uk/>.

Stevens, D. (2005), *The Land of Unlikeness*, (Dublin: Columba Press).

Van Rhijn, A. (Secretary) (1977), *Three Years of Conferences in Holland: A Report and Evaluation* (Bergen: Dutch Northern Irish Advisory Committee).

Volf, M. (1996), *Exclusion and Embrace* (Nashville: Abingdon Press).

Wilson, D.A. (1994), *Learning Together for a Change*, D. Phil. Thesis (unpublished), (Coleraine: School of Education, University of Ulster).

Wilson, D.A. and Morrow, D.J. (1994), *Ways Out of Conflict* (Belfast: Corrymeela Press).

Wilson, D.A. and Tyrell, J. (1995), 'Institutions for Conciliation and Mediation' in Dunn, S. (ed.), *Facets of the Conflict in Northern Ireland* (London: Macmillan Press).

Wright, F. (1987), *Northern Ireland: A Comparative Analysis* (Dublin: Gill and Macmillan).

Wright, F. (1988), 'Reconciling the Histories of Catholic and Protestant in Northern Ireland', in Falconer, A. and Liechty, J. (eds), *Reconciling Memories* (Dublin: Columba Press).

Wright, F. (1996), *Two Lands on One Soil* (Dublin: Gill and Macmillan and The Understanding Conflict Trust).

Youth Council for Northern Ireland Website <http://www.jedini.com>.

Index